Transforming Public Policy

Transforming Public Policy

Dynamics of Policy Entrepreneurship and Innovation

Nancy C. Roberts

Paula J. King

Jossey-Bass Publishers • San Francisco

Substantial discounts on bulk quantities of Jossey-Bass books are available to corporations, professional associations, and other organizations. For details and discount information, contact the special sales department at Jossey-Bass Inc., Publishers (415) 433–1740; Fax (800) 605–2665.

For sales outside the United States, please contact your local Simon & Schuster International Office.

Quote from *A Return to Love* by Marianne Williamson © 1992 by Marianne Williamson. Reprinted by permission of HarperCollins Publishers, Inc.

Quotes from *Memoirs* by Jean Monnet © 1978 reprinted by permission of Doubleday, a division of Bantam Doubleday Dell Publishing Group, Inc.

Margaret Mead quote from Warner, C. *The Last Word: A Treasury of Women's Quotes.* New York: Prentice Hall, 1992. Reprinted by permission.

 Manufactured in the United States of America on Lyons Falls Pathfinder Tradebook. This paper is acid-free and 100 percent totally chlorine-free.

Library of Congress Cataloging-in-Publication Data

Roberts, Nancy Charlotte.
    Transforming public policy: dynamics of policy entrepreneurship and innovation/ Nancy C. Roberts, Paula J. King.
        p. cm.— (A joint publication in the Jossey-Bass public administration and education series)
    Includes bibliographical references and index.
    ISBN 0-7879-0202-0
    1. School choice—Minnesota—Case studies. 2. Education and state—Minnesota—Case studies. 3. Educational change—Minnesota—Case studies. I. King, Paula J. II. Title. III. Series: Jossey-Bass public administration series. IV. Series: Jossey-Bass education series.
LB1027.9.R62   1996
379.1'11—dc20   95–40116

FIRST EDITION
HB Printing   10 9 8 7 6 5 4 3 2 1

A joint publication in
The Jossey-Bass Public Administration Series
and
The Jossey-Bass Education Series

Contents

To my beloved Kiwi
for his friendship and love

To Uncle Sig and Auntie Lib
for their wonderful inspiration

Preface

Change agents embarking on a project ask themselves five questions: What do we want to change? Who will initiate the change effort? Where do we want to focus our attention and energies? When should we begin? And how are we going to proceed?

Of the hundreds—or thousands—of people who ask themselves these questions on a daily basis, a few stand out. Perhaps their answers to the questions intrigue us. Certainly their successes and their spirit capture our attention and prompt us to learn as much as possible about them and their accomplishments.

This book is a guide to those who intend either to undertake or to study *large-scale system change,* that is, change involving multiple organizations and hundreds of people. Our tutors in the process will be six individuals who successfully introduced just such a change in their home state of Minnesota, in the face of fierce opposition. To recap our five questions and our tutors' answers:

- *What to change?* Public policy in education.
- *Who initiates the change effort?* People outside both the government and the educational system, with the time and freedom to think creatively and challenge the status quo.
- *Where to concentrate?* On the state legislature, where public policy in education is formulated for hundreds of local school districts.
- *When to begin?* In the 1980s, when people were trying to redesign public services for a new era of budget constraint and government downsizing.
- *How to proceed?* Radical change by design, triggering the development of a new way of providing services rather than tinkering incrementally with the old system.

At its core, this book is about radical change, also called *second-order change*. Unlike incremental, *first-order change,* which makes minor modifications to parts of a system but leaves their underlying relationship to one another intact, radical change represents a sharp discontinuity. It fundamentally alters the relationship of parts to the whole, creating an irreversible transformation based on a new set of ordering principles.

Design is deliberative, intentional, and purposive planning and action. Individuals, within limits, can diagnose how a system operates, identify the key leverage points, and develop strategies that lead to dramatic change. Although the final outcome of planning and action is shaped by a complex set of forces unleashed during the change process, we believe change agents can set in motion a transformation of the whole.

We believe radical change by design occurs through the twin processes of entrepreneurship and innovation. Entrepreneurship brings forth a new idea, attracts interest, and mobilizes resources to support it. Innovation moves the new idea through the constraints of the policy process. A new idea does not become *an innovation* until it has passed the hurdles of initiation, development, and implementation. We view the policy entrepreneurs as the energy source for the innovation process—or, as one entrepreneur described it, its midwives.

We examine radical change by design using the case study of public school choice in Minnesota. Public school choice abandons the idea of assigning students to schools in their local districts; instead, it permits (and encourages) them to attend school in any district they choose. By depriving districts of a guaranteed student population, this policy shift prompts a fundamental rethinking of basic premises in public education, and launches second-order transformational change. Chubb and Moe (1990) acknowledge its radical character when they note: "Choice is a self-contained reform with its own rationale and justification. . . . The whole point of a thoroughgoing system of choice is to free the schools from disabling constraints by sweeping away the old institutions and replacing them with new ones. Taken seriously, choice is not a system-preserving reform. It is a revolutionary reform that introduces a new system of public education" (p. 217).

Public school choice in Minnesota was an attractive example for investigation because we were able to follow, in real time, the complete cycle of the innovation process. Such studies are rare. Due to the long time periods normally involved (Polsby, 1984) and the complexity of the process, most policy studies break innovation down into its component parts: policy initiation (Polsby, 1984), agenda setting (Peters and Hogwood, 1985; Nelson, 1984; Cobb and Elder, 1983; Walker, 1977; Downs, 1972), enactment (Reid, 1980; Redman, 1973), implementation (Edwards, 1980; Williams, 1980; Bardach, 1977; Pressman and Wildavsky, 1973), and diffusion (Eyestone, 1977; Gray, 1973; Walker, 1969).

Our purpose in this book is to document how entrepreneurship and innovation interact to produce radical policy change. For change agents, we note the policy entrepreneurs' dilemmas and challenges in charting a course over a five-year period. Documenting their steps, we provide a map to others who may wish to follow their path. We believe the process of radical policy change by design can be learned. For academics, we offer a theory of radical change by design. Basing our work on chaos theory (Prigogene and Stengers, 1984), we conceptualize the policy entrepreneurs as auto-catalytic agents and the idea of public school choice as the rogue event that pushed their educational system into significant perturbations. Our policy entrepreneurs diagnosed choice as a key lever for change. Acting deliberately and intentionally, and building on previous experiments with the idea, they anticipated that cross-district choice would release a flood of other reform initiatives. Taken together, the initiatives were expected to force the educational system to shift to a new order. As with any chaotic system, they realized it was impossible to control the outcome of the process and predict exactly how education would be configured in the future. Nevertheless, they sought to influence the trajectory of change.

We came to the study with a set of questions. How does radical change occur? More specifically, how does radical change occur through the policy process? How can we identify policy entrepreneurs and describe their activities, and how can we characterize the dynamics of policy innovation? What is the relationship between policy entrepreneurship and innovation?

Our aim was to build an understanding of radical change that would be useful for both practice and research. We began with the premise that policy outcomes depend on initial conditions and the nature of the process. We selected a single case because we believed in-depth study affords the best understanding of change dynamics and the greatest opportunity to develop interpretations of value for future researchers and practitioners.

Audience

This book is about change agents and written for change agents and those who study and enhance the process of change. It is designed for those who, rather than accept the world as it is, are perpetually committed to work toward a world that could be. To those who seek paradigm changes (Kuhn, 1970), be they elected or appointed officials, citizen activists, lobbyists, or policy analysts, the book will serve as a personal and professional guide to system-level transformation.

We use public school choice as a lens to study the change process; we neither evaluate it as a policy nor examine its results in the schools. Instead, we take the opportunity to learn about innovation, entrepreneurship, and radical policy change through the legislative process.

Many books have been written about change agents and change agentry. It hardly seems possible that more remains to be said. Yet as our world challenges us with increasing complexity and interdependence, our need to understand the dynamics of change and the people who provoke it also increases. As organizational life grows more complicated, the change business grows more complicated. Once the domain of specialists who confined their work to organizations, change agents now are called to labor in open systems without benefit of clear organizational boundaries. Rather than specialize in organization development, this new generation of change agents sees its field as *system development*.

Defined as a set of parts or elements forming a whole, a system can cross group, organizational, regional, even national boundaries. Businesses, for example, can be transorganizational and transnational in character (Reich, 1992). As networks of customers, workers, suppliers, regulators, and competitors, they are open systems, very permeable to outside influences and relationships. In fact, the concept of organizational boundary has lost much of its former meaning. Where is the organizational boundary when organizations decide to outsource many of their major tasks and jobs, when businesses form joint ventures with their competitors in the same product line, when stores turn over inventory control to suppliers (as Wal-Mart did with Proctor and Gamble) to keep goods stocked on their shelves?

In such a world, there is much to be learned from system-level change agents who go well beyond traditional organizational boundaries. We find evidence of their successful intervention all over the world, from New Zealand to Eastern Europe. Many bring their expertise to bear at the level of government policy. Able to affect the system as a whole, they believe this vantage point gives them the best leverage for change. Despite their dedication to public policy, they have much to teach others who labor in private-sector organizations. It is our hope that this study of their efforts in unbounded policy systems will help illuminate a road for others to follow, both in and out of government.

Methodology

This is an exploratory field study (Kerlinger, 1973). We seek to describe what is, and thereby discover significant variables and their relationships. The purpose is to develop a grounded theory (Glaser and Strauss, 1967; Lincoln and Guba, 1985) that will lay the foundation for later, more systematic testing and analysis in the areas of radical change, design, public entrepreneurship, and policy innovation. We employ multiple data collection methods, both qualitative and quantitative, and follow the requirements for each in analyzing the data.

Field studies such as this are strong on realism and theoretical and social significance, but the theories they generate need more systematic assessment before being accepted as scientific truth. Therefore, our results should be regarded as tentative until they can be subjected to more rigorous testing and control. For those who wish to know more about our methodology, we have provided extensive details in the Appendix.

Organization

The Introduction describes the conceptual foundation and conventions that guide this study. It offers a framework for our examination of radical change, the policy innovation process, and public entrepreneurship.

Part One, which contains five chapters, presents our case study. Chapter One explores the idea of public school choice and the context from which it springs. Chapter Two follows the idea from its introduction to the legislature through its implementation. Chapter Three goes backstage to view the activities of the policy entrepreneurs who sustained the idea through all phases of the innovation process. Chapter Four opens up the team's internal operations for scrutiny, and identifies the network of organizations that supported it. Chapter Five introduces the policy entrepreneurs as individuals, helping us to understand how they came to choose their transformative path and how they bore their successes as well as their failures.

Part Two presents the lessons learned from the study. Chapter Six describes the entrepreneurial identity and the variation we find among public sector entrepreneurs. Chapter Seven introduces the concept of collective entrepreneurship and explains its advantages over individual entrepreneurship in the pursuit of radical policy change. Chapter Eight discusses the trajectory of the innovative idea and notes the importance of managing public attention, meaning, and politics in the policy innovation process. Chapter Nine completes the lessons learned and offers readers some final advice about policy innovation and entrepreneurship, and ways to build capacity in the community to support entrepreneurial activity. It also gives the policy entrepreneurs themselves a chance to speak directly to the reader, and highlight the points they regard as most valuable from what they have learned in their years of experience.

The Conclusion draws on the principles of chaos theory to offer a theory of radical change by entrepreneurial design. We believe it provides an explanation of the radical changes in Minnesota, and can be applied both to future efforts to bring about radical change by design and to future studies of such changes.

Acknowledgments

We first want to thank the six change agents who have given this book its life and form. We appreciate their cooperation and willingness to participate in this research effort. Having gained much insight from watching them work, we felt compelled to share what we had learned with others.

Our thanks also go to the many interviewees who gave so generously of their time—Governor Perpich and his staff, and administrators from the Minnesota Department of Education—especially Ruth Randall, commissioner of education; Dan Loritz, deputy commissioner of education and eventually chief lobbyist to the governor; Robert Wedl, assistant commissioner; and Jessie Montano, project director; as well as many helpful teachers and school administrators, legislators and their staff, and officers and members of various interest groups.

We have others to thank as well. Andrew Van de Ven, director of the Minnesota Innovation Research Program, got us started on this project. We were part of the multidisciplinary research team focusing on innovations as they developed in natural field settings. He was always there with research support, guidance, and boundless energy to help our project along. We benefited enormously from his efforts to bring together innovation researchers and practitioners from all over the world. The conferences, workshops, and meetings he organized created an intellectually stimulating environment that enabled us to learn from one another. We were grateful too for the initial grant from the Program on Organizational Effectiveness of the Office of Naval Research, under contract No. N00014–84–K-0016, that supported the research program in its early years from 1983 to 1985.

Our Minnesota colleagues Stuart Alpert, Harold Angle, John Bryson, Jeanne Buckeye, Lois Erickson, Edward Freeman, Dan Gilbert, Virginia Gray, Stephanie Lenway, Charles Mantz, John Mauriel, Tim Mazzoni, Van Mueller, Mary Nichols, Scott Poole, Peter Ring, and Bill Roering were always there to listen and lend support. We benefited personally and professionally from our interactions with them, and we missed them when we each pursued our separate paths, Nancy to the Naval Postgraduate School in Monterey, California, and Paula to St. Cloud State University in Minnesota.

We also are grateful to members of the public sector division of the Academy of Management and the Association of Public Policy Analysis and Management. Through conference sessions and workshops, we have received excellent feedback on early versions of our research from Robert Backoff, Michael Barzelay, John Elwood, George Frederickson, Les Garner, Arie Halachmi, Marc Holzer, Laurence Lynn, Brinton Milward, Keith Provan, Hal Rainey, and Barton Weschler.

We will be forever in debt to Mark Zegans and the two anonymous reviewers who were engaged by Jossey-Bass to review our manuscript. Their critiques were of great value in helping us shape the final version. Their suggestions have made this a much better book.

Nancy owes a special debt of gratitude to Jerry Porras and David Bradford for the excellent start in change agentry they gave her. For their encouragement and help she remains truly grateful. Special thanks also go to her mentor, Carl Jones, at the Naval Postgraduate School, and to former department chairman David Whipple, each of whom provided her with sound advice and wise counsel. She also extends her appreciation to the Research Foundation at the Naval Postgraduate School for funding her research from 1986 through 1988. Its support enabled her to continue collecting data during a critical period in the change process.

Paula extends her thanks to the Alexandria Women's Consortium, specifically Maria Anderson, Barbara Benson, Linda Capistrant, and Ann Heydt, who helped her to think globally and act locally. Her appreciation and thanks also go to Anson G. MacFarlane, who gave her the gift of time and intellectual space to work relatively free of distractions, and to Libby, who consistently brings joy and wisdom to her daily life. For their love and support she is very grateful.

Lastly, we thank Lynn Luckow, Alan Shrader, Susan Williams, Hilary Powers, and the production and marketing staffs of Jossey-Bass. We appreciate their patience and their expert guidance. Working with them has been a pleasure.

Institute for Whole Social Science   NANCY C. ROBERTS
Carmel, California

Minneapolis, Minnesota   PAULA J. KING
December 1995

The Authors

Nancy C. Roberts is a professor of strategic management at the Naval Postgraduate School in Monterey, California, where she has been on the faculty since 1986. She has a *diplôme annuel* from the Sorbonne (1966), a B.A. degree in French (1967) and an M.A. degree in South Asian and Latin American history (1968) from the University of Illinois, and a Ph.D. degree in education with a specialization in organization development and change from Stanford University (1983).

Roberts has been studying the many facets of change for over fifteen years. Her work has been published in a number of professional journals, including *Human Relations,* the *Journal of Applied Behavioral Science, Organizational Dynamics, Policy Studies Review,* and the *Journal of Public Administration, Research and Theory.* She has served as a consultant to many public and private-sector organizations and has directed change studies both as an internal and as an external consultant.

Roberts has been a visiting professor at the Stanford Graduate School of Business and at the business schools at San Jose State and Santa Clara University, and was an assistant professor of organization behavior at the University of Minnesota from 1982 to 1985. She is a member of the Academy of Management, the Association of Public Policy Analysis and Management, Sigma Xi, and the Inter-University Seminar on Armed Forces and Society.

Roberts resides with her husband Raymond Bradley in Carmel, California. They are co-directors of the Institute for Whole Social Science, an organization dedicated to the creation of a multidisciplinary science of social system dynamics.

Paula J. King recently returned to the private sector as vice president of education and human resources at Gabberts, Inc. Her major responsibilities include organization development and change. As an associate professor of strategic management at St. Cloud State University from 1990 through 1994, she was nominated for the Burlington Northern Faculty Excellence Award in recognition of her exceptional teaching.

Prior to that, King was an assistant professor at Saint John's University, Collegeville, Minnesota. Her Ph.D. degree is from the Carlson School of Management, University of Minnesota, in strategic management and organization with an emphasis in public affairs.

King's research interests focus on public entrepreneurship, large-scale system change, and the development of leadership to lead these processes. Having a strong interest in applied work, King has done extensive consulting with diverse institutions ranging from the National Football League to schools of theology. She has developed executive development training for many Fortune 100 companies and institutions of higher education. She has served on the boards of five nonprofits, two of which she founded. King has numerous publications, and she belongs to the Academy of Management, the Association of Public Policy Analysis and Management, and the World Business Academy.

King resides in Minneapolis, Minnesota, with her daughter Libby.

Transforming Public Policy

Concepts and Contexts for Radical Change

There is nothing more difficult to take in hand, more perilous to conduct, or more uncertain in its success, than to take the lead in the introduction of a new order of things.
NICCOLÒ MACCHIAVELLI, *THE PRINCE* (1532)

Four key concepts will help us analyze our subject: *change type, design,* the *innovation process,* and *public entrepreneurship.* This introduction defines these concepts and provides a framework for their application.

Types of Change

Two general types of change are described in the management, organization, and policy literatures. (See, for example, Levy, 1986; Golembiewsky, Billingsley, and Yeager, 1976.) *First-order change* describes modest adjustments to an existing system—slight variations in a system that itself remains unchanged (Watzlawick, Weakland, and Fisch, 1974). Researchers have assigned many names to the concept: branch change (Lindblom, 1959), evolutionary change (Greiner, 1972), single-loop learning (Argyris and Schön, 1978), continuous change (Meyer, Goes, and Brooks, 1993), incremental change (Tushman and Romanelli, 1985), and momentum

---

Note: The sections defining the innovation process and public entrepreneurship are drawn from Roberts (1992).

change (Miller and Friesen, 1980). All refer to incremental modification of an ongoing social system.

In contrast, *second-order change* refers to basic change in the system itself instead of a modification of one of its parts (Watzlawick, Weakland, and Fisch, 1974). Second-order change is characterized by a discontinuity and a jump from an initial system to a new one, and thus represents a qualitative rather than a quantitative shift in the way things are done. Again, it has many names: root change (Lindblom, 1959), radical change (Tushman and Romanelli, 1985), revolutionary change (Gerlach and Hines, 1973), transformation (Hernes, 1976), double-loop learning (Argyris and Schön, 1978), and paradigm change (Sheldon, 1980).

Embedded in every innovation, implicit in every new idea, is the concept of change. It is probably best to think of first- and second-order change as anchoring two ends of a continuum, with incremental change on one end and radical change on the other, and degrees of incrementalism moving into degrees of radicalness. Somewhere on the continuum, we can locate any innovative idea based on the type of change it implies (Kanter, 1988; Nord and Tucker, 1987).

The dominant models of policy making have been useful in helping us understand first-order change in public policy (Lynn, 1987). Rather than focusing on major shifts, the primary research interest has been in explaining the continuity of public policy and the relatively small adjustments made to the status quo (Lindblom, 1959; Cobb and Elder, 1983; Ripley and Franklin, 1991). This emphasis is not surprising. As Kaufman reminds us, "The logic of collective life has a conservative thrust; it lends authority to the system as it stands" (1971, p. 10).

Yet transformations, second-order changes, do occur in public policy. British and Swedish welfare policy was fundamentally altered during the first several decades of this century (Heclo, 1974). During the mid 1970s in the United States, there were major policy shifts concerning clean air (Jones, 1975), tobacco (Fritschler, 1989), deregulation (Derthick and Quirk, 1985), pesticides (Bosso, 1987), and nuclear power (Campbell, 1988).

Taking a historical perspective, Baumgartner and Jones (1991) note that policy often shows long periods of stability punctuated by short periods of dramatic change. They believe that the "grand lines of policy" are set, sometimes for decades, in these critical periods of disequilibrium when radically new policy values and assumptions challenge and displace old ones.

How do these transformative shifts occur? What breaks the stability of the old policy order and permits a qualitatively different policy to take its place? These are the central questions of this research. We offer the theory of radical change by entrepreneurial design as one possible answer.

Design

As a concept, *design* entails deliberate, purposive planning. When someone sets out to alter government policies to meet specific objectives—and succeeds—it shows that intentions can play a central part in radical change. We do not disagree that deliberate action is bounded, constrained, and limited by many factors in the change process. But we argue that it is possible for individuals to make a difference, if they apply their energies to the proper point in the chaotic system around them.

Typically the domain of policy analysts (Bobrow and Dryzek, 1987), design is concerned with drawing causal links between a problem and its solutions so as to shape a policy outcome. Its basic assumption is that designers can anticipate how bureaucracies and other groups will react, and can find the levers to pull to produce desired effects (Schneider and Ingram, 1990; Weimer, 1995). The levers are tools of government action adapted to various policy purposes: direct service delivery, project grants, formula grants, loans, loan guarantees, interest subsidies, social regulation, contracting out, tax expenditures, vouchers, government corporations, franchises, price supports, entry restrictions, and many more (Salamon, 1989).

In our view, policy entrepreneurs engage in the same planning function as others in the policy design process (Ingraham, 1987). They determine the nature of a problem and its causes, the range of possible solutions, and the strategy most likely to achieve a desired outcome given the available resources. The Minnesota experiment with public school choice illustrates how social actors can consciously mold public policy by intervening in the policy system.

Many aspects of the Minnesota policy entrepreneurs' change strategies were comparable to other reports of those who seek policy change by design:

- They employed rhetoric, symbols, and analysis to frame the policy problem in a way that promoted their views and their preferred solution (Baumgartner and Jones, 1991; Riker, 1986; Stone, 1980).
- They studied the policy process and the way bureaucracies, courts, legislatures, and interest groups functioned, so they could introduce and promote their ideas smoothly and counter the resistance that was likely to occur (Schneider and Ingram, 1990).
- They sought out the most favorable venues for their ideas to give them the most leverage for change (Baumgartner and Jones, 1991; Schneider and Ingram, 1990).
- They developed and chose particular strategies that would assist them in building support for their innovative ideas, including changes in institutional rules and norms to further their cause (Baumgartner and Jones, 1991).
- They tried, whenever possible, to avoid opposition. But when that was not possible, they developed strategies and tactics to overcome resistance, including active participation by the media (Gifford, Horan, and White, 1992).
- They built coalitions, drawing support from elites who were effective in persuading other interests to participate (Baumgartner and Jones, 1991).
- They selected tools designed to induce policy-relevant behavior (Salamon, 1989).

In addition, we will also reveal a number of other lessons learned from their approach to designed change:

- They covered the entire process, from creative and intellectual work through strategic planning to mobilization, execution, administration, and evaluation.
- They built an entrepreneurial team to coordinate their activities and those of a growing constellation of supporters.
- They developed an ecology of organizational support to sustain their entrepreneurial ventures over time.
- They mobilized grassroots support—not just elites—in the pursuit of their goals.
- They chose collective over individual entrepreneurship, to distribute their burdens and responsibilities.

- They shared an entrepreneurial identity that sustained them through the frustrations and difficulties of their effort.
- They learned how to manage attention, meaning, and politics by developing a set of heuristics—rules of thumb—for action.

Design is not the only explanation for radical change in the literature; we found three competing theories that attempt to cover it. In contrast to the design perspective, which treats political actors as capable of deliberately framing radically new public policies, these alternatives view radical change as occurring by chance (Kingdon, 1984), by learning (Sabatier and Jenkins-Smith, 1993), or by consensus (Coyle and Wildavsky, 1987). We paid careful attention to these theories in our analysis, and will revisit them in the Conclusion, after presenting the case study and the lessons learned from it, to see which theory or theories have greater explanatory power in describing the events in Minnesota.

Innovation Process

Policy change in government, radical or incremental, is treated as policy innovation (Polsby, 1984). The *innovation process* begins with an innovative idea: a new technology, a new service, a new product, or even a new administrative process or procedure (Daft and Becker, 1978). The central element of an *innovative idea* is its departure from existing practice: it supplants standard operating procedures. In economic terms, it combines factors in a new way or it carries out new combinations of things (Schumpeter, 1939, p. 88).

New ideas can be described as representing various *levels of innovation,* a phrase referring to their source (Peltz and Munson, 1982). No matter whether we invent brand new ideas ourselves *(level: origination),* retool ideas that originate with others for use in our own situation *(level: adaptation),* or even use ideas directly from others *(level: borrowing),* we are innovating when we introduce the ideas to our context for the first time. What determines whether an idea is innovative is not the source, but the current context and the perception of people in that context. Asking whether something is a new idea in a context is different from asking the source of that idea. While both are important, it is the former that becomes the defining characteristic of an innovative idea. Thus, a *new idea* is defined as "any idea, practice, or material artifact perceived to be new by the relevant unit of adoption" (Zaltman, Duncan, and Holbek, 1973, p. 10).

Having a new idea, whatever its source and degree of radicalness, is our first step in the innovation journey. Our next step is to fashion the idea into something more concrete and tangible. If it is a product, what does the product look like? Do we have a model or prototype to examine? If it is a service, what are the details? That is, who gets the service, how is it delivered, when and with what costs? Any innovative idea has to be given some kind of form and shape before it can begin to influence people. Some ideas come with specific plans, instructions, and cost estimates, while others are only vaguely outlined, the details to be filled in later.

Suppose our innovative idea has survived to this point and we have fleshed it out on paper or have a working model to show. And most importantly, we have built enough support to begin testing. We are ready to take our idea into the field to evaluate its promise. Questions left over from our early sketches and designs will be addressed, and features of the idea will be modified and revamped as necessary. We will do what it takes to put idea into practice. If, after some tinkering, testing, and evaluation, we find that the idea works or is acceptable, the innovation journey is complete.

There is some consolation for those whose innovative ideas are discarded before the end of the journey. Despite our heroic efforts, we know that not all ideas can work in the real world. Some are not economically viable or politically feasible. Many have unanticipated problems or unintended consequences that prevent full-scale use. Others suffer from poor timing and get forced off center stage by competing innovative ideas. And most seriously, an idea can provoke so much resistance and threaten the status quo that it is dismissed before it is given a chance. Just because we have developed an innovative idea into a form we can pass on to others, we cannot expect everyone to appreciate or support it. New ideas are not automatically accepted into practice. It is important to remember that there are risks on the innovation journey and that it can end well short of full implementation.

Phases of the Innovation Process

A way to characterize this innovation process is to group its activities into a set of logically related categories. Like others, we conceive the innovation process as having stages or phases (Angle and Van de Ven, 1989; Gross, Giaquinta, and Berstein, 1971; King, 1990; Lambright and Teich, 1979; Peltz, 1985; Peltz and Munson, 1982; Pressman and Wildavsky, 1973; Rogers, 1983; Scioli, 1986; Tornatzky and others, 1983; Zaltman, Duncan, and Holbek, 1973). Although there are many ways of viewing the process, we have settled on four phases we believe capture its essence no matter what the innovation: creation, design, implementation, and institutionalization.

Creation marks the emergence and development of an innovative idea and the association of the idea with some need, problem, or concern. The linkage between innovative idea and problem or need produces a candidate solution that then competes with other candidate solutions in the marketplace of ideas. In the public arena, one usually can find many innovative ideas that lay claim to meeting some need or solving some problem.

Polsby (1984) describes this phase as *policy initiation*—"the politics of inventing, winnowing, and finding and gaining adherents for policy alternatives before they are made part of a 'program,' and likewise the politics of moving alternatives from the unlikely to possible to probable candidates for inclusion on an agenda for enactment" (p. 3). Because we wish to emphasize the creative aspects of defining a problem and putting forth solutions, we prefer the term creation. We consider the terms to be equivalent, however, and will use them interchangeably throughout the book.

Design translates our innovative idea into a concrete form so that those in authority have something tangible to review. Perhaps we present a position paper and circulate a description of our idea to potential advocates suggesting how it can meet a need or solve a problem. Perhaps we actually develop a prototype or model so we can examine it and experiment with it. However the new idea is presented, we must first win the support of the power holders who control the critical resources the idea needs for implementation. There are always gatekeepers, and progress is very difficult when they ignore or oppose an innovative idea.

Implementation brings the innovative idea into actual practice. Feedback from the implementation process answers several crucial questions: Does the idea work as anticipated? Does it have to be modified to fit organizational conditions—and if so, how? Do those who use the idea support it or want to block it? Does the idea meet the need or solve the problem as promised? Is it worth the expenditure of time and resources? Is it better than what we have already? As these questions suggest, we view testing as part of the implementation process.

Institutionalization, also referred to as incorporation, routinization, or diffusion (Yin, 1979; Lambright, 1980; Zaltman, Duncan, and Holbek, 1973; Tornatzky and others, 1983), marks the coming of age of the idea. Having passed the hurdle of implementation and survived testing and evaluation, it moves into the realm of accepted practice. No longer questioned in terms of its viability, the once-innovative idea is incorporated into the routines of normal operations. The debate over its viability and survivability have been settled, and the idea is no longer viewed as something new.

Figure I.1 represents the process graphically. There are partitions for each temporal phase: creation, design, implementation, and institutionalization. As the figure illustrates, each phase of the innovative process has a different by-product. The *innovative idea as solution* evolves from the creative phase. The *prototype* develops from the design phase. *Innovation* itself emerges from the implementation phase. *Accepted practice* derives from institutionalization.

Conceptualizing the innovation process in these terms has some advantages. It makes it clear that an innovation is more than a new idea. It is a new idea that has been turned into a prototype, taken into the field for experimentation and evaluation, tested and successfully implemented, and accepted into common practice. Innovation, therefore, is not just a process from creation through implementation; it is also a by-product that emerges from that process (Kimberly, 1981).

Assessing the Process

Viewing innovation as the outcome of this series of phases does not assume that an innovation is always something good. Since an innovation emerges from a difficult process, the assumption is that it has addressed some problem or met some need, at least to the satisfaction of those using it. New ideas that are not viable are considered *mistakes* (Van de Ven and Angle, 1989, p. 13), or failures that did not hold up under scrutiny. No judgment about the inherent goodness of an innovative idea is implied. The only judgments

Figure I.1. Phases and By-Products of the Innovation Process.

Creation	Design	Implementation	Institutionalization
↓	↓	↓	↓
New Idea	Prototype	Innovation	Accepted Practice

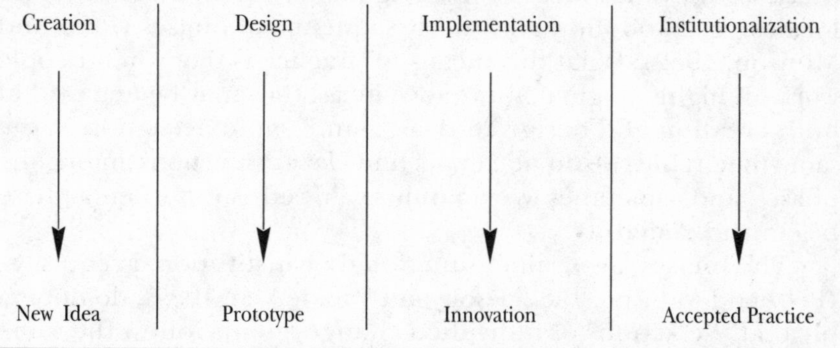

Source: Roberts, N. C. "Public Entrepreneurship and Innovation." *Policy Studies Review,* Spring 1992, 11(*1*), p. 58.

made are those concerning the new idea's survivability over time. Taking this perspective thus enables us to interpret innovation as an act of creative destruction (Abernathy and Clark, 1985; Schumpeter, 1934). In introducing something new, we often displace or destroy what is in its place. Depending on our perspective, this may be a benefit or a disaster.

Another important point to remember is that the innovation process follows a fixed sequence—creation always preceding design and so on. The four phases represent constraints of the process; unless an idea survives the hurdles they represent, it will not become a full-blown innovation. Working within these constraints helps us to conceptualize the innovation process in *global terms*. We understand what a fully developed innovation looks like and how we must move through the phases to achieve it.

Although we group the temporal order into four phases, we should not assume that the phases represent or require an equal amount of time. Creation and design may take a long time, perhaps decades, while implementation may be relatively short. Peltz and Munson (1982) found that the duration of each phase varies depending on the originality of the innovation. The more original the new idea, the more time it requires in all phases.

Change agents also should be advised that an idea's trajectory through the innovation process often does not flow neatly from one phase into the next. We know, for example, that the more novel an innovative idea, the more overlap there tends to be among the phases. Innovative ideas of low originality, borrowed from other locales, tend to follow an orderly sequence of phases (Peltz and Munsons, 1982). What this means in practice is that when people work on highly original, innovative ideas, they may be engaged in both creation and design or design and implementation at the same time. Thus, we do not always find clear distinctions among the phases, and sometimes we can only say in retrospect when a phase began and ended.

The phases, also called functional or institutional requisites (Peltz and Munson, 1982; Poole and Van de Ven, 1989), do not imply that the actions of individual change agents follow the same sequential logic. To assume that a change agent or innovator would be expected to go through a predefined set of activities, such as creation, design, and implementation, and in that order, confuses the phases of the innovation process at the global level with the innovator's decisions and actions at the individual level. These are two very different issues.

The phases or requisites of the innovation process describe innovation in global terms, stating the necessary conditions for innovation to occur. If a new idea is not created, designed, and implemented, it will not be able to attain the developed status we attribute to innovation. On the other hand, change agents can go through a much messier process that follows no predetermined set of activities (Lambright and Teich, 1979; Van de Ven and Angle, 1989). As Kingdon reminds us, "events do not proceed neatly in stages, steps, or phases. . . . Participants do not first identify problems and then seek solutions for them; indeed, advocacy of solutions often precedes the highlighting of problems to which they become attached" (Kingdon, 1984, p. 215). In fact, some would advocate this messiness, by encouraging change agents to work implementation issues while they are creating and designing new policy (Pressman and Wildavsky, 1973).

Public Entrepreneurs

We refer to innovators who promote new public policy as *public entre-preneurs*—individuals who introduce, translate, and implement an innovative idea into public practice. Characterized as tenacious and persistent, they are willing to work long hours to reach their goals, try new ideas even when it means taking risks, and be unconventional (Kingdon, 1984; Lewis, 1980). They are described as highly creative, self-confident, hardworking, charismatic, decisive, energetic, and dedicated to translating their ideas into reality (Ramamurti, 1986b). They have a claim to a hearing (Kingdon, 1984) and they have valuable political connections (Kingdon, 1984; Lewis, 1980). They have a "capacity to engage in systematic rational analysis, an ability to see new possibilities offered by the evolving historical situation, and a desire to 'make a difference'—to throw . . . energies and personal reputation into the fray in order to bring about changes" (Doig and Hargrove, 1987, p. 11).

Public entrepreneurs are sometimes difficult to identify with complete confidence. We know in general terms that individuals who carry out innovations are entrepreneurs and that the function of the entrepreneur is innovation (Schumpeter, 1939). But as Schumpeter notes, "It is not always easy to tell who the entrepreneur is in a given case." It is not due to our lack of understanding of the entrepreneurial function, "but simply the difficulty of finding out what person actually fills it. Nobody ever is an entrepreneur all the time, and nobody can ever be only an entrepreneur" (p. 103).

We have developed the logical tree in Figure I.2 to help us distinguish public entrepreneurs from other participants in the policy innovation process. We begin with the question in the lower left corner. Does the individual develop or initiate a new idea in the context and is the new idea linked to a problem or need? If we answer yes, we go on to the next question. Does the individual design and translate the innovative idea into some prototype or proposal? If yes, we ask whether the individual's idea has been implemented into practice and whether the implementation has survived evaluation and testing? If we answer yes to all of these questions, we identify the individual as a public entrepreneur.

Answering no to any of these questions distinguishes others engaged in the policy process from public entrepreneurs. For example, at the bottom of the tree, those who do not invent or develop new ideas are identified as *system maintainers*. Their function is to keep systems working in their present form.

Those who generate innovative ideas but do not engage in design work are called *policy intellectuals*. They are the source and stimulus of

Figure I.2. Logic Tree.

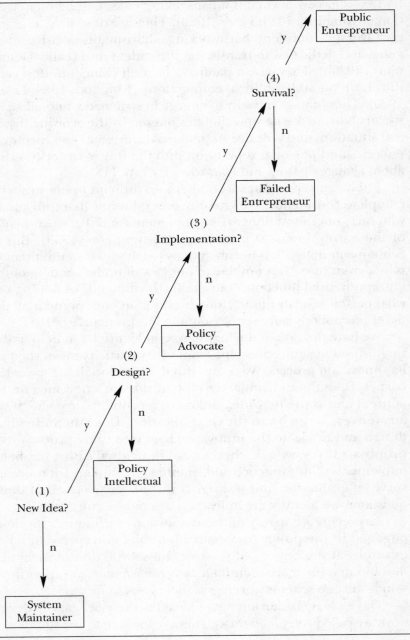

new ideas, although they do not engage in the translation of ideas into more formal proposals, statements, or prototypes. Idea advocates rather than proposal advocates, according to Wilson (1981), they are not the authors of particular policies. Instead, they provide the "conceptual language, the ruling paradigms, the empirical examples . . . that become the accepted assumptions for those in charge of making policy." They frame and to a large degree conduct "the debates about whether this language and these paradigms [are] correct" (p. 33). Their orientation is thought and analysis, not action.

Policy advocates are individuals who not only contribute to invention or develop innovation ideas, but extend their work into the design phase. Their function is to mold an idea into a proposal, and to press for its acceptance. They are more action oriented than policy intellectuals; their ultimate goal is to initiate new public policy rather than to theorize about it. However, as advocates of proposals and bills they hope to get fashioned into administrative procedures or legislation, their work stops at the design phase. They do not implement policy; they are its proponents. This conceptual distinction helps us separate public entrepreneurs who engage in all three active phases of the innovation process from the policy advocates who are involved only in the creation and design phases.

The final branch category in Figure I.2 is that of *failed entrepreneur.* Having an innovative idea and translating the idea into a proposal or bill are two of the necessary steps to public entrepreneurship. The trials and challenges of implementation pose the final test. We call those who succeed public entrepreneurs; those who do not we call failed entrepreneurs. And we note in making this distinction, as mentioned earlier, that no judgment or evaluation of the goodness of the idea or its prototype, nor the person proposing it, is implied here. A failed public entrepreneur is someone whose innovative idea, for whatever reason, did not survive the implementation process. This designation is not considered permanent because a person could be a failed entrepreneur for one idea and a successful entrepreneur for another.

Other Participants

There are other actors in the innovation process whom we need to identify. Some individuals are involved in the design and implementation phases, but not in the creation phase. Others focus their work only on implementation. Figure I.3 gives us a more complete way to categorize participation in the process.

Policy champions are those involved in both the design and implementation phases of the innovation process. In this case of policy innovation, they are a governor, key administrators, and legislators who participate in the various design steps to initiate a proposal, set the agenda, or carry the bill through enactment. While they may not directly administer the new programs, processes, or procedures specified in the law, they monitor the progress during implementation, sponsor hearings when appropriate, and attempt to assess the workability of the program as it is being implemented.

Policy champions have their counterparts in business (Peters and Waterman, 1982; Pinchot, 1985). According to Angle and Van de Ven (1989), a champion typically is an individual who "commands the power and resources to push an innovative idea into

Figure I.3. Participants in the Policy Innovation Process.

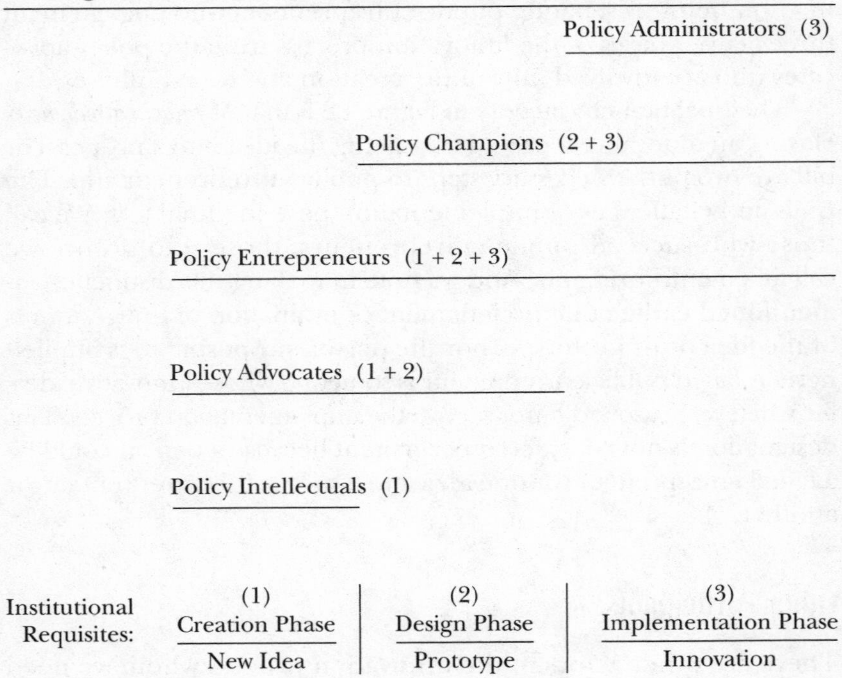

Policy Administrators (3)

Policy Champions (2 + 3)

Policy Entrepreneurs (1 + 2 + 3)

Policy Advocates (1 + 2)

Policy Intellectuals (1)

Institutional Requisites:	(1) Creation Phase	(2) Design Phase	(3) Implementation Phase
	New Idea	Prototype	Innovation

Source: Roberts, N. C., p. 62.

good currency." He is a person who "'carries the ball' as an advocate for the innovation" (p. 680) when resources are allocated. The same can be said of policy champions in the public sector.

Policy administrators complete our set of policy actors involved in the innovation process. Their involvement is limited to the implementation of the law. They take the sometimes very general statements of purpose and intent in the law and specify procedures to make the law come to life. They are a critical link in the innovation chain. As Pressman and Wildavsky (1973) have demonstrated, innovative ideas often fail because they are unable to bridge the gap between promise and performance. Linking ideas and execution, word and deed, policy administrators combine the necessary conditions of successful innovation by joining the formulation of innovative ideas with their execution.

Typology of Public Entrepreneurs

It is important to make one final distinction about public entrepreneurs. We have found descriptions of all sorts of entrepreneurs in the literature. Researchers identify policy, program, political, bureaucratic, administrative, issue, executive, and paper entrepreneurs, but there is little consensus on the meaning of these terms. We developed Figure I.4 to help us describe the six public entrepreneurs in this study and compare them to other public sector change agents.

The questions in Figure I.4 allow us to recognize four mutually exclusive types of public entrepreneur: *policy entrepreneurs,* who do their work without holding formal positions in government; *bureaucratic entrepreneurs,* who work in government in nonleadership positions; *executive entrepreneurs,* who hold appointive government leadership positions; and *political entrepreneurs,* who hold elective office. (See Roberts, 1992, for an in-depth discussion of the types of public entrepreneurs.) For simplicity, we have excluded consideration of what we refer to as *crossovers*—public entrepreneurs who come from one sector of government to work for innovation in another. For example, a government employee could work for innovation by legislative design rather than pursuing innovation by management design on the job. Similarly, a legislator could work with interest groups to press for innovation by judicial design or bureau design.

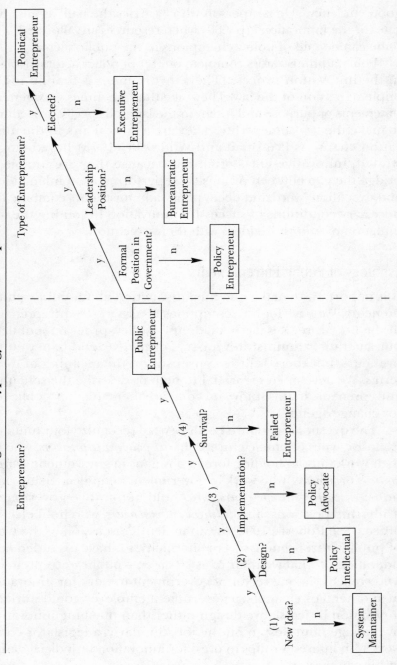

Figure I.4 Typology of Public Entrepreneurs.

Source: Roberts, N. C., p. 63.

The typology of entrepreneurs provides several advantages. First, it helps us track the movements of public entrepreneurs as their roles change over time. We can document their histories, evolutionary paths, and learning experiences more clearly if we anchor them to categories in the innovative system.

In addition, we can expect an association between an entrepreneur's behavior and base of power. Knowing that power is contingent on resources (Pfeffer and Salancik, 1978), and that position in a system is one element in the calculus of resources (Pfeffer 1981), we postulate that entrepreneurs' resources and position will influence their strategies, tactics, and modes of operation. Decisions are always deeply affected by the position and relative power of those who make them. It is possible that in linking a public entrepreneur to a position in the policy system, we might better understand how the sponsor's resources and position help the innovative idea survive over time.

Based on our typology, we identify all the individuals in our study as policy entrepreneurs. The group included the executive director of a public affairs think tank, the head of a business lobbying and policy development group, the president of a nonprofit organization, a professor in a public policy school who was also an elected public official, a policy analyst and former think tank executive director, and an author who also worked as an educator and consultant. Five of the six came from positions outside government. The sixth was, during this study, both a political entrepreneur and a policy entrepreneur. As a legislator, he held a formal position in government, but as a faculty member, he also held a position outside government. However, he considered himself an outsider, a person who owed his allegiance to ideas rather than a constituency. He was unwilling to engage in what he called "political horsetrading," as his own values and principles were more important to him. Despite his position as a legislator, he saw himself (as did others) as a philosopher who willingly challenged conventional wisdom and operated at the periphery of the legislative system rather than at its core. This shared perception of him led us to see him more as a policy entrepreneur than a political entrepreneur, and he agreed with this assessment.

We chose not to identify these individuals by name to protect their confidences. The promise of confidentiality was especially important in this case due to the controversy and debates surrounding the concept of choice. We also collected sensitive psychometric data, as reported in Chapter Six. The participants requested anonymity and we honor that request. Although we recognize that it is standard procedure in policy studies to name the individuals involved, we made this trade-off so as to be able to collect sensitive information about the individuals, especially their plans, strategies, and tactics, while following the innovative idea in real time.

Part One

Change Agents in Action

A Case Study in Educational Reform

Chapter One

The Innovative Idea and Its Context

*We seem to be going through, in public life, the kind of
"revolution" described in 1962 by Thomas Kuhn after
his study of the major shifts in scientific thinking:
A prevailing view is confronted with facts which it cannot
handle; these produce a crisis for the existing theory; so
new ideas are put forward; conflict occurs between the
old view and the new; finally the conflict is resolved, not
because one group persuades the other but as people adjust
their sense of what problems it is important to have solved.*
—A POLICY ENTREPRENEUR

Innovation begins with a new idea. For the Minnesotans in our
study, the new idea was cross-district public school choice or open
enrollment. The aim was to give parents and students the option of
finding a school district that met their needs better than the one
where they lived. Rather than determining school attendance based
on real estate, attendance would be based on student requirements.
"Kids are different," said one proponent. "Not every child learns
best in a traditional atmosphere . . . our schools must be different
because the learning needs of students vary."

Student movement from school district to school district was
expected to create a market for educational services. Parents would
be able to shop around until they found a district that suited their
children. Seeking to retain students, districts would begin to compete with each other. Compelled by market forces, each district

would be prompted to introduce innovative, high-quality, individualized programs to keep its students. Thus, school districts would have an incentive to change.

Districts and schools that responded to consumer demand would flourish by drawing students to their programs and classes. Less effective educators, administrators, and schools would be compelled to improve or risk loss of state foundation aid, decline in student enrollment, and potential state receivership. Incentives, both positive and negative, would serve as market regulators. Consumer sovereignty and expanding opportunities for educators would provide a self-correcting lever to introduce innovations, improve performance, and ensure accountability.

Implicit in the idea of public school choice was the belief that the responsibility for teaching and learning rests with parents, students, the community, teachers, local schools and districts, and the state—in that order. Rather than having the state assume more and more of the burden to regulate and mandate school activity, proponents believed that the state should eliminate most controls, decentralize authority to those most closely involved in the learning process, and rely on market forces to correct deficiencies in the system.

The existing system gave schools little incentive to change. Innovative programs and improvements relied on the good will and high energy of dedicated individuals. Few rewards existed to diffuse innovative ideas beyond the confines of their inventors' classrooms. And equally serious, problems and abuses evoked few sanctions. What happened when schools decided they could not afford to offer special programs or advanced training? And what happened when districts continued to employ teachers and administrators who were ineffective in helping students learn? Very little, argued the proponents of open enrollment.

Policy entrepreneurs believed an important part of the answer to these questions was to eliminate most state mandates while increasing the state role in two major areas—the requirement of statewide achievement tests for all students and the assignment of state financial aid to the child and not to the district where the child lived. The purpose of such action was the public comparison of all schools to reveal how well they fulfilled their charge. Not only would the state be able to take corrective action in districts that performed poorly, but parents could make informed choices about which public school districts were more appropriate for their children. Choice gave parents the clout because state dollars allocated to each child would follow the child wherever he or she went. If parents believed a school and its teachers were not meeting their child's needs, they had the right to find another school beyond district boundaries.

Rationales for Public School Choice

Policy entrepreneurs offered four different rationales in support of public school choice. The first, *public service redesign,* affirmed the need to change the way the public sector was organized. Rather than continue the traditional formulation of government services, advocates called for a distinction between government as a provider of services and government as a producer of services. Government-as-provider entails deciding what should be done collectively, for whom, at what level of government, and with what method of financing. By contrast, government-as-producer entails the establishment of ongoing operations to offer specific services. Proponents argued that the public sector needed to separate the two functions and put more emphasis on the first—government as a skillful buyer, leveraging producers to serve its policy objectives. This would create a competitive situation in which a policy body charged with providing services could call on two or more suppliers—public, private, or a combination of the two. The responsibility for selection of supplier would rest with the eligible users of the service in question through "a free choice of vendor (or voucher) arrangement." To make this system work, users would have to be able to evaluate supplier quality and to be free to choose among the competing suppliers.

Applying this logic to the educational system, advocates of redesign saw public school choice as the driver of change. Giving parents the freedom to select a school district would establish them as buyers in search of suppliers to meet their children's educational needs. Competition for students and student dollars would give schools incentives to offer quality education to all students, forcing a shake-up in the educational establishment. To make this work, however, unnecessary state mandates would have to be eliminated and decision making decentralized to the districts and schools. Without deregulation and decentralization, schools would have little leeway or incentive to experiment and innovate. And innovation was essential to ensure that the best educational services would be delivered to all who needed them.

The second rationale, *expanding opportunities,* held that public school choice was a right parents should have in a democracy. In fact, the freedom to choose a school district was likened to voting— all should be accorded the opportunity, not just those who could afford it. Advocates of this rationale cited authorities such as Raywid (1984), who argued that school choice would empower those who participated. Families would become agents rather than pawns of the system, opening up new options and possibilities for them.

Benefits of parent-student choice were many, according to the proponents of expanding opportunities. Parents who selected a school would feel better about the school system. Students would improve their attitudes and thus achieve more in school. Principals and teachers would feel better about their work when they were able to create different kinds of programs for the families they served. And lastly, high-quality programs of choice among public schools would result in more integration, with more mixing of kids from different racial and economic backgrounds. Thus, public school choice became a vehicle to achieve three ends: equality of opportunity for all learners; individualized options to meet students' unique needs, styles, and preferences; and empowerment of parents in the education of their children.

The *community perspective* offered a third rationale for public school choice. Central to this view was the belief that public school choice would return a much-needed sense of control and belonging to the schools and districts. Said one proponent, "government, as currently organized, is important but cumbersome and ineffective. It has major responsibilities but should carry out much of its work through institutions close to home, through communities." The sense of community was expected to restore "an inspiring conviction on the part of students, teachers and parents that they are cherished and efficacious, that they belong and have a say over events at their school," he asserted.

Advocates pointed to school research to support their arguments. (See, for example, Bickel, 1983, and Coleman, 1981.) Effective schools, they noted, shared five attributes: strong leadership, orderly environment, effective basic skills instruction, high standards, and *sense of community*. They also cited management theorists such as Barnard (1938), who held that the need for communion (feelings of belonging and connection) was the basis of informal organization and essential to the operation of every formal organization. Establishing a sense of community was as important for schools as it was for any organization.

Promoting a sense of community ultimately led advocates to demand that lawmakers stop fostering bureaucracy and instead fashion laws supporting "family, community, clan, and polity." Proponents maintained that reform and excellence in education would not come from greater public expenditure, but instead would be rooted in a new design that replaced bureaucracy with community as the organizing principle for public institutions.

The fourth rationale for public school choice centered on the theme of *accountability*. The educational system suffered from "flawed accountability," according to proponents of choice. They cited the way districts measured teacher performance by degrees acquired and number of courses and training sessions completed, and measured student performance by the amount of time students sat in class. Although some standardized performance tests that did attempt to assess what students learned in school had been introduced recently, most measures of performance tracked inputs and resources rather than results. There was little information about the effectiveness and efficiency of student learning, so it was reasonable to raise questions about the effectiveness and efficiency of the schools. Advocates of accountability recognized that the schools were working with an increasingly complex mission and student population and with a steadily tightening budget, but argued that it was essential for the public to know if public funds were being allocated appropriately.

Proponents of accountability were willing to believe that all was well with education as long as the few indicators of student performance (Scholastic Achievement Test, American College Test) maintained consistent levels. But when national scores began to decline, and when businesses, colleges, and the military began complaining that public school graduates lacked the habits, skills, and knowledge necessary to be contributing members of society, some began to insist on greater accountability for the schools. As one advocate said, we "are going to have to move to a system that relies much more firmly on paying a price for failing to do something different. In other words, there's got to be a price paid for failure."

Accountability advocates called for a measurement of learner outcomes rather than an assessment of inputs to the educational process. It became more important to know what the students had learned than to count the per-pupil expenditures or calculate the student-teacher ratio. If students could demonstrate learning on statewide tests, and particularly if they could show progress over time, the public would have greater assurance of a school's effective performance and fiscal accountability. These changes, combined with decentralized school decision making, control at the local school site, and the relaxation and streamlining of state mandates, would give communities a way to make informed judgments about their educational system. Poor test scores would alert the community and the state that something was amiss in their classrooms or in the community and that changes were needed. If a school refused to make the necessary adjustments to facilitate student learning, comparative test data on student performance in other schools would prompt parents to make alternative arrangements for their children.

Tracking learner outcomes was the most important but by no means the only tool to rationalize education. Critics believed that educators should develop mission statements, establish objectives, and decide on strategies and tactics, as well as use performance data from student tests to drive educational reform. In essence, educators were expected to develop strategic planning models for their districts similar to the models used in business and industry. With a watchful eye on student performance and a strategic planning process to correct deficiencies as they surfaced, proponents of reform argued that educational change at the district level would be possible.

Contextual Forces

Every new idea springs to life molded and shaped by its context. To fully understand an innovative idea, then, we must appreciate the forces that generate it and sustain it over time. We found three factors that seem to have prompted the appearance of public school choice and nurtured its development: a crisis in educational performance, a worsening national and state economy, and a search for a new concept of governance.

Education Crisis

Hints of a decline in educational performance began appearing in the early 1970s. Building over the next decade, distress over education reached a crescendo in April 1983 with the publication of *A Nation at Risk,* a report issued by the National Commission on Excellence in Education. The commission, appointed by the secretary of education, warned that U.S. education was threatened by a "rising tide of mediocrity." Statistics from the report sent shock waves across the country:

- By the simplest test of everyday reading, writing, and comprehension, some twenty-three million adult citizens were functionally illiterate.
- Scores on the College Board Scholastic Aptitude Tests declined from 1963 to 1980, with average verbal scores falling over fifty points and average mathematics scores dropping nearly forty points.
- Average achievement of high school students was lower on most standardized tests than it had been when Sputnik was launched twenty-six years before.
- Many seventeen-year-olds did not possess the higher-order intellectual skills expected of them. Nearly 40 percent could not draw inferences from written materials; 80 percent were unable to write a persuasive essay; and 66 percent could not solve a mathematics problem requiring several steps.
- Between 1975 and 1980, remedial mathematics courses in public four-year colleges increased by 72 percent. They constituted one-quarter of all mathematics courses taught in those institutions.
- Business and military leaders spent millions of dollars on costly remedial education and training programs in basic skills such as reading, writing, spelling, and computation.

Intentionally confrontational, the report tapped a nagging fear that the United States was slipping hopelessly behind other industrialized nations and losing its ability to compete in yet another area—education. With stark and provocative language, the report included a call to arms: "If an unfriendly foreign power had attempted to impose on America the mediocre educational performance that exists today, we might well have viewed it as an act of war. As it stands, we have allowed this to happen to ourselves. . . . We have, in effect, been committing an act of unthinking, unilateral educational disarmament" (National Commission on Excellence in Education, 1983, p. 5).

Performance declines at the national level were evident even in states like Minnesota, which had enjoyed a reputation for excellent schools (Citizens League, 1982). Scores on national tests, such as Preliminary Scholastic Aptitude Test (PSAT) and the American College Test (ACT), were declining faster than the national average. Minnesota colleges had to provide substantial remediation in mathematics. High school seniors who planned to specialize in education had lower mean verbal SAT scores than all but three of twenty-seven other occupations, and lower mean math SAT scores than all but two other occupations. The proportion of respondents rating public school performance as good or excellent dropped from 63 percent in 1974 to 36 percent in 1979 (Citizens League, 1982, p. i). And both employers' complaints about the skills of their new employees and students' complaints about the emptiness of their high school experience added to the chorus of concern (Minnesota Business Partnership, 1984).

These and similar statistics from around the country on the dismal state of educational performance touched off what Ernest Boyer, former U.S. commissioner of education and president of the Carnegie Foundation for the Advancement of Teaching, described as the "most serious and sustained [educational reform] movement we have had in this country, certainly this century and maybe longer" (Vobejda, 1988). In the months and years that followed, reports on the status of education blanketed the country. Coming from commissions, task forces, and committees set up by virtually every interested party, a search was on to explain and solve the performance declines. By 1985, over 350 separate reports were issued (Gross and Gross, 1985, p. 17). Scholars added their voices of concern in highly publicized books on the status of the schools. Examples include *A Place Called School* (Goodlad, 1984), *High School* (Boyer, 1985), and *Horace's Compromise* (Sizer, 1984). This flurry of activity came to be known as "The Great School Debate" on the status of U.S. education (Gross and Gross, 1985). Why had these declines occurred and what was the nation going to do about them? The public wanted answers.

Public school choice offered one answer. It promised to challenge an educational bureaucracy grown complacent and unresponsive. By virtue of the freedom to choose, parents and students would become change agents. Hundreds of their daily decisions would force school districts to adapt and innovate—or to relinquish their business to those who could. Policy entrepreneurs argued that there was no need for the state to mandate changes in curriculum, teacher education, or student-teacher ratios, nor was there any need for a costly bureaucracy to administer such mandates. Performance deficiencies would be corrected as parents and students had choice and schools had the freedom and the incentives to adapt.

Worsening Economy

The United States in the early 1980s was slowly recovering from the wounds inflicted by backbreaking recession and double-digit inflation. During the 1970s, the U.S. economy had lost 23 percent of its share of world markets, representing $125 billion in lost production and loss of at least two million industrial jobs ("Reindustrialization," 1980). From Wall Street to Main Street, people were questioning whether major industrial sectors were fit to compete with other countries, especially Japan, Korea, and West Germany. The national psyche took a beating as people debated causes and cures for the loss of competitive strength.

With the rate of economic growth declining and international competition increasing, it became more and more difficult to draw money from the private sector to fund the public sector. Indeed, by the end of the 1970s, an array of tax-limitation measures had passed in states and localities across the nation. Besides California's much-heralded Proposition 13, 1978 was notable for the beginning of a decline in federal support to state and local public sectors. These trends, along with increasing interstate competition for economic development, kept state fiscal systems under pressure. All levels of government were finding it harder and harder to support programs that had flowered in the period of sustained growth after the Second World War. Education suffered along with housing, health care, social insurance, welfare, civil rights, conservation and environmental improvement, and rural and urban development. Especially after 1980, retrenchment was a byword in the public sector. Under siege from all sides, government seemed unable to sustain its commitment to services, including education. For a growing number of people, the only alternative appeared to be smaller government and lower spending.

Public school choice mapped well with this trend. According to policy entrepreneurs, it held out hope for reduced expenditure while promising to improve educational performance. Money could be saved by minimizing costly mandates and scaling down expensive bureaucracies that administered them. If parents and students held the levers of change at the local level, there was less need for state-level intervention. And if schools were judged on their students' performance, then accountability could devolve to the local level. The advantage was that districts had greater knowledge of their students and could develop programs to fit their special needs. Under these conditions, it was possible to have both lower spending and increased educational performance.

Search for a New Concept of Governance

Signs were visible in the early 1980s that signaled some major rethinking in the United States about the role of government. The public, concerned about the effectiveness, responsiveness, and cost of government, and less interested in an activist, progressive government bent on social reform, elected Ronald Reagan as president in 1980. His presidency offered a new policy agenda, including (among other points) supply-side economics and an effort to balance the budget through deep cuts in social programs, along with deregulation of key industries and reduced protectionism to promote competition (Stockman, 1987).

Hoping to stimulate the growth of the economy and shake the country out of its lethargy, the president and his supporters envisioned a new role for the government. Under the banner of *New*

Federalism, the goal was to free the government from the social service burdens it had acquired from Roosevelt's New Deal to Johnson's Great Society. Obligations best handled at the national level, such as defense, would be retained, while other programs better left to the states, such as education, would be dismantled or reduced. State and local governments, much closer to the needs of their communities, were expected to assume more responsibility for the funding and delivery of social services.

Key economic sectors such as transportation, financial services, telecommunications, and health care were to be deregulated. Market forces would substitute for government controls in these areas, providing the fiscal accountability lacking in most government-regulated programs. Profit and loss figures were far better signals of organizational health than compliance with governmental regulations, so the argument went. Thus, the themes of decentralization, deregulation, and fiscal accountability were the defining elements of the New Federalism.

Public school choice fit in well with New Federalism. The push for decentralization from federal to state and local levels paralleled Minnesota school choice proponents' push to free districts from state controls and to make districts and schools the focal point of educational decision making. Proponents expected deregulation of education to increase competition among schools (paralleling then-recent experience in the financial services and transportation sectors), and ultimately to ensure greater accountability in the educational system.

The search for a new concept of governance was evident even in Minnesota, a state with a reputation for supporting populist causes and Democratic candidates. However, it took a very different turn from the national New Federalism. Against conventional proposals to do less, and against the other side's equally conventional proposals to do more, what surfaced in Minnesota communities, nonprofit organizations, and policy research institutes were proposals to do things differently. Although not yet clarified as a coordinated strategy for change in the public sector, the new thinking about the role for government and public services did offer a new vocabulary. Phrases such as "alternative service delivery," "load-shedding," "contracting," "vouchers," and "co-production" reflected the search to find new ways of conducting public business.

The Citizens League was a leader in this exploration. In 1980, this nonprofit policy analysis organization issued a statement that set forth a new perspective on public services and called for consumer solutions to public problems. While not denigrating traditional public administration and design, it argued that citizen-users of public services should have power to do more than simply elect public officials. They should have an expanded role, an option to withdraw if the services did not fulfill their expectations, and a voice to articulate how services should be run more effectively and efficiently. Thus, the League envisioned a market-driven public service system governed by consumer sovereignty and regulated by market pricing.

Public school choice was one example of how this new market-driven public service system could work. Parents would have the option of choosing schools for their children outside their local districts. Their choice of districts and schools would register their preferences in an educational market where parents, not district officials, would be sovereign. Loss—or potential loss—of students would prompt school officials and teachers to offer improved and innovative programs. Thus, Minnesota's search for a new concept of governance and public service was opening up an alternative path for public education.

Battle Lines Forming

Minnesotans' positions on public school choice depended, for the most part, on how they explained student performance declines. Those favoring *improvement* believed performance problems were temporary, or could be temporary. They attributed the performance declines to the tremendous social changes and economic dislocation of the times, and they insisted that the trends could be reversed and student learning could be improved with an infusion of funds and public support. Others, convinced that the performance declines were indicative of far more serious global and national problems, believed that the only solution was to *redesign* the schools. All aspects of U.S. society were being fundamentally altered in the postindustrial age, and the schools must follow suit.

Improvement Approach

During the 1980s, proponents of what we refer to as the improvement approach to Minnesota educational reform maintained that the state had a quality public school system. Judged by recent studies (Peek, Duren, and Wells, 1985), they believed it had earned its national reputation for excellence. In 1982, Minnesota spent 122 percent of the U.S. average for education: $572.77 per capita, compared to $468.34 in the country as a whole. The state had one of the highest high school completion rates in the nation (second only to North Dakota). Ninety-one percent of students graduated from high school. The figure exceeded President Reagan's goal of a 90 percent completion rate by 1990. The historically high SAT scores compared favorably with other states. Although occasional news stories provided anecdotes about problems with a given district, school, or teacher, for the most part the general consensus was quite positive, with 79 percent of the people polled ranking the schools as good or excellent in 1984 (Peek, Duren, and Wells, 1985).

Relying on various reports, those in the improvement approach concluded that Minnesota's schools were not at risk. Rather, they were at a "turning point where the most thoughtful decisions must be made about the future" (Anderson and Grossman, 1984, p. i). The educational system had to "cross new bridges to the future" to handle the social, economic, and political forces that threatened delivery of a high-quality educational product.

There was no doubt that environmental forces were having a dramatic impact on education. Budget cuts caused an abrupt halt to reform efforts in special education, school financing, technology in the classroom, early childhood services, and community education. From summer 1980 to the end of 1982, the state suffered severe revenue shortfalls. As of 1981–82, the state share of school revenues was 71 percent; by 1982–83, it reached a low of 45 percent (Minnesota Department of Education, 1986a). From 1980 through 1984, the Minnesota economy lagged the national recovery from the recession. Unemployment rates on the Iron Range, in the northern part of the state, reached record highs when taconite mines closed and firms were forced to downsize due to intense competition from low-cost foreign steel manufacturers and

U.S. minimills. The farm economy experienced the most serious depression since the 1930s, with bankers and farmers locked into a deadly dance to see who would survive. During this period, inter-state competition for new jobs was becoming especially keen, and there were a growing number of complaints about Minnesota's business climate. The state's largest employer, Minnesota Mining and Manufacturing (3M), transferred 1,600 jobs to Austin, Texas. It cited Minnesota's high unemployment compensation, income, and property tax burden as one of the main reasons for the move. The policy agenda was full of issues of job creation, tax reform, and fiscal management. As one legislator put it, "The state economy almost collapsed in 1980 and '81. The Iron Range is dead. The Feds have cut the rug out from under us in a dozen different ways and the South and Southwest are draining our potential reorga-nization capital by the costs of energy while they kidnap our indus-try. Sure we care about schools. It's the biggest chunk of our state budget if nothing else. But there were and are a hell of a lot of things we talk about first in Minnesota, and I don't just mean in the legislature" (Wilhelm, 1984, p. 212).

To add to the budgetary distress, federal aid to education was consolidated into a block grant during this period, and a number of programs were cut back. The Reagan administration philosophy toward federal aid to domestic programs hit programs for the dis-advantaged, child nutrition, and vocational education the hardest (Peek and Wilson, 1983).

Declining enrollment of school-age children also drained crit-ical resources (Peek, Duren, and Wells, 1985). Between 1972–73 and 1982–83, enrollment dropped 21 percent. This compared to the average national decline of 14 percent. The contraction of enrollment had a ripple effect through the entire education sys-tem: schools closed, districts consolidated, teachers and staff were laid off. Minnesota lost over one-tenth of its classroom teachers during the decade. The Carnegie Foundation for the Advance-ment of Teaching pointed out that only four other states (Mich-igan, Delaware, New York, and Maryland) and the District of Columbia lost a greater proportion of their teachers during this period (Feistritzer, 1983). Rapidly rising school costs also con-tributed to the bleak picture. Inflation rose by almost 120 percent during the 1973–74 to 1982–83 period in Minneapolis/St. Paul, just at a time when demand for new programs and services increased. Schools were required to foster racial integration, eliminate sex discrimination, improve access for the handicapped, minimize fiscal disparities among districts, and broaden the age groups they served (Peek, Duren, and Wells, 1985). These expectations came at a time when demands for new technology also increased. Teachers needed computers, software, and staff development to retool for the information age. These were costly add-ons in a period of retrenchment, and it became increasingly difficult to achieve economies of scale. Declining enrollment, underutilization of buildings and classrooms, rising inflation, and new services, programs, and technology drove up per-pupil costs (Peek, Duren, and Wells, 1985).

Proponents of improvement were quick to point out that the changing social fabric also contributed to the deterioration of student performance. Minnesota children and youth lived in families that had changed dramatically. By 1980, 58 percent of married women with children worked outside the home. As a result, more preschoolers were reared outside the home, and more children spent time alone or unsupervised before or after school. While it was difficult to tie poor student performance directly to the dramatic increases in the divorce rate and the number of blended and single-parent families, out-of-wedlock births, and female-headed households, the argument was a compelling one for both educators and the public. Children from five to eighteen years old were spending 11 percent of their lives in school and 89 percent outside of school; if they were not learning, it was important to look beyond the school to find the major causes.

Improvement advocates also cited other possible contributors to educational decline: widespread use of alcohol and drugs, increased sexual activity at an early age, greater reliance on television and decreased time spent reading books and doing homework, and a greater number of students who worked during the school year (Peek, Duren, and Wells, 1985). These trends, they explained, all worked to reduce the efficacy of the schools and increase the difficulty of their task. Teachers had to cope with the changing nature of the children. From the perspective of those in the improvement approach, fiscal exigencies, declining enrollments, explosive costs, changing social fabric, and new youth culture were all responsible for the deterioration of student performance. To counter these trends, and make up for ground lost due to harsh economic realities, they urged the state to require higher standards from its students and teachers, and to pump more resources into the educational system—more money for better-trained teachers, updated technology and curricula, new services, and more modern facilities. Their goal was to restore historic levels of funding so the state could respond to the tremendous social changes and maintain its competitive edge in education (Peek, Duren, and Wells, 1985).

Implicit in this approach to educational reform was the belief that the ultimate responsibility for teaching and learning rests with state government. State constitutions were viewed as the source and legal embodiment of the obligation to provide education for state residents. While a state could discharge this obligation in whatever administrative and organizational manner it liked, a state possessed the authority to define what education was and determine how it should be delivered to the citizenry. For example, a state established the number of days in the school year, the minimum qualifications for teachers and educators, the core subjects to be taught, and the list of textbooks from which schools were to make their selections.

Historically, these responsibilities were exercised at a distance. States relied on local school districts to discharge the legal obligation to the public. But the steady increase of school consolidation since World War II, the pressure for states to subsidize local expenditures, and the school finance reform movement (requiring states to equalize education funding among districts), led states to take on a larger role in education to ensure a higher quality of education for all of their citizenry.

Redesign Approach

The policy entrepreneurs wanted fundamental change. Not content with "tinkering around the edges," as they called improvement solutions, they demanded a total revamping of the educational system. For them, education could not be substantially better without being significantly different. They pursued the same goal as the improvement advocates—educational excellence for the state of Minnesota—but they differed greatly in their definition of the root causes of the decline and their recommendations for correcting the deficiencies. Although they acknowledged the impact of external forces, the policy entrepreneurs focused their attention on what they saw as the structural flaws inherent in the system, and the inertia that inhibited a mature bureaucracy from responding to the external forces. The educational system needed to be efficient, flexible, innovative, and supportive of diversity to be able to respond to the changes in society. The entrepreneurs believed that it lacked this capacity, and so they advocated far-reaching redesign.

Citing the noted theorist Anthony Downs (1967), they drew parallels with other mature bureaucracies. The educational system, they claimed, suffered from the same ills: structural inertia; excessive rules and regulations; attempts to stake out, defend, and expand policy territory; goal inconsistency; inaccurate information about performance; protective self-interest; and reduced flexibility and responsiveness to those served. They argued that the current educational system would not be able to respond to the challenges it faced because there were too many entrenched interests to protect the status quo and keep the system from adapting.

Then, too, advocates of improvement offered policy makers only two choices—either pay more for services rendered or reduce the quality and quantity of services delivered. Neither alternative was attractive to the entrepreneurs. For them, the challenge was to find methods to change the system without adding more burden to the taxpayers and business community. Calling strategies to improve education "well meaning but misguided and costly," they insisted more had to be delivered for less.

Proponents of redesign believed policy makers were growing resistant to spending tax dollars without clear proof that the funds spent would yield a commensurate return. For example, per-pupil expenditures in the nation's schools had actually declined in 1980, after adjustment for inflation, for the first time since the National Center for Education Statistics began tracking them in 1968 (Citizens League, 1982). In Minnesota, the legislature had raised the per-pupil formula by the lowest percentage in a decade, dropping educational spending per capita from 125 percent of the national average in 1967 to 109 percent in 1981 (Citizens League, 1982). And educational research supported this fiscal restraint, finding "no relationship between expenditures and the achievement of students" (Hanushek, 1981, p. 19).

Advocates of redesign expected financial conservatism to continue in the 1980s. States were preparing for huge deficits due to the economic recession, faltering federal assistance, and increasing welfare costs. A Citizens League report (1982) warned of national and state reluctance to spend more on public services. It cited a 1981 Gallup poll finding that 60 percent of the respondents in Minnesota would vote against a tax increase if local public schools said they needed more money.

Two organizations were particularly forceful in building interest and momentum for education redesign. The first was the Citizens League, whose 1982 report, *Rebuilding Education to Make It Work,* took on conventional wisdom by declaring: "It will not suffice to merely pump more money into the same old system even if there were a willingness to do so. Instead, the system itself must be rebuilt" (p. i). The report recommended a new structure for education that must:

- Give parents—who should be the key decision-makers in buying education—more choice in what to buy. To put it another way, public educational dollars should follow parents' choices about which schools or educational services to use.

- Place more authority for shaping education at the place where it happens—the individual school.

- Remove artificial barriers to excellence and encourage innovation, competition and entrepreneurship. Somehow, people in education must have the chance to break out of their stifling constraints, and others with new techniques and new technologies must have the chance to apply them to education [p. i].

The intended audience for this report was the Minnesota legislature. Although the report advised continued state control over policy issues of equity in access, enrollment, and operations, it did ask the legislature to remove all bars to open enrollment and allow students to cross district lines to select schools of their choice. To implement open enrollment and finance choice, the state would issue vouchers to each student. In addition, the report recommended school-site management and decision making decentralized to the local schools, reduction in state mandates, and encouragement of entrepreneurial activities among students, teachers, and administrators.

In 1983, another prestigious group, the Minnesota Business Partnership, threw its considerable status and weight into the educational debate by commissioning an independent study of the K-12 public school system. Founded by chief executive officers of major Minnesota corporations, the Partnership wanted its own independent assessment of the schools. How well were students prepared for college, work, and citizenship? What were the costs of the K-12 system? What were the problems and needs of elementary and secondary schools, particularly in areas amenable to public policy or private assistance? And could a plan be formulated to strengthen Minnesota education?

The consultants who conducted the study reported that Minnesota had "a good system that [could] be much better" (Berman and Weiler, 1984, p. iv). In fact, they warned that the state's track record for excellence was a mixed blessing that could just as well "lead to a false sense of confidence and complacency" (p. 1). "Despite its strengths, Minnesota education . . . has reached its limit of effectiveness. Adding more money will not help. Nor will tinkering. It is time for major restructuring" (p. 18).

The consultants felt that proposals relying on measures such as raising state requirements, policing the teaching profession, and increasing the funding for K-12 education would not solve Minnesota's shortcomings in education, which they defined as youth learning well below their potential and failing to master higher-order skills needed for the increasingly complex world. Instead, the report recommended restructuring or deep reform in the organization of instruction and the system's responsiveness to change. Three proposed alternatives to existing educational practice were particularly noteworthy: student choice for eleventh and twelfth graders, allowing them to use state-funded stipends for educational programs offered by either public or private vendors; decentralized authority, allowing school sites to make decisions on school governance and management; and statewide tests to measure student performance, assessing how well students had mastered learning in core courses based on individualized instruction.

To the redesign advocates, the challenge was clear. Reversing the declines in educational performance required a restructured school system, not higher levels of expenditure. A cluster of solutions would support the cause: *deregulation* of state mandates, to reduce red tape, permit more local control over the schools, and encourage creativity, innovation, and change; *decentralization* of decision-making authority to local school principals, teachers, and parents, to empower those most intimately involved with student learning; and increased *accountability* for students in what they learned and educators in the services they offered, to ensure the delivery of quality education. The mechanism to deliver a redesigned system based on deregulation, decentralization, and accountability was the innovative idea of parent-student choice. For the redesign advocates, choice would provide the motive power to drive all other changes, by giving educators the incentive to change.

Viability of the Innovative Idea

Explaining performance declines and proclaiming the need to redesign the schools is one thing, but implementing public school choice as the means to accomplish it is another. The issue in Minnesota as elsewhere was whether people would listen and act on the recommendations, especially when the new idea had to compete with many alternative solutions. Those in the improvement mode did not view the performance declines as reason for fundamental redesign of the school system. For them, declining indicators illustrated what happens to education when budgets are cut and critical resources are denied. It was not necessary to resort to radical solutions such as choice to rectify the situation as far as they were concerned. They believed the current educational system was basically sound; it just needed an infusion of money to cope with the changing needs of students and restore a funding base battered by recession.

Thus we understand that innovative ideas can be viewed as alternative solutions to what the public defines as a problem (Dery, 1984). The intriguing question is how any innovative idea gains currency as the preferred solution, making it more attractive than other alternatives. Would educational redesign and public school choice solve the problem of performance declines or would educational improvements and increased funding be the more viable policy option for Minnesota to follow? To begin to answer this question, we return to the context that gives shape to the debate.

Momentum for Educational Improvement

Despite the interest in market incentives in Minnesota and the wave of New Federalism, it would be a mistake to think that school choice would automatically win in the contest of ideas. Currents in the national, state, and local context ran in many directions. Choice was compatible with New Federalism and the incentive approach to public services, but there were other forces that could shift the course and direction of the policy agenda. As the momentum for school choice built over time, so did an equally powerful momentum for incremental improvement.

Within a few months of the release of *A Nation at Risk* in 1983, we find major improvement efforts underway in states around the country. A U.S. Department of Education survey (1984) found sweeping attempts at educational reform. For example, curriculum reform had been initiated in forty-two states, stiffer high school graduation requirements had been proposed in forty-four, and statewide testing had been introduced in thirty-five. Incremental in nature, these measures aimed at improving the current system by beefing up standards and upgrading the quality of teaching and leadership. Said one noted educator and writer, we are "in the throes of an educational reform movement of epochal proportions" (Finn, 1985, p. 75).

It would have been natural for Minnesota to join, even lead, this surge of improvement, since "scarcely any state government had shone more brightly than Minnesota on education" (Peirce and Hagstrom, 1984, p. 52). The state had long enjoyed a reputation as an educational leader, stemming in large measure from the part education played in the lives of early Scandinavian settlers. Their passion for learning, handed down through successive generations, continued to manifest itself as a strong commitment to public education.

Educational leaders and legislators, seeking to add Minnesota to the list of states in search of educational improvement, were poised for the 1985 legislative session. The Minnesota Education Association had issued its *Agenda for Educational Excellence: A Teacher*

Treatise (1984). Senators Jim Pehler and Tom Nelson and Representatives Bob McEachern and Ken Nelson on the major education committees in the legislature had prepared a report titled
*Initiatives for Excellence: Continuing Minnesota's Commitment to Educa-
tional Improvement* (1985). Both reports urged support for reform
following the improvement path in order to regain the fiscal
ground education had lost due to recession and revenue shortfalls.

Besides these endorsements for educational improvements,
mainstream educators criticized radical proposals to reverse the
declines in student performance. Some warned that movement
toward educational redesign was a cover for the real issue—a
national shift toward conservatism that marked a return to states'
rights, increased competition between public and private schools,
the administration's support for tuition tax credits and vouchers,
and a shift in federal policy from equity for all students to excellence for the elite (Pincus, 1985). Others felt the debate on education to be worthless because it ignored more fundamental issues,
such as government policy, social problems, economic growth, and
the price tag for the recommended changes (Rossides, 1985;
Shanker, 1985; Shapiro, 1985; Singer, 1985).

Improvement advocates also were quick to criticize reports like
that of the Minnesota Business Partnership. The proposal was not
well linked to Minnesota data, they said (Duren and Peek, 1984).
Nor was the report internally consistent. Prior to publication, a
panel of experts, four of whom were principal readers of the chapters dealing with Minnesota, found a poor linkage between the
data in the first volumes and the general conclusions of the summary, which in their view were not justified by the study's results
(Giroux and others, 1985).

And there were disputes about the very existence of a crisis
in education. According to some, *A Nation at Risk* and other high-
profile reports were "political documents consisting of a litany of
charges [made] without examining the veracity of their evidence
or its sources" (Stedman and Smith, 1985, p. 84). Critics challenged three aspects of *A Nation at Risk:* the quality of the evidence
for the poor state of education, the claim that the U.S. educational system is inferior to those of foreign countries, and the
assumption that a high-technology revolution is sweeping the
economy. "In particular, the commissions made simplistic recom-

mendations and failed to consider their ramifications. They proposed increasing time without altering pedagogy, instituting merit schemes without prescribing procedures, and adopting the 'new basics' without changing old definitions. They ignore numerous problems—teenage unemployment, teacher burnout, and high dropout rates—that must be solved before American education can be considered sound" (Stedman and Smith, 1985, p. 102). The countercurrent to educational redesign was running strong and deep.

Thus, by the mid 1980s in Minnesota, we see the emergence of two currents in the river of educational reform. One attempted to shift the course of the river, while the other sought to improve the existing riverbed with an increased flow of monetary support. Although it was difficult to navigate on waters with such crosscurrents, at least the two alternatives were becoming easier to read. The course Minnesota actually charted is the subject of our next chapter.

Chapter Two

An Idea Becomes Law

The Legislative History of Reform

*The question was: where to begin? Once again, I realized
that this was the only question that mattered. Once you
have made a start, all you need do is continue. But in
order to begin, one needs to have clear ideas and decide
on the simplest way forward.*
—JEAN MONNET, *MEMOIRS*

Minnesota Governor Rudy Perpich joined the policy entrepreneurs
on the redesign side of the Great School Debate, becoming the
champion of public school choice. This chapter follows the governor's proposal through four legislative sessions, 1985 through
1988, documenting major events as the idea cycled and recycled
through enactment, implementation, and evaluation to become
the first statewide public school choice program in the country. In
Chapter Three, we will see what the policy entrepreneurs did to
bring this result about.

1985 Legislative Session: Agenda Setting

In a preemptive move on January 4, 1985, several days before his
State of the State address, Governor Perpich unveiled his proposal,
Access to Excellence. His dramatic announcement began what the
news media would characterize as his crusade for education. His
selection of the Citizens League forum was a choice that was both

symbolic and strategic. Fifteen years earlier at a Citizens League meeting, gubernatorial candidate Wendell Anderson had endorsed equalized school financing—an idea known eventually as the Minnesota Miracle. Perpich wanted his own Minnesota miracle, but one driven by the vision of educational quality and not just financial equity. Here are the major elements of Perpich's proposal:

- *Increased state responsibility for school funding*—up from 63 percent to 80 percent, reducing the burden on property taxes.
- *Complete state responsibility for evaluating school results,* mandating the Department of Education to define what students should know and to measure "learner outcomes" at three grade levels. (Tests would be developed in conjunction with teachers, parents, administrators, and school board members, and results of these tests would enable everyone involved in education to identify areas for improvement or concentration.)
- *Near or total elimination of all other statewide mandates.* Local districts would set their own programs to meet their students' needs, guided by student demand and test results.
- *State-provided management assistance programs* to help local districts identify their areas of need and to make improvements in their management and organization.
- *Competition among schools for "model school" designation.* (A statewide School for the Arts and district-run magnet schools for mathematics and science would serve as two distinctive patterns.)
- *Parent and student choice among schools.* Starting in the 1986–87 school year, all eleventh and twelfth-grade students would be able to attend any public school or postsecondary institution and bring their share of state aid with them. By 1988–89, the choice of public school would be extended to students in any grade.
- *Increased state funding* (amount unspecified) to local districts for staff and curriculum development.

Access to Excellence was a bold initiative. Perpich was passionate about public education, which he regarded as his own passport out of poverty. He spoke of the "single theme of accountability" and called on the state to become more accountable in its chief areas of educational responsibility: providing equal funding to all students, setting quality standards, evaluating performance, and providing technical assistance when necessary. School districts should also become accountable for determining what programs met the particular needs of their students and designing the best staff development for their teachers. Parents should be more accountable too in their area of expertise: making informed decisions about their children and selecting a public school appropriate for them.

Rather than move with the nationwide trend of increasing state mandates to local districts, the governor's intent was to reduce regulations and encourage more local control of education. Although the state of Minnesota would assume a greater percentage of the financial burden, and establish statewide standards and testing, local districts would retain control over what should be taught and how it should be taught, beyond the state-required minimum. As the nation was moving to deregulate certain industry sectors and decentralize authority from the federal government to the states, so too was Minnesota making an effort to deregulate and decentralize its educational system to encourage greater innovation, differentiation, and flexibility among the schools. The mechanism was parental choice, coupled with state foundation aid awarded to each student to attend the public school district of his or her preference. Perpich's proposal also included money to help school districts make the transition to choice.

The governor's announcement was hailed as "historic" and "magnificent" by some members of the Citizens League audience, but not all were so enthusiastic. "The idea of choice was greeted like an explosion," said Perpich (Randall and Geiger, 1991, p. 156). Educational leaders and some lawmakers, alerted only one day before his announcement, predicted chaos in the public schools. A newspaper headline the following day captured their reaction: "Perpich School Plan Meets With Caution, Rejection and Confusion" (Foley, Smetanka, and Sturdevant, 1985, p. 8A).

Leaders of the two teachers' unions, long opponents of voucher financing, voiced strong opposition. "A voucher system would be the end of public education," commented Ed Bolstad, executive secretary of the Minnesota Federation of Teachers. The president of the Minnesota Education Association, Marty Zins, expressed similar concerns. Not only was student movement from district to district disruptive of staffing and program design, but the requirements of state tests, most likely multiple-choice tests, would not address or measure critical thinking skills, "and that might be the most important learning that goes on in a school" (Foley, Smetanka, and Sturdevant, 1985, p. 8A).

Legislators added their reservations. Tom Nelson, chair of the Subcommittee on Education Aids, said "They've got a lot of work to get done before we can act on this. The choice idea will meet with a lot of resistance in the Legislature. There's going to have to be a lot of clarity brought in" to win followers (Foley, Smetanka, and Sturdevant, 1985, p. 8A).

Enlisting Policy Champions in the Legislature

Keenly aware of the political risks he faced by advocating a package of educational reforms opposed by mainstream educational groups, the governor urged his staff to begin a search for policy champions in the legislature to introduce and carry the bill. Resistance came from several quarters. Some lawmakers objected to the choice provisions, others resented the governor's intrusion into the domain of educational policy—normally the province of a few legislators on key committees, their staffs, experts from the Department of Education, and representatives of educational interest groups. By initiating a proposal without consulting the traditional actors, the governor (in a traditionally weak-governor state) challenged legislative power and violated policy making norms. At a deeper level, what was at stake, said one legislator, was who would set and control state education policy. Partisan politics was also an issue. A former chair of a key education committee refused to sponsor the bill because the opposition party was asked to introduce it first. He did not want to be on the second team. He was especially incensed that the governor did not consult with legislators in the development of his proposal, and did not seek support from his own party (Democratic-Farmer-Labor, called DFL) before he went to the opposition (Independent Republican, IR) even though his party was in the minority in the House at that time. For a while, it looked as if the proposal would founder for lack of a policy champion in the legislature. As one astute observer of the legislative process in Minnesota commented, "You can set the agenda, and you can move an issue forward, but you can't really exercise any political muscle unless you have the Speaker and Majority Leader as a strong proponent willing to help you out. That's where the trading is going to take place . . . in terms of getting things in the bills, and advancing things that legislators might want during the session" (Mazzoni, 1986, p. 63).

After some negotiation with Perpich and his staff, House Majority Leader Connie Levi (IR) agreed to be the chief House sponsor of the bill. There were several advantages in attracting her support. She had a history of success with legislation similar to the governor's. In 1982, she had drafted a law that permitted school districts to enter into agreements with postsecondary institutions to allow students to enroll in postsecondary courses. Although some districts took advantage of this option, most did not. Disappointed with the response, she drafted revisions to the bill in 1984, but again she was frustrated with the lack of action. She viewed the Postsecondary Enrollment Options of the governor's bill as an extension of her earlier efforts—and one that had a better chance for success because it gave parents and students, rather than districts, the choice for postsecondary enrollment. Also, as House Majority Leader, she was in a good negotiating position, well aware that Perpich, a DFL governor, needed her support and cooperation in order to pass his legislative agenda in the IR-controlled House.

The principal Senate champion was Senator Tom Nelson (DFL), the chair of the Subcommittee on Finance. He was described as "trusted and popular," "one of the best," "very fair," and "always accessible" by his colleagues and the lobbyists with whom he had contact (Sturdevant, 1985a, p. 9C). Yet he faced the distinct disadvantage of introducing a bill without the backing of his party's Senate majority leader, nor of its most senior member, a well-respected former chair of the Education Committee. Worse still, the latter became a chief sponsor of an alternative bill that eliminated Perpich's controversial choice options for students, and the majority and minority leaders in the Senate became co-sponsors (Wilson, 1985).

Despite these handicaps, Nelson and Levi joined forces with the governor to champion open enrollment in the schools. They unleashed what some described as a legislative free-for-all and pushed the question of public school choice into headline news.

Implementation Concerns

In the ensuing weeks, educational leaders and interest groups began a concerted attack on the proposal. Writing op-ed pieces for local and metropolitan newspapers, they decried the idea of public school choice. Leading the charge was a coalition of four major groups: Minnesota Education Association (MEA), the Minnesota Federation of Teachers (MFT), the Minnesota Association of School Administrators (MASA), and the Minnesota School Boards Association (MSBA). Together with the Minnesota Association of Secondary School Principals and the Minnesota Association of Elementary School Principals, two groups more supportive of open enrollment, they formed a coalition referred to as 6M. "Odd bedfellows," retorted veteran lawmakers, who realized the significance of these old adversaries joining forces despite their long history of sparring and conflict at the legislature.

Members of the coalition confronted Education Commissioner Ruth Randall, a Perpich appointee, over their exclusion from the staff group that advised the governor. Angry that they had not been asked for input prior to his announcement of a major education policy statement, they chided her for excluding them from the deliberations (Randall and Geiger, 1991, p. 172). Eager to incorporate their views, especially their expertise in policy implementation, the commissioner formed a task force to study ways to make choice viable if and when it became public policy, and assigned a team from the department, headed by Robert Wedl, to staff it. The twenty-one-member task force (invited for strategic reasons, according to an executive agency official) consisted mostly of educators. It included superintendents, principals, counselors, teachers, representatives from the 6M coalition, the PTA, and concerned citizens.

The commissioner credited this task force with sorting out some of the logistical problems and difficult issues surrounding the implementation of public school choice, such as questions on integration, transportation, accreditation, and funding, and with providing language for the bill that later became law (Randall and Geiger, 1991). Others, however, were not as complimentary. Said one critic, the task force took its time and "dragged its feet." Much of the time during its six-week deliberation, participants debated the question of public school choice, not how to implement it, their original charge. And this delay unfortunately gave opponents a highly visible platform to vent their displeasure with the governor's initiative, enabling them to slow the bill's momentum and delay its formal introduction at the state legislature until late February, 1985. Having bypassed traditional educational groups to craft his policy, Perpich now had to wait for their input.

Planning and Coordination for Enactment

Planning and coordination for the open enrollment campaign "came directly from the governor's office" (Mazzoni, 1986). His staff brought in, on a regular basis, the advocates of public school choice—representatives from the Minnesota Business Partnership, the Citizens League, the Department of Education, policy entrepreneurs, educators, and special interest groups that supported open enrollment. The goal was to coordinate the actions of this growing coalition and to plan some common strategy to build support among the public and the legislature.

The group eventually came up with a three-pronged strategy. They encouraged the Minnesota Business Partnership to form a group of visible, big-name leaders to promote the ideas and lend credibility to the plan. One of the policy entrepreneurs formed a grassroots organization, People For Better Schools, to begin the campaign at the local level. The third component of the strategy focused on the media. Enlisting and keeping their interest became a high priority to gain credibility, visibility, and support for redesign ideas.

The governor was personally very involved beyond these strategy meetings. Often accompanied by the commissioner, he visited some twenty high schools in less than three months to champion his initiative. His media campaign also included a five-city, outstate tour in April with then 3M CEO Lewis Lehr, the head of the Minnesota Business Partnership's task force on K-12 educational reform. It too received excellent press. A good media fight with the opponents of choice also made headlines, as the debate between the governor and the education establishment heated up. Media coverage was extensive in the Twin Cities and throughout the state. Besides these attempts to galvanize public support for open enrollment, Perpich waged an insider's campaign to lobby key power brokers within the legislature, especially those members who would review his bill in the various House and Senate committees. In one case, "Perpich thought he was one vote short of the six he needed to get the proposal through its crucial first test. So he went to work. One by one, Perpich called six of the ten members of the Education Aids Subdivision to his office for a little personal lobbying. One of these was DFL Representative Ken Nelson, a critic of the idea. . . . Hours later, Nelson, a leading member of the Committee's DFL minority, told the Subdivision that he changed his mind. He said afterward the conversation with Perpich made a difference" (Sturdevant, 1985b).

The two other policy champions, House Majority Leader Levi and Senator Nelson, were also hard at work. Despite resistance to open enrollment among the leaders in his party, Nelson was successful in the first couple of committees. The most controversial element of the bill, K-12 open enrollment, passed the Senate Tax Committee, the Senate Education Aids Subcommittee, and the Senate Education Committee, only to be defeated in the Senate Finance Committee. It was estimated that it lacked four votes to keep it alive (Sturdevant, 1985d, p. 1B). The House majority leader achieved her first victory when the House Education Aids Subdivision got the open enrollment proposal accepted by a close voice vote. However, she was quick to credit the governor and the Minnesota Business Partnership for their lobbying efforts. "I'd say the governor's office and the Minnesota Business Partnership made the difference today" (Sturdevant, 1985b, p. 9A). Her views were shared by other observers as well. The ties between the Independent Republican legislators and the business leaders gave the plan more credibility than it might have had coming from a DFL governor (Sturdevant, 1985b, p. 9A). The next go-round in the House Education Committee was not as successful. Despite vigorous lobbying, the K-12 open enrollment proposal was defeated by a 14–13 vote. Levi's assessment was that K-12 "open enrollment may have died for this session" (Sturdevant, 1985c, p. 11A). And she doubted that any effort to put the option back into the House bill would succeed. Even if open enrollment stayed in the Senate version, "the chances of bringing it back from conference committee are very slender" because the most likely House conferees oppose it (Sturdevant, 1985c, p. 11A). "We gave this a good shot," she said. But the proponents of open enrollment were up against "probably the most powerful lobby in the state. . . . I'm pleased that we did as well as we did" (Sturdevant, 1985c, p. 11A). What Levi did not mention, however, was that although K-12 open enrollment failed, the postsecondary enrollment options provision ("her baby," as others called it) had passed. Not only were eleventh and twelfth-grade students able to take courses in Minnesota state postsecondary institutions for both high school and college credit, but state dollars would follow the students. This provision received little media attention, however.

The final deliberations on the governor's education bill took place in what some analysts have referred to as the "Third House," the conference committees that reconcile differences between House and Senate versions of a bill. Bills coming out of conference committees are negotiated settlements among caucus, committee, and issue leaders, and the governor, and take the form of a non-amendable report (Hanson, 1985).

In this case, however, agreement was not forthcoming. The DFL-controlled Senate and IR-controlled House were deadlocked in conflicts in May and June over school funding, questions of distribution, and the governor's demand for a state arts high school. Levi's earlier assessment had been correct. There were too many opponents of open enrollment on both committees to reinstate K-12 open enrollment.

However, when discussions had completely broken down between the two groups, Levi stepped in as a mediator. She teamed up with the DFL leader and co-chair, Nelson, and together the original sponsors of the governor's initiative worked out a compromise. Postsecondary Enrollment Options, originally excluded in the Senate and passed in the House, would not only remain, but incentives were added to encourage the participation of colleges and universities (Mazzoni, 1986, p. 124). In addition, a state high school for the arts and a testing program to assess student learning, both from the governor's original proposals, were also included in the compromise.

The Postsecondary Enrollment Options Act (PSEOA) was signed into law at Anoka Ramsey Community College in late June 1985, as part of the 1985 Omnibus School Aids Action, a $2.53 billion funding package for K-12 education. Calling attention to his favorite aspect of the law, the option for high school students to take college classes at state expense for both high school and college credit, the governor invited student participation in the program on either a full-time or part-time basis.

Aftermath of 1985 Legislative Session

The media hailed the law as a true innovation—"landmark legislation" ("More Options," 1985). The law also received national press coverage, catching the attention of Governor Lamar Alexander (R) of Tennessee, chairman of the National Governors' Association, and other governors who became interested in public school choice as a policy option.

In the meantime, officers of organized Minnesota interest groups continued to be vocal in their opposition. The law was not sound policy as far as they were concerned. Although never formally announcing their strategy, educational groups were expected to try to gut the law during the next session.

For his part, Perpich, who "hadn't worked for anything this hard," (Thomma, 1985, p. 12A), and had announced after the vote in the Senate Finance Committee that he would not seek nor would he accept the endorsement of the teachers' unions because of their opposition to change, decided to offer an olive branch to those who opposed his choice initiative. Although things "really got mean" (Randall and Geiger, 1991, p. 153) during the legislative debates, it was time for some fence-mending. Since educators had been angry about being left out of the policy formulation process, Perpich and his staff created a forum where all sides could meet and discuss the next steps. He challenged the K-12 educators who objected to his initiative to come up with their own plan for Minnesota education.

Governor's Discussion Group

Perpich and Randall convened the Governor's Discussion Group (GDG) in August 1985 with a charge of developing a "visionary plan" for state education. The GDG included sixty-one participants representing twenty-four groups with a stake in educational reform. Members represented the 6M coalition as well as redesign proponents, businesses, and community groups. The intention was to generate creative ideas in the hope of giving the governor a new proposal that all stakeholders could support, not just those who wanted educational redesign. Immediately, the GDG became the place to be if one wanted to influence educational policy in Minnesota. (See Roberts and Bradley, 1991, for a more complete assessment of the group and its activities.)

Implementation of Postsecondary Enrollment Options Act

At the same time, the Minnesota Department of Education, in conjunction with the Higher Education Coordinating Board (HECB), created mechanisms and processes to implement the new statewide Postsecondary Enrollment Options Program. The department provided guidance to districts, information to students and parents, and direction to postsecondary institutions. The Department was also responsible for developing and coordinating the program evaluation mandated by the legislature.

Due to the length of conference committee deliberations, the implementation was telescoped into a very brief period during the summer. The department had less than three months to develop plans, policies, and procedures for the open enrollment program. This would not have been a problem except that everyone involved was in uncharted territory. Many questions were unanswered: Would a mass exodus from school districts occur as the critics had predicted? What would the loss of state aid do to the school districts? What types of students would use the program? Would student leaders be siphoned off to take advantage of college credits? How would student readiness for the program be assessed? The open enrollment program demanded new roles for many stakeholders, including high school personnel, parents, students, and postsecondary institutions.

Initially, the Postsecondary Enrollment Options Program was managed by then-assistant commissioner Wedl, who had been involved with the legislation since its inception. During the summer of 1985, Jessie Montano, a long-time Department of Education staff member, was made project director. Working both nights and weekends, they got the program ready to go.

- The Minnesota Department of Education distributed the first set of program guidelines to all school districts by August 7,

1985. The guidelines addressed such issues as participant eligibility, reimbursement costs, transportation aid, and awarding academic credit.

- The department distributed a fact sheet to the public explaining open enrollment and how take advantage of it.
- The department set up a toll-free number to answer questions from the public. Over fifteen hundred calls were received in August alone.
- The department sponsored nine regional workshops to explain how to establish an open enrollment program and to respond to school district concerns.
- In response to parents' questions, the department distributed another fact sheet and a booklet titled *Choosing Wisely, Choosing Well.*
- Randall held four news conferences to share information about the program. In addition, department staff participated in a number of radio and television programs to discuss implementation of open enrollment.

Evaluation of 1985 Postsecondary Enrollment Options Program

Although the Postsecondary Enrollment Options Act required the commissioner to give the legislature a full evaluation report by January 15, 1987 (after the program had been running for a year), program advocates expected a rearguard sabotage attempt in the 1986 legislative session. They believed the program would be in trouble without objective evaluation data. With a positive preliminary evaluation, the House and Senate Education Committees would be more likely to support program continuation until the formal evaluation could be completed in 1987.

There was a major hurdle to overcome in this initial evaluation effort, however. Although student users of the program might well provide rich, anecdotal information, advocates could not get participants' names to mobilize their support. Federal confidentiality law prevented Randall from releasing their names to the general public. She did agree—somewhat reluctantly—to host a meeting of all program participants on the condition that an invitation to the meeting be extended to all members of the GDG to avoid showing favoritism to anyone.

About seventy students participating in the program attended the meeting, which was well covered by the press. Students reported numerous barriers to participation: "Some high school counselors, principals and superintendents are resisting or nearly 'sabotaging' students' efforts to enroll in the classes. . . . A mother from Montgomery said 'there has been a lack of support from the school district and hostility from the superintendent. We feel we're pioneers in this area'" (Carlson, 1986, p. 13C).

In view of these complaints and concerns, the legislature called for a preliminary evaluation report to be issued in February 1986, to supplement the mandated final report that was due in 1987. Planning for the preliminary report began in October 1985. The commissioner appointed a task force to direct this initial evaluation, and several choice advocates and policy entrepreneurs were appointed as members.

Funding was the first challenge confronting the task force. The 1985 Act had not provided adequate resources for either preliminary or final evaluation research. Levi and other choice supporters initiated contacts with the U.S. Department of Education for low-cost evaluation assistance. Pelavin Associates, a Washington D.C. independent consulting firm under contract with the U.S. Department of Education, eventually provided technical assistance to staff from the Minnesota Department of Education and the task force. Together they developed a research design that called for a telephone survey of two groups. The first consisted of 1,000 students who were not participants in the program. The survey reached approximately 92 percent of these students. The second consisted of the 1,679 participants in the program, and the survey reached approximately 90 percent of them (Minnesota Department of Education, 1986b).

The preliminary evaluation report released by the Department of Education revealed that during fall 1985, 1,679 students from 226 districts participated in open enrollment. Sixty-one percent were female and 39 percent were male. They attended sixty-seven colleges, universities, and vocational institutes. About 70 percent attended postsecondary institutions full time. Those who had participated in the Postsecondary Enrollment Options Program were overwhelmingly satisfied with the experience and planned to take more courses (Minnesota Department of Education, 1986b). Parents seemed to be very pleased, said Barbara Zohn, Minnesota State PTA president. And when asked by the commissioner to tell about his participation in the program, one young man responded: "I'm a high school dropout. I'm now attending the University of Minnesota. This past semester I received two A's and a B. And I'm contesting the B" (Randall and Geiger, 1991, p. 31).

Continued Concerns over Implementation

In November 1985, after the first students were enrolled in post-secondary institutions, the department held eleven regional work-shops to present the revised application form, introduce the evaluation study that had begun in October, and clarify procedural questions such as transportation aid for low-income students, trans-fer of credit from postsecondary school to high school, and other difficult issues.

The burden of district level implementation fell on the school guidance counselors, many of whom were reported feeling caught in the middle between parents and students on one hand, and prin-cipals and teachers on the other. Because of confusion at the district level, many questions were redirected to the Department of Educa-tion. Program director Montano received about twenty to thirty phone calls a day from parents, school counselors, principals, and postsecondary advisors. She spent a great deal of time advising par-ents of their rights, listening to school district complaints, and inter-preting the guidelines to the participating postsecondary institutions.

1986 Legislative Session

Educational policy making during the 1986 session continued to be an interest-group free-for-all, according to one interest group member, although others in the GDG saw it as a time for deliber-ation and discussion. Supporters of redesign realized that 1986 was not a session to expand their agenda. But they were prepared, if necessary, to check any effort to dismantle the Postsecondary Enrollment Options Program. To protect the law, the governor and his staff, the policy entrepreneurs, and the legislative policy cham-pions—including an additional supporter in the House, Repre-sentative Ken Nelson—developed a simple strategy. According to a Department of Education official, their goal was to hold the Post-secondary Enrollment Options Program, maintain its integrity, and allow for a meaningful full-year test. It was a practical strategy during an election year (with only six weeks for the legislative session) and it enabled all participants to maintain a positive atmosphere in the GDG.

The legislative hearings on the bill were similar to those in 1985. Representatives from traditional education groups that had originally opposed the legislation now described abuses and misuses of the program. Local school district responses were mixed—ranging from enthusiastic endorsement to subtle sabotage of students' efforts to exercise their options. One student was dropped from eligibility in the National Honor Society because he entered college full time. Two juniors, after they chose to participate in the post-secondary enrollment options program by taking college classes part time, were told they obviously didn't appreciate their teachers or they wouldn't have left high school for a local college. Pictures and biographies of some high school students were excluded from their yearbooks because they attended college classes. Asked for a reason, the school official said "the students no longer 'belonged' to the school" (Randall and Geiger, 1991, pp. 63–64).

Advocates of Postsecondary Enrollment Options provided accounts of success and motivation on the part of students allowed to attend postsecondary institutions. Student testimony was particularly compelling. Advocates had organized some of the students in the Postsecondary Options Program into what an observer called "a formidable force at the legislature." One student became a legislative intern for a policy entrepreneur, while others became ardent and convincing lobbyists on behalf of the law. The students told upbeat stories of renewed enthusiasm for learning and the benefits of taking challenging classes not available at their high schools. Their heartfelt testimony convinced some skeptical legislators that the law should not be repealed or significantly revised in 1986. One hard-core legislative opponent changed her stance when she talked to two young students from her district who had had very positive experiences with the program.

Results from the February 1986 preliminary evaluation added to these positive impressions. Fears of mass exodus from the high schools proved to be unfounded. Said the assistant commissioner of education, "course offerings [have been] expanded in every school district in the state without constructing one new school building, without buying one new school bus, and without hiring one new administrator or teacher" (Wedl, 1985). Thus, the hearings in the House and the Senate resulted in no substantive revisions of the original act during its first year of implementation and evaluation. The hold-and-maintain strategy had succeeded.

Governor's Discussion Group

The GDG had a deadline of December 19, 1986, to produce its visionary plan. Continuing its regular meetings through the 1986 legislative session, the GDG still saw public school choice as the major point of contention. Traditional education leaders objected to it and advocates supported it. "Either choice is in or we don't play the game," declared one of the policy entrepreneurs. Deadlock loomed under the scrutiny of the local media in a series of intense meetings during fall 1986. Ultimately the visionary plan was signed by all members, but only after an extremely tense and volatile meeting as the clock ticked toward the deadline.

Although the plan was not as visionary as Perpich had anticipated (Roberts and Bradley, 1991), it did include a compromise about many of the redesign elements the governor advocated. The final proposal included a voluntary K-12 open enrollment options program, the expansion of school choice to at-risk students, school-site management, and testing for student performance. And the very act of signing it had a dampening effect on interest-group politics. The document wedded disparate, adversarial stakeholders into a strange and unstable alliance, said one legislator. It became tangible evidence of a tacit agreement to support the concept of increasing public school choice for Minnesota students in principle, even though groups like the Minnesota Education Association and the Minnesota School Boards Association did not agree with expanding choice in practice. Signing the document created a new social contract among GDG members, who considered themselves bound to support the plan—or at least not to actively sabotage it.

Final Evaluation of Postsecondary Enrollment Options

After the legislative session ended in June 1986, Randall convened a second task force to help the department complete its long-range evaluation study of the Postsecondary Enrollment Options Act. This task force included representatives from all the major education groups, but not the policy entrepreneurs—who were excluded, according to a department official, as a fence-mending gesture to the education establishment.

Since the 1986 legislative session had allocated no money for an expanded evaluation study, the Minnesota Department of Education again turned to the U.S. Department of Education. Technical assistance for the final evaluation report came from Decision Resources Corporation, another Washington D.C. consulting firm under contract to the Department of Education.

The final report, published in February 1987, evaluated substantive issues such as student performance and satisfaction, parental opinion, and perceptions of the school districts and postsecondary institutions. Additionally, the study examined several critical policy issues such as admissions standards, advanced placement, postsecondary-high school cooperation, use of postsecondary options for summer school, non-public-school participants, comparability of high school and postsecondary courses, counseling services, credit appeals processes, and compulsory attendance (Minnesota Department of Education, 1987, p. iv).

Results showed that during the 1985–86 school year, 3,668 students from 330 high schools in 272 districts participated in the program. They tended to be children of well-educated parents. Students indicated that while high school counselors were the major source of information about the program, parents were the major source of encouragement. The main reasons given by 88 percent of the participants for using the program were "to get a head start on college and an interest in the educational opportunities provided by the program" (Minnesota Department of Education, 1987, p. ii). The average revenue reduction per district as a percentage of total operating revenue was slightly more than one-tenth of one percent, and the average revenue reduction as a percentage of Grade Eleven and Twelve foundation aid was only about eight-tenths of one percent (Minnesota Department of Education, 1987, p. iii).

Randall issued her final report to the legislature in February 1987. Noting results indicating high user satisfaction and support for the program and small fiscal impact, she praised the program for providing greater academic opportunities for high school students. Newspaper headlines proclaimed: "Fears About the College Program Groundless" (Smith, 1987b). Walter Munsterman, vice president of the state's largest teacher union and a member of the evaluation task force, said, "It seems to be working and the 'bugs are being taken out of it.'" He also noted that the predicted mass migration did not materialize, "partly because many school districts have strengthened their curricula in the last two years. . . . More and more college-level courses are available in high school buildings, some provided by colleges and others by high school teachers with special credentials" (Smith, 1987b).

1987 Legislative Session

The dynamics of the 1987 legislative session were qualitatively different from 1985 and 1986 for several reasons. Senator Randy Peterson was successful in focusing attention on the issue of education finance. Single-handedly, he analyzed data, wrote a bill on revenue equity, and shepherded the bill through enactment. Education finance, as a consequence, pushed public school choice off center stage as the most visible action agenda item. The positive evaluation report of the Postsecondary Enrollment Options Program and the signing of the GDG "Visionary Plan" also reduced interest group struggles. By creating a tacit agreement to support public school choice, politics at the legislature around education issues became less partisan, commented one legislator.

Policy Champions in 1987

Education remained Perpich's number one priority, according to a member of his staff, and extending public school choice was still a major goal. In particular, his focus was on the extension of choice to at-risk learners. Chairing the National Governors' Association Task Force on Dropouts, his investment of time and political capital in education was growing as he became more active at the national level. In February 1987, at a speech at the National Governors' Association meeting in Washington D.C., he announced that he would ask the Minnesota Legislature to give school dropouts "the option to attend the school of their choice, regardless of residence." He also "urged the other states to follow suit and provide alternative programs to keep young people in school and give dropouts a 'second chance'" (Wilson, 1987, p. 1B).

Joining forces with the governor to expand public school choice were Senator Nelson, Senator Peterson, Senator Pehler, Representative Nelson, and Representative McEachern. Together with policy entrepreneurs and redesign advocates, they were successful in enacting three additional choice laws in 1987 as part of the Omnibus Education Bill—the Voluntary K-12 Enrollment Options Act, the High School Graduation Incentives Act, and the Area Learning Centers and Alternative Programs Act.

New Laws

The K-12 Enrollment Options Act was a voluntary program to expand open enrollment to all students, not just those in their junior and senior years in high school. By voluntarily adopting a formal school board resolution, districts could allow resident pupils to enroll at other participating districts. Soon after the law was enacted, the governor sent personal letters to 160 well-respected school superintendents. His message was simple: "If you know you have a superior district, why are you afraid of choice?" (Randall and Geiger, 1991, p. 180). According to the *Minneapolis Star and Tribune,* Perpich put a "full court press on Minnesota's school district superintendents . . . urging them to adopt a model open enrollment policy" (Smith and Parry, 1987, p. 1B).

Pundits anticipated that at most 25 districts would adopt voluntary open enrollment, so there was great celebration when 96 out of 435 districts joined the program (Randall and Geiger, 1991, p. 102). Although large metropolitan districts such as Minneapolis and St. Paul elected to take part, some key suburban districts with excellent track records, such as Edina, did not. An article in the *Minneapolis Star and Tribune* reflected a more subdued assessment, cautioning that open enrollment was still limited to a select few students. Even though districts with a combined enrollment of 226,000 had adopted open enrollment and would allow students to transfer in or out of their districts, fewer than 100 students were expected to use the option, according to state officials (Doyle, 1987, p. 1A).

Additional redesign legislation passed in the 1987 session included the High School Graduation Incentives Act, championed by Representative Bob McEachern, and the Area Learning Centers and Alternative Programs Act, championed by Senator James Pehler. These bills were designed to help students at "the other end of the spectrum"—dropouts—who had failed in the educational system. While the Postsecondary Enrollment Options Act was thought to help top students take advanced placement and college-level courses, these programs were aimed at increasing opportunities for students who were failing traditional programs.

Students had several options under these acts. Area Learning Centers and special alternative programs were established to enable qualified students from age twelve to twenty-one to earn a high school diploma in an alternative educational setting designed to meet their individual needs. In addition, dropouts could also attend other public high schools and postsecondary institutions. Even persons over the age of twenty-one could participate if the local school board had passed a resolution to that effect. By 1989, there were twenty Area Learning Centers and about forty state-approved alternative programs throughout the state that enabled students to attend on a full-time or part-time basis (Randall and Geiger, 1991).

By the end of the 1987 legislative session, with these three laws on the books, public school choice became part of the policy mainstream in Minnesota, attaining what Schön (1971) has described as good currency. Convinced that public school choice was hard to oppose, fewer lawmakers called it radical. Perpich and the legislative champions were clear winners as their redesign agenda was slowly gaining acceptance. While there had been some disappointments, and representatives of the Minnesota Business Partnership were unhappy because their favored initiative (statewide competency testing) was not enacted, advocates on the whole were optimistic. The changes that had seemed so controversial only a few months before had sailed through the 1987 legislature. The governor's plan was no longer viewed as the threat the education establishment once feared. One newspaper columnist attributed the calm to the proposals being optional rather than mandatory (Smith, 1987a).

1988 Legislative Session

Speaking publicly to the School Boards Association prior to the 1988 legislative session, Perpich announced he would not be pushing for a further expansion of public school choice. He said that if choice was a good idea, it would run its own natural course. He did not want a fight and would not be using the "bully pulpit," as one executive agency staff member explained it. The governor's comments left educators unprepared for what followed in the upcoming legislative session. In the waning hours of the session, lawmakers enacted the first statewide mandatory K-12 open enrollment law in the country. It required "every school district to release students to attend public schools in any district by the 1990–91 school year. The state's larger schools would have to meet the open enrollment requirement in the 1989–90 school year" (Wilson, 1988, p. 1B).

The silent bill, as one legislative observer called the open enrollment legislation, passed without the visible presence of the governor or his staff. Yet behind the scenes, advocates worked without fanfare in a very low-key and quiet way to secure its passage. Before the session, the governor conferred with Senator Peterson and both agreed that it would be a good year to pass mandatory K-12 open enrollment legislation. There was bipartisan support, the evaluation reports on the optional choice programs had been good, and there was a growing sentiment around the state in support of passage. Since the House was facing an election year and there was opposition from lawmakers in rural districts fearful that K-12 open enrollment would force school closures, the Senate was the likely place to carry the bill. The governor had shared his strong support for mandatory open enrollment with Representatives McEachern and Nelson, but there was no strong lobbying effort on his part. Nelson did not believe the bill could go anywhere in the House, but was willing to co-sponsor the bill for discussion. Instead, the House took up other education initiatives for the governor.

The surprise legislation came from Senator Ember Reichgott. Originally carrying the bill that sought to extend public school choice to all eleventh and twelfth graders, her discussions with Peterson and Pehler convinced her that the time was right to push for mandatory open enrollment for all grades. It "was simply the next step," she said. "Why don't we just do it and take advantage of the opportunity?" Encouraged and supported by Peterson, she championed amendments to the Omnibus Education Bill that included the K-12 Mandatory Enrollment Options Act. Watching as the amendment moved through the various committees in the Senate, Reichgott noted little debate or negative reaction. Discussion was explanatory, with few lawmakers in opposition. Even the educational groups that had once been so vocal in opposition were mute. They had to be encouraged to testify before the education committees. A motion to eliminate the amendment when it reached the Senate floor was overwhelmingly rejected on a voice vote.

The dynamics in conference committee were more complicated. Enmeshed in debates over other initiatives and over increased funding for education, the K-12 Mandatory Enrollment Options Act looked to some as though it was "going down." While testimony had been excellent in favor of open enrollment, especially from parents who were disappointed that their school districts had not opted for voluntary participation, the conference committee faced an impasse. At this point, the governor's director of governmental relations and chief legislative lobbyist, Dan Loritz, entered and (with shuttle diplomacy) succeeded in negotiating a compromise—a phased-in mandatory open enrollment program that gave additional time for smaller districts to manage the costs and changes.

Thus on May 6, 1988, at his hometown high school in Hibbing, Minnesota, an ebullient Perpich signed the $38 million Omnibus Education Bill that established the nation's first mandatory K-12 school choice program. With his immigrant parents at his side, he told a crowd of 1,800, "The passage of this bill represents the crowning achievement of the 1988 legislative session. . . . This bill itself justifies the work of the Legislature this year" (Cook, 1988, p. 9A).

In his short speech, which received several standing ovations, Perpich recalled how the proposal provoked an uproar from legislators, educators, and parents when he first suggested it in 1985. He talked about how hard it is to change education and quoted Senator Nelson, who said "it [getting open enrollment passed] was a little like trying to rearrange a cemetery" (Cook, 1988, p. 12A). He also called the law "a historic reform, and a model for the nation. . . . It compels our schools to be more responsive to the people they serve. . . . And it reinforces our status as the brainpower state of this nation" (Wilson, 1988, p. 11B).

Open enrollment was immediately hailed as an innovation by the national and international press and as a major victory for Perpich. The plan was almost identical to the one he first proposed in

1985. It prohibited school boards from preventing interdistrict student transfers, except in cases where the transfers would upset racial desegregation efforts, and it ensured that state per-pupil school aid would follow students to their new districts.

Thus, over four legislative sessions, public school choice across district lines became a reality in Minnesota. In the words of U.S. Secretary of Education William Bennett, "the idea [had] won" (Snider, 1987, p. C2). Bennett praised the plan and predicted that many states would be likely to follow, concluding that greater educational choice was not crazy—it was legitimate. Chester E. Finn, special counselor to Bennett, concurred. Parental choice had triumphed. "I have no sympathy with the notion that people should be made to go against their wills to bad schools with bad teachers" (p. C2).

The Actions Behind
the Headlines

*I knew from experience that change can only come from
outside, under the pressure of necessity. . . . Statesmen are
concerned to do good, and above all to extricate themselves
from awkward corners; but they do not always have either
the taste or the time for using their imagination. They are
open to creative ideas, and anyone who knows how to
present such ideas has a good chance of having them
accepted.*
—JEAN MONNET, *MEMOIRS*

The headline news in Chapter Two told the surface story of open
enrollment in Minnesota. But there is much more that merits our
attention. Beyond the glare of the press and noise of public debate,
we found individuals who had already spent years working for
school redesign. Politically astute and strategically well placed,
these policy entrepreneurs eventually succeeded in attracting a following and prompting the governor and his administration to take
on their cause. It is their work that this study set out to analyze, but
before we can understand how they functioned, we need to fill out
the historical record with the details of their accomplishments.
This chapter maps their activities around the phases of the innovation process (creation, design, and implementation) to illustrate
how they went about the daily business of policy entrepreneurship.
In so doing, we fill in some important pieces of the story, such as

---

Note: This chapter draws on Roberts and King (1991).

how Perpich came to champion educational redesign and how the proponents of public school choice were able to succeed against the powerful forces pushing for educational improvement.

Creative Phase: 1978–1984

It is difficult to pinpoint the beginning of the process. We know that two of the policy entrepreneurs met informally with other educators and change agents as early as 1978 to discuss concerns about the declining quality of Minnesota and U.S. education. They began to brainstorm about educational problems, and about strategies and solutions to deal with them.

Problem Framing and Problem Definition

Problem framing and definition took shape by way of analogy. The policy entrepreneurs borrowed liberally from trends and events in the private sector. Education, they declared, was like steel or textiles or any other declining industry. Said one entrepreneur, "If they are ailing, they ask for protection . . . they want import quotas, they want tariffs, they want anything to reduce the amount of competition in the system so that they can sell their product in the marketplace." Despite what industry claimed to want, however, better results could be obtained from deregulation, decentralization, and fiscal conservatism.

Policy entrepreneurs also drew from educational and social theorists in making analogies between mature bureaucracies, regulated monopolies, and education (Downs, 1967). Education suffered from the same ills, they claimed. Performance declines could be attributed to inertia, protectionism, lack of either accountability or competition, excessive rules and regulations, inconsistent goals, and inadequate concern for performance and the customer. Innovation and change would not be possible without breaking the monopolistic hold school districts had on students. The system—designed for an earlier industrial age—had been pushed to its limits and could no longer adapt to the challenges of the information age, and it was time for a major overhaul.

Mainstream educators bristled at these analogies. The president of the Minnesota Educational Association flatly rejected them, countering, "Look what has happened to those deregulated industries such as airlines—lost baggage, delays, and frustration. Lots of good deregulation did them." Nonetheless, the entrepreneurs persisted in framing the problem as an outmoded institution unable to cope with the challenge of change. As they continued to search for solutions within that problem framework, they pointed out how educators and families would benefit from the expanded opportunities derived from cross-district choice.

Idea and Solution Generation

As writers, authors, analysts, researchers, and teachers, the policy entrepreneurs were all in the idea business. They firmly believed in the power of ideas to shape the direction of history. One of them, an economist by training, quoted verbatim from John Maynard Keynes in *The General Theory of Employment, Interest, and Money* to illustrate the difference ideas can make: "The ideas of economists and political philosophers, both when they are right and when they are wrong, are more powerful than is commonly understood. Indeed, the world is ruled by little else. . . . I am sure the power of vested interests is vastly exaggerated compared with the gradual encroachment of ideas."

Their search for new ideas started without constraints. Challenging the underlying assumptions of education, they took nothing as given. School district boundaries, teacher education requirements, tenure practices, certification procedures, district governance structures, state core curriculum, length of school day and year, differentiated staffing practices, and accountability systems were all called into question. The policy entrepreneurs wanted a school system that would suit postindustrial society and every aspect of the existing system received scrutiny.

Ideas came from two sources. Some were *adapted* from other policy domains. Observing deregulation in industry, for example, policy entrepreneurs believed that education would derive similar benefits from competition. As choice broke the stranglehold of unnecessary mandates and protection in transportation, so too it would provide the leverage for change in education.

Other ideas were *original.* A participant in a brainstorming session credited one policy entrepreneur with a new discovery: "We were holding a meeting with teachers and [the policy entrepreneur] asked them, 'Who do you work for?' The teachers were unclear about whether they worked for the kids, the district, or the school. However, one thing was clear: they did not work for themselves. This made them sad. In a flash of insight, he determined that teachers were the only professional group that did not have a choice to be either employed or in private practice. They had to be employed. [The concept of] teachers-in-private-practice was born."

Lawyers, psychologists, and physicians all have the option to form legal partnerships to pursue private practice, and so should teachers. Teacher partnerships could operate like any professional association. The partnership could have the option of offering an array of services such as teaching specialized subjects, writing curricula, or working with students with special needs. It would give teachers greater autonomy and flexibility to determine their own staffing, budgets, and resource utilization. The concept as envisioned was a possible way to bring back talented teachers who had left education for more lucrative and professional work.

After many sessions similar to this one, the informal group of policy entrepreneurs and change agents centered their discussions on nine ideas they thought were worth pursuing: parent-student school choice, school-site management (which involves assigning decisions about curriculum, budget, and personnel to the schools rather than the school districts), teacher partnerships (teachers-in-private-practice), shared facilities, a model schools program, technology for tomorrow's schools, alternative pathways to a teaching career, and new career advancement patterns for teachers (Public School Incentives, 1984a). Group members drafted position papers on all these ideas, but devoted the most attention, time, and energy to parent-student choice, school-site management, and teachers-in-private-practice.

Demonstration Projects and Funding

Excited about their ideas, but lacking funding and official support, the informal group decided to form a 501(c)(3) nonprofit corporation called Public School Incentives (PSI) in 1981. The purpose of the group was "to translate innovative, high potential ideas into demonstration projects to test their efficacy and potential for success in Minnesota schools" (Public School Incentives, 1984b). Successes from these projects could be used to argue for widespread dissemination, and failures or problems would help refine the ideas and avoid trouble on a larger scale.

Since resources were needed to translate ideas into testable programs, PSI also served as a fiscal agent for foundations willing to support innovative projects in education. A total of $1.2 million was eventually funneled through the organization, some of it supporting innovative ideas such as school-site management and parent-student choice. For example, in 1983, PSI received a $135,000 grant from the McKnight Foundation to look at public school choice and study various family-choice arrangements both locally and nationally. One policy entrepreneur joined PSI as part of the McKnight grant. Within a year, he revised his book on educational reform, which was widely disseminated at the state and national level (Minnesota Senator David Durenburger gave a copy to each of his Senate colleagues). The book summarized parent-student choice models and described examples such as magnet schools, choice within and between districts, and private school voucher systems.

PSI also actively worked for expanding choice in Minnesota. A voucher bill, advocating a limited voucher system for low income families, was moved along by testimony of PSI representatives. Choice, in their view, had the potential to break the hold of the regulated monopoly of schools because it permitted students to seek out the learning opportunities that best met their needs and goals.

Information Dissemination and Networking

Policy entrepreneurs engaged in a continual effort to spread their ideas as widely as possible. They wrote books, position papers, and journal and newspaper articles to publicize the new policy options they were designing, and sought feedback from their audience. By encouraging press coverage of events and issues, the policy entrepreneurs also got help from the media in publicizing their ideas. On occasion, they drafted speeches or parts of speeches for politicians, and served as guests on local and national radio and television programs. One policy entrepreneur was even a host of a local public television public affairs program.

Despite this array of mass-media channels, one entrepreneur complained that it was difficult to get a hearing. "There are not enough forums. At the national level, there is *The Public Interest* or *The New York Review of Books*, but at the state level, they are very hard to find. . . . However, it is not as difficult in Minnesota compared to other states. We have an unusual number of citizen groups. The Citizens League performs a very valuable service. You can offer proposals that seem to be weird and the League encourages, blesses, and gives the ideas legitimacy."

The policy entrepreneurs also employed face-to-face meetings (both formal and informal) to promote their ideas and attract support. They gave speeches on a variety of public policy issues to a wide range of audiences. They taught courses in leadership development programs and graduate programs in public affairs to help shape the attitudes and behaviors of students who would enter public service. They were in constant touch with a large network of people who cited their phone calls and personal contacts, and the articles and documents they sent, as factors keeping them updated on ongoing policy debates. The policy entrepreneurs even created forums to discuss redesign topics, bringing together national education experts with state and local political and education leaders. Commenting on a policy entrepreneur at one such occasion, an amazed observer said: "He is phenomenal—the most effective organizer I've ever run into. . . . He just makes a couple of phone calls to people and says, 'Gee, I'm having a little gathering at my office. Would you like to come?' The governor shows up, the commissioner shows up—everybody shows up."

As time passed and their ideas became better known, the policy entrepreneurs began to enter the national arena. One accepted a job to coordinate a major project for the highly visible and active National Governors' Association, which had decided to investigate the current state of education. Although he continued to take part at the state level, this entrepreneur's new obligations drew him more and more into national education circles, spreading the team's ideas as he went. Thus, information channels and networks began to develop well beyond the confines of local and state government.

Cultivation of Bureaucratic Insiders

The policy entrepreneurs were aware that their innovative ideas would be difficult to initiate from outside state government. Although one team member was in the legislature, he did not view himself an insider, and none of the others had any formal position in government. Strategically placed insiders would be important not only to initiate their ideas, but to carry the ideas during the later phases of the innovation process. Two noteworthy examples illustrate how the policy entrepreneurs developed and cultivated a governmental network of like-minded reformers.

First, policy entrepreneurs worked to get district superintendent Ruth Randall the opportunity to present a speech at the legislature. Her "Horizon" speech attracted the governor's attention, and—with some additional encouragement from the policy entrepreneurs and others—the governor nominated her to be his commissioner of education. As a self-proclaimed change agent who shared some of the entrepreneurs' ideas, the new commissioner's very visible and proactive reform stance helped disseminate the ideas of educational redesign to an even wider audience. She was described as the first commissioner in modern memory with an agenda to change anything, and her advocacy was critical in moving ideas to the decision agenda. Said a policy entrepreneur, "Without Ruth Randall at the helm, no significant change in policy would have occurred." Her outspoken support of innovative ideas eroded her slim base of support among mainstream educators, but she provided invaluable expertise in formulating legislative proposals and administrative procedures, especially in the design and implementation phases of the innovation process.

In the second case, a policy entrepreneur cultivated a relationship with a Department of Education staff member who took part in a university-sponsored leadership development program the entrepreneur led in 1980. This initial contact exposed the strategically placed insider to the entrepreneurs' ideas and convinced him of the logic of their arguments. The policy entrepreneur stayed in touch with him throughout his tenure in office through phone calls, meetings, and discussion groups, often sending him articles and readings to keep him abreast of the latest developments in education. He, in turn, provided inside information on department activities, keeping the policy entrepreneurs up-to-date on the critical developments. As we shall see, his help was invaluable during the legislative sessions.

Collaboration on Major Studies with High-Profile Groups

To gain greater credibility for their ideas, the policy entrepreneurs often worked with and through other organizations and groups, especially those with high visibility and good standing within the larger community. The objective was to urge these groups to sponsor studies on the status of education and to propose recommendations for change. They were successful in collaborating with two important organizations, the Citizens League and the Minnesota Business Partnership, both of which issued reports recommending dramatic educational reforms consistent with, or in a some cases identical to, ideas espoused by the policy entrepreneurs. Four of the six policy entrepreneurs either provided expert testimony or served on the committee that produced *Rebuilding Education to Make It Work,* the controversial 1982 Citizens League report endorsing educational restructuring and school choice. And when the Minnesota Business Partnership commissioned a $250,000 study on the state educational system, several policy entrepreneurs provided input. In fact, one of them helped set up the study and delimit the design and parameters for the team hired to conduct the research. As the policy entrepreneur described his involvement:

> We [MBP] spent a lot of time negotiating with them [Berman and Weiler, the research team] about our expectations that were exactly—almost completely contrary to their previous work. . . .
> We felt in the California work that the data assessment part of it was excellent. We wanted to replicate that here, that is, to really come in and critique and analyze what was happening here. That part of it of course was going to be identical to California. But the strategies that were appropriate here are *dramatically different* than California. . . . How do you spend money more effectively [we asked,] and how do you manage a more effective school system at a time of conserving resources? We explicitly said to them in our negotiations that spending more money was off the list.

Given the policy entrepreneurs' level of involvement, it was not surprising that the recommendations in both reports paralleled their ideas. Equally significant, the reports signaled to the larger community that educational restructuring and school choice were viable options. No longer consigned to the fringes of policy debate, the new ideas had the endorsement and advocacy of two very credible and influential organizations.

Initial Legislative Efforts

The policy entrepreneurs' earliest efforts to introduce reform and educational choice to the legislature came during the 1983–84 session. The 1982 Citizens League report met with resistance from policy makers who refused to endorse its voucher plan—the controversial proposal that opened up the issue of public aid to private education. No one in the legislature was willing to endorse the report or sponsor it as a bill. However, a state representative (and later a policy entrepreneur) ultimately introduced a modified version that recommended a voucher option for students of low and moderate income families. These vouchers, according to the bill, could be cashed in any private or public school that met certain selection criteria set up by the state. The bill gave the topic of vouchers visibility. It received support from a broad coalition of people of color, low-income whites, and others who worked with low-income families. Although the House held hearings on the bill, neither proponents nor opponents called for a vote. "Nobody ever expected that bill to pass but everyone expected it to stir up a thoroughly interesting conversation about how you were going to change things," said one insider (Wilhelm, 1984, p. 257).

According to some observers, however, the bill did have an impact. While it did not sell the idea of vouchers, it enhanced the legislators' awareness of major educational reform and made them more receptive to change (Wilhelm, 1984). It also created a loose quasi coalition of minority people, the disadvantaged, and discontented educators seeking alternatives to the present system, and thereby laid a groundwork for reform that had the potential to be activated in the future.

Strategy and Coordination

The policy entrepreneurs tended to organize themselves into a core group for the purpose of preparing a road map for change:

grand strategy to guide their efforts and *tactical political strategies* to cope with day-to-day changing political realities. As one policy entrepreneur noted, grand strategy provided the overall direction of the change effort. Tactical political strategy required a more short-term focus, often centered on the legislature and the shifting political mood. The tactical strategy was often modified to fit the evolving political context, and to clarify what was attainable given the political mood. As one policy entrepreneur summed up the activity: "What we're doing . . . is identifying both short-term tactics and long-term strategies . . . or how we make this happen. Nothing like this happens that isn't orchestrated. This doesn't fall into place. You've got to decide where to push, when you push, and what your position is."

The group usually met once a week, although attendance at the meetings was fluid depending on the agenda. Any of the six could call a meeting. Strategy meetings normally involved only the core group. Informational sessions also drew in outsiders—strategically placed midlevel Department of Education managers, legislative staff members, education consultants, foundation staff members, representatives of business firms, lobbyists, and sympathetic members of the education establishment—who would be asked to share their insight and provide up-to-date feedback on the inclinations of key legislators, the governor, and education groups.

Search for a Policy Champion

Despite the successes of the policy entrepreneurs up to this point (1984), and the credibility and support they had built with some major constituencies, there still was a great deal of opposition to school choice and educational redesign. To move the ideas beyond discussion and onto the decision agenda, the entrepreneurs needed a policy champion, someone who had visibility, credibility, and clout. Assessing the political climate, one policy entrepreneur commented: "It was very clear . . . with the strength education groups—the organized groups—enjoyed in this state, we weren't going to get anywhere without a major, popular political leader making it his policy. It was absolutely of basic importance to find out if the governor would undertake this cause" (Mazzoni, 1986, p. 33). The opportunity came along in the fall of 1984.

The Department of Education had begun planning for improvement in the summer of 1984, and department representatives had proposed numerous ideas that were rejected by the Department of Finance and the governor's executive team. The ideas were dismissed as too costly in a period of budget constraint, and as failing to provide an integrated educational package. Finance Commissioner Gus Donhowe, who also had close ties with the policy entrepreneurs and the Citizens League, wanted something new. He opposed throwing more money at education, which was already the largest item in the state budget. As one member of the education department expressed it, there was a "fundamental communication problem." Department of Education representatives did not understand the executive team's budget philosophy and the executive team did not respond favorably to the policy recommendations coming from the Department of Education.

The stalemate wore on through late 1984, exacerbated by the department's lack of access to the governor's team. One Department of Education member voiced frustration and concern. "We can't get in. The executive team just blocked us out. We can't get at them."

Then, on December 6, 1984, there was a very important phone call. A policy entrepreneur tracked down an education department representative who was out of town on agency business. He asked his contact, with whom he had developed close ties over the years, how things were going. Did he need some help? Was the department going to have any new proposals? The representative explained the department's difficulties and why it was impossible to get their ideas before the executive team. He remembered his words to the policy entrepreneur this way: "We're not going anywhere—we're just dead, finished. The budget's got to be done and Finance makes the decisions and we can't get to the executive team."

When asked if the policy entrepreneur should try to help, the department representative recalls that he responded,

> Yes, if you can get into that [meeting] you could do something. . . .
> If you want to change education policy in this state at this moment in
> time, you have to get to the executive team. You have to get to their
> meetings and you have to come with a fair amount of force and
> bring people with you. . . . You'll have to represent us [Education]

because we can't be there. . . . We're dead—just finished—can't move. The executive team blocked us off. In fact, they not only blocked us off, they're ridiculing us. . . . We can't get anywhere. You'll have to break it open or something.

The policy entrepreneurs already had access to the meeting, though the Department of Education official did not know of it at the time. After the fall legislative elections, a policy entrepreneur had attended an evening program for newly elected legislators at the Citizens League, an orientation set up to get them acquainted with one another and with the League. At one point in the evening, the policy entrepreneur sat down next to Tom Triplett, who at that time was director of the State Planning Agency. Triplett indicated that the governor's people were "in the market for an education program" and invited further discussion.

So on December 7, a select group of policy entrepreneurs set up a meeting with the governor's policy team, which included Triplett along with Lani Kawamura, deputy director of planning, Keith Ford, the governor's chief of staff, and some other key players. The education department insider described the results as they were later recounted to him: "For whatever [the policy entrepreneur] did after we talked, he arranged to get a select group of people and they had an audience with the executive team. And [he] sold them on choice. I mean, to the point where . . . [a member of the Finance Department] loved it so much he couldn't stop talking about it. So now all of a sudden, the door's open for us."

The meeting continued for about two to three hours. As Deputy Finance Commissioner Jay Kiedrowski said, it "altered Minnesota's education agenda." Said another attendee, "That meeting probably turned around the willingness of the governor's policy team to introduce something. . . . I think it probably pretty well excited most of the group present."

By December 10, the Department of Education formally heard from the executive team that "we have found life." And by December 17, members of the finance and education departments, with the policy entrepreneurs' input, had pulled together a package to brief the governor.

The governor's response surprised even his closest advisers. Said one member of the Finance Department: "When we went in—

in fact we talked about how we would approach him on this issue—and we went in, in a very quiet, soft, easy [way]. 'Here's the kind of steps you've been taking. We're interested in this kind of thing.' And frankly, *he* jumped on the bandwagon. The bandwagon started moving quicker than we thought possible. He liked it so much, he started dragging us. Honest to God, he started dragging us."

Ignoring the warnings of an adviser that public school choice was so controversial that he could blow his reelection supporting it, Perpich told the group to go ahead and draft a formal proposal for him to introduce to the legislature. Commented a Department of Education official: "We got the green light on all of the ideas—learner outcomes, testing—we got the green light on everything. And off we went. And I mean, that was the quickest four days you'll ever see. . . . This was not planned change. This was serendipity. It just happened to be at some given time all the right things came together and it was sold entirely on an informal network. There's no formal procedure in that whatsoever."

Design Phase: 1984–1988

The policy entrepreneurs understood their good fortune. As one said, "people with ideas are a dime a dozen, they are always around. What is not around is a major elected official to pick up an unpopular idea and press it." Working under a tight deadline, the policy entrepreneurs and the governor's policy advisors had to prepare the proposal before his State of the State address.

The Governor's Initiative: *Access to Excellence*

Perpich wanted a separate announcement to dramatize the central role educational reform was to play in his administration. On January 4, 1985, he unveiled *Access to Excellence*. As described in Chapter Two, he proposed to phase in parent-student choice between the 1986–87 and the 1988–89 school years and to provide state aid to whatever public school (or, for eleventh and twelfth graders, postsecondary institution) each student attended. Other aspects of the proposal included greater state financing, state evaluation of student outcomes, and reduction of state mandates. The package was virtually identical to the basic ideas on education redesign that had been recommended by the Minnesota Business Partnership and the policy entrepreneurs.

Enlisting Policy Champions in the Legislature

The governor's announcement created the expected uproar. His more cautious advisors had been accurate in their assessment; resistance came from all quarters. Traditional education groups predicted chaos in the schools, and legislators from both parties resented his intrusion into the domain of educational policy making. Ironically, the first person to support the proposal was former governor Al Quie, whom Perpich had defeated for the governorship. But finding policy champions in the legislature was difficult under these circumstances. Without someone to sponsor the governor's ambitious educational policy agenda, no initiative could be introduced to the legislature.

The bureaucratic insider and ally of the policy entrepreneurs knew that Representative Connie Levi of the Independent Republican Party had sponsored a bill to permit high school juniors and seniors to attend college while continuing in high school. Realizing that her legislation was similar to the governor's proposal, he recommended her to Perpich. After some negotiation, she agreed to champion the bill in the House. The governor also picked up support from Senator Tom Nelson, a member of the governor's party. Thanks to these two legislators, Perpich could introduce his controversial initiative.

1985 Strategy and Planning

Gearing up for the 1985 legislative session, the policy entrepreneurs stepped up the pace of their meetings. Said one observer, "[They meet] much too often. . . . [One of them] stops by here at least twice a week to fill me in." Yet this pace was necessary to coordinate the growing number of groups attracted to the debate, such as the Minnesota PTA and the League of Women Voters. The team also wanted to keep abreast of the activities of the opposition, the 6M consortium of established education groups. As the governor and his staff became directly involved in the strategy sessions, the coordination and strategy group expanded to include representatives from the Minnesota Business Partnership, the Citizens League, and the Department of Education, as well as educator and special interest groups.

In the initial discussions, the governor's staff was worried about two things: damage control and mobilizing support for the divisive initiative. To fend off political flak, a three-tiered support strategy developed, and the policy entrepreneurs were central to pulling it all together. Reasoning that political clout and name recognition would provoke interest and capture media attention, the policy entrepreneurs recommended attracting well-known figures. Elites, or *thought leaders,* as one policy entrepreneur called them, were important to cultivate for the innovation process. "If you got elites committed, the rest would fall into place." "Big name types" then could form one lobby group as the first element of the strategy while another advocacy group could organize the grassroots supporters as the second line of attack. The policy entrepreneurs also recommended a media campaign. Redesign advocates needed to gain and keep media interest in order to activate and build public support. Public support, in turn, would likely allay some of the fears legislators had about school choice. The policy entrepreneurs provided some of the coordination to make sure that things happened as planned.

Lobbying Activities

Following their three-tiered strategy, the governor's staff asked the Minnesota Business Partnership, with the help of several policy entrepreneurs, to form a high-profile lobbying group. The resulting Brainpower Compact included business leaders, four past governors of both political parties (one, Quie, a nationally recognized leader in education), state educational leaders, and the mayor of St. Paul. With funding from Partnership member firms, the Brainpower Compact hired a lobbyist and a public relations specialist to support the governor's initiative for the 1985 legislative campaign. Meanwhile, the Partnership conducted a letter-writing campaign in support of the bill, and sponsored personal appearances by Lewis Lehr (then CEO of 3M) to endorse the governor's initiative. Under the guidance of its lobbyist, the Partnership was reportedly persuasive in creating initial legislative momentum for the bill (Sturdevant, 1985b).

The grassroots strategy was rolled out with flourish. At the request of the governor, a policy entrepreneur organized the first meeting of what was eventually to be known as People for Better Schools. Held at the State Capitol in St. Paul, Minnesota, at twenty-four degrees below zero (it was February 2), this grassroots meeting attracted some of the original members of Public School Incentives (citizen-activists who supported the initial choice bill in 1983–84), the governor, his key advisers, and the media.

Opening the meeting in hushed tones, the policy entrepreneur created an aura of anticipation and promise: "I was on the telephone this morning with *Time* magazine and I told the journalist on the line that 'this is the most important meeting in the state today—maybe in the country—on behalf of kids, parents, and taxpayers.'" Another dramatic moment came when a former president of the PTA, a well-known voucher opponent, challenged Perpich to state whether or not the meeting was about vouchers for private schools. Perpich answered by pledging support for *public* school choice. Satisfied, the PTA activist agreed to help the governor, and encouraged the state PTA to join with him—which it did.

The thirty-five people at the gathering, most of them teachers, superintendents, principals, or school board members, eventually formed the nucleus of a growing statewide network to support public school choice. They began a campaign to influence legislators, blanketing newspaper editorial columns with favorable letters. Up against the teachers' unions, two of the state's most effective lobbying groups, People for Better Schools sought to build a real movement to oppose the education establishment. By March 1986, they had 780 members across the state, many of whom personally lobbied for the legislation and were the base of support beyond the Twin Cities of Minneapolis and St. Paul.

The founder of People for Better Schools went on to orchestrate a tireless lobbying effort at the legislature. He and other group members often visited the capitol to deliver information on choice to lawmakers and their staffs, and to create a visible presence at hearings. They were most successful in obtaining testimony of credible supporters, including principals, superintendents, school board members, and students, on behalf of school choice. One legislative analyst noted their impact: "This has been one of the few issues in all the years I've been here that I've seen develop that way. . . . This developed almost in textbook fashion. The testimony was convincing! People came in support of that idea that you never would have expected—the principals' organization for example" (Mazzoni, 1986, p. 67).

Media Relations

Throughout the legislative session, every effort was made to get media coverage of the deliberations and testimony. Reasoning that it was important to help push their ideas forward and to keep the issues visible, policy entrepreneurs worked very diligently to get and keep press coverage. Enticing media attention took a lot of effort, as one policy entrepreneur explained. "The educational establishment thought we had the press in our pockets but we had to work very hard to get the press involved. . . . We called, we begged . . . we worked closely with the press to get people interested and to keep [our ideas] on the agenda." Capitol reporters were unimpressed with the initiative when the governor presented it. They knew the major education groups were opposed, and concluded nothing would come of it. "Why cover stuff that wasn't going to be happening?" It was only after the bill cleared both houses of the legislature that they became interested.

Media attention was expected to increase public awareness and support for the ideas and to convince recalcitrant legislators of the merits of the governor's bill. It also was needed to counter the strength of the 6M group's opposition, especially the Minnesota Education Association (MEA). Thus, identifying good stories for the press and encouraging reporters to print them became an important entrepreneurial tactic, especially "David versus Goliath" stories that attracted journalists who liked to cover a fight.

The policy entrepreneurs' efforts did not go unnoticed. Members of the education establishment criticized a major paper for lack of objectivity in reporting on the educational issues and dismissed one policy entrepreneur's media interventions by saying, "He has excellent access to the media. . . . In fact, the *Minneapolis Star and Tribune* has lost its perspective in news coverage. . . . They like to focus on change and controversy."

There were close ties between the policy entrepreneurs and the media. One, a former journalist and editorial writer, was close to the editor of a local business publication—an association that dated back to their work on the *Minneapolis Star and Tribune*. They also lived near each other and talked regularly about education issues. This policy entrepreneur also worked closely with the wife of one of the *Tribune*'s editorial writers. A second policy entrepreneur was linked with WCCO television and with an editorial writer of the *St. Paul Pioneer Press and Dispatch*. The writer called the policy entrepreneur a close friend. There were also ties to Minnesota public radio.

These relationships raised the hackles of traditional education establishment members, who complained that the policy entrepreneurs had a "distinct advantage with good media connections and knowing how to manipulate these relationships." One admitted that educators did not know how to use the media effectively, stating that "6M doesn't use the media . . . except the MEA—they like to deal aggressively with the media."

Strategy and Planning II: 1986–1988

When most of Perpich's ambitious proposal failed to pass during the 1985 legislative session, the governor changed his strategy. He asked his Commissioner of Education to invite former adversaries to join the Governor's Discussion Group (GDG) and develop their own visionary proposal for state education. As the forum shifted, so did the policy entrepreneurs' strategy and coordination efforts.

From August 1985 through the 1987 legislative session, the GDG was the focal point for educational policy debates. Working closely with Commissioner Randall and her staff, policy entrepreneurs helped shape the GDG's monthly agenda to keep redesign ideas prominent. They made the case that evaluation of education's operating assumptions and givens would be a good starting point, and thus the GDG began by examining the status quo—and by implication questioning education's relevance for a postindustrial society. Policy entrepreneurs also volunteered to write rough drafts of GDG policy statements, which ultimately became the framework for the visionary plan.

This proactive stance kept educators off balance and forced some of them to defend the status quo. In so doing, it reinforced the perception that educators were averse to change and lacked new ideas. The press took note—as did the public, which was kept up-to-date with reports of GDG activities and progress.

Other tactics were less transparent. Meeting for breakfast before the monthly GDG session, and conferring by telephone as needed, the policy entrepreneurs developed a game plan for each meeting. Said one: "There was a clear attempt to control the agenda. . . . There was a good bit of discussion of what was going to happen at the meeting. . . . We sounded out the arguments that we expected to get back in rebuttal, we tried to consider the tactics that might be employed. . . . We tried to be alert to the sensitivities of the players from the commissioner and her staff to the governor. . . . We planned ahead."

The game plan also involved various policy entrepreneurs and supporters taking specific roles in the debate. One or another would agree to be the "bad guy" who launched an attack, the "mediator/negotiator/compromiser" who sought common ground and mutually agreeable solutions, the "questioner" who tried to direct the flow of the discussion, or the "orator" who gave impassioned speeches about the urgency of reform and the importance of the restructuring agenda. "At some meetings, somebody said, 'I'm going to be the bad guy today.' . . . Somebody else said, 'I'm going to get out there on the edge and push and start talking in more threatening terms.' . . . And somebody else said, 'I'm going to look more like a mediator.' . . . The roles were never assigned but happened instinctively."

Judging from the comments of GDG participants, most were unaware of this background scripting. The three or four who were aware did complain of the policy entrepreneurs' undue influence and expressed their dissatisfaction with the GDG's group process, agenda setting, leadership, and criteria for membership (Roberts and Bradley, 1991). Little was done to alter the process and procedures, however. Although the commissioner attempted to run the meetings in even-handed fashion, she found it difficult both as the manager and facilitator of the GDG to contain the policy entrepreneurs' determined and focused behavior.

As the policy debates shifted from the legislature to the GDG, relationships among the policy entrepreneurs, the governor, and key bureaucratic insiders changed as well. They had followed a unified strategy for the 1985 legislative session, but their paths began to diverge. Perpich decided he now needed the participation and involvement of the educational establishment. He invited educational groups to join the GDG, and chose to take a less visible stance while awaiting the group's recommendations in 1987. "This time, we'll do it together," he is reported to have said.

To the policy entrepreneurs, the governor appeared to be retreating from his stand on public school choice. His apparent turnaround created chaos among supporters. They believed he gave mixed signals when he reversed an earlier announcement and sought political endorsement from the MEA, a powerful teachers union. Frustrated with this apparent backpedaling, a policy entrepreneur discussed his concerns with an influential *Minneapolis Star and Tribune* writer. Soon afterward, a scathing editorial appeared:

> Like the astronomy establishment of Galileo's day, the public-education establishment disliked such innovation [school choice]. But before they could grade and correct Perpich's composition, he passed it around out of class. He let other students read it, and the student council, and other grown-ups who pay taxes and even business and professional people. . . . [The members of the educational establishment] were miffed. They reminded Perpich that student compositions are supposed to be OK'd first by the proper authority. They told him he was too independent, that his attitude was dangerous. . . . Just as Galileo abjured his heretical writings, Perpich told his tormentors that he would stop pushing for open enrollment. Perpich's now-muffled opinion is right; his recanting is wrong. Bolder astronomers soon vindicated Galileo. . . . bolder would-be governors should soon vindicate Perpich ["Perpich Sort of Recants," 1986].

The editorial writer readily admitted he was in contact with the policy entrepreneurs, who "fed ideas and information about the Governor's Discussion Group" to him. He was adamant that the editorial was his, however.

By May 1987, becoming increasingly frustrated with what they considered the governor's and commissioner's lukewarm advocacy of the GDG visionary proposal, the policy entrepreneurs decided to make their criticism public. They communicated their displeasure in a letter signed by ten of the non-education-group members of the GDG. They also took the letter to a reporter at the *St. Paul*

Pioneer Press and Dispatch. In reporting the story, the paper led with the headline: "Reformers Claim School Bill Gutted." Sections of the letter were quoted in the article: "We are looking at a disaster in terms of significant change in this state's system of education. Virtually everything we proposed for a strategy of incentives and opportunities has disappeared from the bills" (Dalglish, 1987).

According to a staff member, the letter made Perpich furious. Key sponsors of the redesign legislation were also irritated. One expressed incredulity that the policy entrepreneurs would broadside their strongest supporters. (The letter had also criticized Randall for substituting more palatable language in the bill.) "Acting out of school" and not discussing the matter with the governor, commissioner, or supportive lawmakers caused a rift between the policy entrepreneurs and their legislative allies. Said one legislator: "It was very inappropriate. . . . They didn't speak to us first . . . They shouldn't do this without advance warning. They just went to the press. You don't publicly accuse or embarrass those who are trying to help you. They . . . did a disservice to say that little or nothing was happening. . . . It was unfair."

Indeed, the policy entrepreneurs had not been privy to Perpich's strategy. He had been working behind the scenes to ensure the passage of additional school choice legislation. Although he did not want a fight, before the 1988 legislative session Perpich made it clear to key lawmakers that the legislation was very important to him and he did not want it held hostage. Loritz (his lobbyist) was to take a low profile and "be ready to go in when and if" public school choice legislation "got in trouble."

Although the governor held a meeting to address the letter, and dispatched Loritz to reassure the policy entrepreneurs that something would happen with the visionary proposal in 1988, they were skeptical. They became even more alarmed when the legislative conference committee met, and senators began sending out warnings about trouble for open enrollment, and calling up policy entrepreneurs and telling them to come and help. Loritz cautioned them to stay away from the legislature, however. Certain groups like the Minnesota Business Partnership were "a real problem for some people," he said. And, according to a close observer, Loritz was especially concerned about one policy entrepreneur, who had been arguing with a key legislator over taking credit for open enrollment. Loritz did not want him threatening the delicate negotiations.

The policy entrepreneurs did not understand how delicate the negotiations were, as they had alienated themselves from their allies and were no longer receiving confidential interpretations of the governor's actions from bureaucratic insiders. The House was expected to pass one set of initiatives for Perpich while the Senate passed a set that was completely different, especially regarding open enrollment. In their attempts to reconcile the different education bills, conferees would be forced to trade and negotiate with each other, giving both houses some of what they wanted. Eventually conferees understood the governor's strategy: "We take a beating, we kill each other, and you [Perpich] get everything." Indeed, according to Loritz, the governor had used this strategy since 1985 to get his program passed. The House would pass part of his package and the Senate the other part and he would get most of what he wanted. Half in admiration and half in irritation, a teacher union lobbyist concurred: Perpich had rewritten the book on strategy.

Pursuing a media-centered, confrontational strategy focused on the educational establishment, the policy entrepreneurs had misread and misinterpreted Perpich's intentions. Without the behind-the-scenes operations and skillful shuttle diplomacy of the governor's lobbyist, all might have been for naught, at least in 1988. As it was, mandatory open enrollment passed, the first legislation of its kind in the country. The policy entrepreneurs' strategic miscalculations and missteps had not been fatal.

Implementation Phase: 1985–1988

The policy entrepreneurs were at a decided disadvantage when it came to implementing and evaluating public school choice. Their intellectual and political talents had won them a hearing during the creative and design phases of the innovation process. The distant and dispersed duties of administration were more difficult to influence. Educational policy once enacted into law is turned over to the Department of Education. While the legislature retains oversight responsibility, day-to-day management is the job of the department. Even if department staff meant to apply the law exactly as intended (which research studies indicate is a big assumption; see Pressman and Wildavsky, 1973), implementation in 435 school districts throughout the state is difficult to manage, monitor, and evaluate.

So in contrast to their hands-on and active involvement in the first two phases of the innovation process, the policy entrepreneurs had to stand aside and watch the educational establishment implement school choice. Now on educators' turf, the team had less access to the process, and they had to revise their strategy accordingly. Fortunately, their close ties with the commissioner of education afforded them opportunities that they would not otherwise have had. With the commissioner as ally, the policy entrepreneurs intervened when and where they could to leverage their resources and protect the idea of school choice. The measures they took have been described partially in Chapter Two, but it is useful to look at them again in a new context.

Facilitate Program Administration

The commissioner's task force on implementation had tackled many of the issues prior to the 1985 legislation, so the Department of Education had a head start on establishing the program. In a matter of a few months, it devised a comprehensive plan for public school choice. When the department needed to inform the schools and the public of the new open enrollment program, the policy entrepreneurs were there to help with mass mailings. The department was under a great deal of pressure to implement the program quickly, and was grateful for the support.

Organize Student Users

Concerned that implementation might not be going as smoothly as they hoped, and fearful that traditional educators would attempt a rearguard effort to sabotage the law, policy entrepreneurs were anxious to hear firsthand how the program was faring. They asked the commissioner for the names of students in the Postsecondary Enrollment Options Program and permission to contact them in person. Permission was refused due to federal confidentiality law, but the commissioner did agree to host a meeting with the GDG for all program participants.

According to one policy entrepreneur, the purpose of the meeting with the students was twofold: "To get positive media coverage of the students who were using the Postsecondary Enrollment Options Program, and to obtain the names of the student users to make them available to members of the Governor's Discussion Group." As GDG members, the policy entrepreneurs went one step further. They organized and coordinated the interested students into a lobbying force at the legislature. And by all accounts, the resulting testimony and lobbying efforts were impressive—they were responsible, in large measure, for reversing some lawmakers' opinions on school choice.

Task Force Funding and Evaluation

Minnesota lawmakers wrote mandatory program evaluation into the school choice law—but they provided no funding to the Department of Education to carry out the charge. Policy entrepreneurs, who by this time had developed an extensive national network, called contacts at the U.S. Department of Education in search of low-cost evaluation assistance. An evaluation team from a consulting firm under contract with the U.S. Department of Education was eventually sent out to work with the Minnesota Department of Education.

Several policy entrepreneurs, appointed by Randall, also joined this first evaluation task force. In this capacity, they were able to influence, design, oversee, and evaluate the statewide implementation of open enrollment. Limited by their positions outside government and prevented from direct involvement in implementation activities, they were able to monitor the program from this excellent vantage point. While there is no evidence that this participation skewed or biased the evaluation results, some educators feared potential bias, and the commissioner decided not to reappoint the entrepreneurs to the second evaluation task force. By that time, however, the initial results were in. The Postsecondary Enrollment Options Program was a success, and momentum was growing to expand its application to others besides high school juniors and seniors.

Thus we conclude with a list drawn from our earlier work (Roberts and King, 1991, p. 168) that outlines the complete activity structure of the policy entrepreneurs.

A. Creative/Intellectual Activities
   1. Generate Ideas
      • Invent new policy ideas
      • Apply models and ideas from other policy domains
   2. Define Problem and Select Solution
      • Define performance gap
      • Identify preferred solution alternative
   3. Disseminate Ideas
B. Strategic Activities
   1. Formulate grand strategy and vision
   2. Evolve political strategy
   3. Develop heuristics for action
C. Mobilization and Execution Activities
   1. Establish demonstration projects
   2. Cultivate bureaucratic insiders and advocates
   3. Collaborate with high-profile individuals and elite groups
   4. Enlist support of elected officials
   5. Form lobby groups and coordinate efforts
   6. Cultivate media attention and support
D. Administrative and Evaluative Activities
   1. Facilitate program administration
   2. Participate in program evaluation

Chapter Four

The Players Behind the Scenes

The Entrepreneurial Team and Its Network

Never doubt that a small group of thoughtful committed citizens can change the world; indeed it is the only thing that ever has.
—MARGARET MEAD

The policy entrepreneurs operated collectively, pooling their resources rather than working independently to achieve their ends. The group gave each member strength for maneuvering through the complex terrain of educational policy making. Yet team entrepreneurship has problems as well as benefits. Setting goals and choosing strategies, coordinating activities, and managing disputes over personal preferences are acquired skills. It takes time to learn to work together, complement one another's talents and preferences, trust one another's advice and recommendations, and create a culture of support. Opening the door to the group's internal operations, this chapter shows the challenges of forming and maintaining a viable team.

Recall that the team consisted of six core members, all of whom worked outside government. Meeting informally during the late 1970s, they began attracting support from a growing circle committed to public school choice. Such prominent citizens as former Governor Quie, known as "Mr. Education" for the legislation he sponsored in the House; Roger King, vice president of a Fortune 1000 firm; and Steve Lindgren, former state senator and lob-byist for the Brain Power Compact all joined their ranks when the debates over open enrollment heated up in the legislature. The participation of these well-known Republicans gave public school choice bipartisan support during the very important deliberations in the legislature.

Group Identity

The group originally developed its identity as a behind-the-scenes operation working to effect what one member called a *paradigm shift* in educational policy. Concerned about prematurely activating opposition, which they knew would occur soon enough, they preferred to maintain a low profile and keep their strategic and well-coordinated activities off the record.

Group members gave several reasons for working together. They shared a sense of purpose built on their unified interest in educational reform. All considered themselves action-oriented change agents who found interaction with like-minded reformers rewarding. As one said, "people are here to make things happen." They also learned from one another—sharing ideas and information and exchanging notes about past experiences, especially about change strategies that had worked or failed. Mutual support and reality checks kept morale and spirits up during difficult times.

Group members also found that working together helped them maximize their impact. As one noted, "no one person has all the requisite skills or resources needed to engage in large-scale policy change and we need each other to distribute the workload." Said another, "it is inconceivable to consider such a large-scale endeavor without a network of committed individuals willing to work long and hard for policy change." Still another added that "one of the reasons why it [policy change] has worked is because there were enough of us doing it. . . . There was nearly always somebody pushing it. . . . You know there was always somebody turning some dial or turning some lever or talking to somebody. And if you didn't like what we were doing, it probably seemed like we were busier than we were."

Summing up their victories (some of them had worked together in other policy domains over the years), members believed they had the right ingredients for success. "We have the ability to see the big picture . . . and have our eye on major structural change. . . . We have achieved success together, I guess that's why we stick together. We are a winning combination."

Meetings

Meetings in the late 1970s and early 1980s were designed to gain insight, broaden understanding, test perceptions, and eventually identify a set of innovative education policy ideas that members could rally around. Deliberations began with no fixed agenda and no preset assumptions in mind, only a loose framework for redesigning public service. Attendance at meetings was fluid. Broadening their dialogue to include teachers, students, parents, business leaders, elected officials, and administrators as the occasion warranted, the group eventually evolved and prioritized a series of ideas to redesign education and improve performance. The idea of public school choice led the vanguard of change, while the complementary ideas of school-site management, teachers-in-private-practice, educational performance measurement, and charter schools were to follow. Working and reworking these ideas, the group eventually succeeded in getting their proposal for educational redesign and public school choice accepted and championed by the governor. At that point, the pace of their meetings accelerated. During the 1985 legislative session, for example, the group met at least once a week, with a similar pattern of activity during the ensuing years.

Structure

The group members shared an antibureaucratic bias. They preferred a lean, nonhierarchical arrangement to keep their interactions fluid and flexible. One member characterized it as "a very loose thing" with "no particular structure or chairman or any kind of pecking order or authority." They hired no staff, had no formal organization chart (even when their numbers grew to involve more individuals and groups), and created no rules or procedures to constrain member action. "There was a feeling that we didn't need to put a structure in place to keep the momentum of what we were doing moving ahead. In fact, I can't remember the suggestion or thought even passing through my own mind," said one. Nonregular members of the group were welcomed at meetings. However, if anyone tried to direct the conversation or even to delegate responsibility, the team creatively maneuvered to redirect his attention. "Nobody was impolite," a member reports, but they let it be known that such activity didn't fit. For example, one nonmember came to the group and attempted to assume leadership during a meeting. He was given the onerous task of taking formal notes and minutes (not something that was usually done at all), and "that's how we got [him] to stop chairing and that worked very well. Everybody was happy. . . . [People] kind of got the message that [rules and controls] were neither necessary or desirable."

Although the team did not regard itself as a formal entity, it did serve as the locus of organization, strategy formulation, and action for the change effort. One member described the group as the core in a constellation of groups and people devoted to educational reform. Another commented, "I don't want to be misleading, but we're providing whatever coordination is happening. . . . [We're] an umbrella group that doesn't have a name." Cultivated over a number of years, the constellation connected the group with national organizations such as the U.S. Department of Education and state organizations including the Minnesota Business Partnership, the Citizens League, and Public School Incentives. Exhibit 4.1 categorizes the major organizations in this constellation and provides a short description of each.

Coordination in this extended network of organizations revolved around task-specific activities. Someone had to call meetings, prepare loose agendas, and extend invitations so network members could caucus on particular issues. Someone had to keep people up-to-date about developments on the national, state, and local scenes, and prepare and distribute whatever written documentation the group might need. Someone had to adapt plans and strategies to suit the changing political climate. Someone had to hammer out specific tactics and assign roles for legislative sessions and Governor's Discussion Group meetings. Someone had to negotiate with the opposition and establish and maintain linkages with others who shared similar objectives.

Two factors were important in determining who performed which task: the skills required and the time available. Some members gravitated toward writing, some acted as spokesmen and negotiators,

Exhibit 4.1. Constellation of Organizations.

Government Organizations

1. **Minnesota Department of Education.** Responsible for the state's educational system and the implementation of educational policy. Headed by reform-minded Ruth Randall, commissioner of education, throughout this study (1983–1988).
2. **Minnesota Department of Finance.** Responsible for the state's budget and the allocation of state money. Headed by the commissioner of finance, Gus Donhowe, and the assistant commissioner, Jay Kedrowski.
3. **Minnesota Governor's Office.** The support office for the executive branch.
4. **Minnesota State Planning Agency.** Responsible for the state's long-range planning as well as policy analysis and new policy initiatives. Led by Tom Triplett, director of state planning, and Lani Kawamura, deputy director.
5. **United States Department of Education.** Responsible for educational policy and its implementation throughout the country. Funded evaluation studies of choice legislation in 1985 and 1986 at the request of the Minnesota Department of Education.

Nonprofits

6. **McKnight Foundation.** A private grant-making foundation established in 1953 by William L. McKnight and his wife, Maude L. McKnight. Its primary mission has been to assist people who are poor and disadvantaged, to advance public understanding of important issues, and to encourage citizens to participate in decisions that affect their lives and communities. Grants are made principally to nonprofit organizations in Minnesota.
7. **Northwest Area Foundation.** Founded in 1934 by Louis W. Hill, son of James J. Hill, builder of the Great Northern Railway. Its mission is to "promote the public welfare" with private means. Using Public School Incentives as the fiscal agent, the foundation funded $1.5 million in school-site management pilot projects throughout the upper Midwest.
8. **Citizens League.** A public affairs research and education organization in the Twin Cities metropolitan area founded in 1952.

Volunteer research committees of League members study policy issues and problems in depth and advocate specific solutions.

9. **Public School Incentives.** Organization formed by a group of concerned citizens, educators, administrators, and activists in the late 1970s. At first a discussion group, it evolved into a 501(c)(3) nonprofit organization. Its mission was to be a "design shop" where "high-potential" ideas could be developed and tested. It became the fiscal agent for the Northwest Area and McKnight Foundations.

10. **Minnesota Business Partnership.** An association, formed in 1977, of the chief executive officers of ninety-five of Minnesota's largest corporations. Its mission is to promote a healthy economic and social environment for all Minnesotans by attracting and keeping quality jobs in the state. In 1983, it commissioned a study and hired Berman-Weiler Associates to assess the performance of Minnesota's schools and make recommendations for change.

11. **Hubert H. Humphrey Institute of Public Affairs.** This graduate school of public affairs at the University of Minnesota serves in part as a nonpartisan resource to help empower citizens, communities, and organizations for effective participation in the public policy arena through technical assistance, consultation, seminars, and forums on vital issues.

12. **Parent-Teacher Association.** Parent-teacher group, headed by Barbara Zohn, formed to support the public schools. The association endorsed public school choice and worked closely with People for Better Schools to advocate school choice, parental involvement, and educational equity and excellence.

13. **League of Women Voters, Minnesota.** Nonpartisan organization that encourages the informal and active participation of citizens in government and influences public policy through education and advocacy.

14. **Spring Hill Regional Conference Center.** A regional conference center and think tank funded by individuals and foundations to study policy issues.

Lobbyist Organizations

15. **Brainpower Compact.** A lobby group formed in 1985 under the aegis of the Minnesota Business Partnership to support

Exhibit 4.1. *(continued)*

Governor Perpich's education initiative, *Access to Excellence.* Consisted of "elites" who supported public school choice, including four former governors, the mayor of St. Paul, and other business and political leaders. The Compact, with Minnesota Business Partnership funds, hired a public relations consultant and a lobbyist to support the governor's legislation.

16. **People for Better Schools.** A grassroots organization formed in February 1985 with the encouragement of Governor Perpich and his policy team. Its purpose was to support the governor's initiative and demonstrate widespread support for his ideas. By 1986, the group had grown to 780 members, including students, parents, teachers, superintendents, principals, and other citizens.

Consulting Organization

17. **Berman-Weiler Associates.** A California consulting firm hired by the Minnesota Business Partnership to conduct a $250,000 study of Minnesota education. The firm's report, *The Minnesota Plan: The Design of a New Educational System,* was released after ten months of investigation and contained recommendations for student choice.

---

and others became grassroots organizers working at the legislature during its sessions. Commented one, "some people can do certain things that other people can't do. . . . I mean, some people can write. Some people can go talk to politicians better than other people can . . . or some people have status that other people haven't got." Thus, some created proposals, others developed long-term and short-term strategies for change, and still others labored to build interest groups and lobby the legislature. If a member was unable to do one thing because of time constraints, he was expected to do something else to aid the overall effort. It was acceptable, as an example, for those with full-time jobs to attend meetings, offer their views, and leave the day-to-day tasks to others whose schedules and responsibilities allowed them to work full time on reform.

Leadership

Group members regarded leadership as shared, although they did defer to Quie, if he were present, out of respect for his past experience and leadership. The position of chair tended to rotate depending on who called the meeting, who set the agenda, and who was present. As one member put it, "We are all leaders. . . . No one dominates, there is sharing and respect for ideas. There is no gavel and [our meetings] are very free-flowing." Said another, "If you were to ask me who was the leader in the group, I'm not sure I could answer that question for you. . . . I'd have to say that function fluctuated over time. Probably every one of the group had the occasion to want to convene the players at one point or another during the course of the process and did." This shared leadership experience led another member to conclude that "the group has been remarkable for its leaderless character."

Although these responses show that the group acknowledged no formal leader, some informal leadership did exist. Two members were identified as the driving force behind the group's efforts. Veterans of many policy battles over a thirty-year period, they provided important information and guidance on steering policy change. The most senior entrepreneur called himself a mentor to the other and his closest friend. "We complement each other and we are the informal glue that holds this whole thing together. In fact, we are the heart of the team in transportation, education, healthcare, and metropolitan government issues." Sharing previous experience and policy successes with the group, they often took the lead in determining when to meet and what to discuss. Neither of the two appeared to have a need to be in control at meetings, judging by the other members' comments, but their actions did provide direction for the group that several of the members found very satisfying and effective.

Culture

The team members saw themselves as a cohesive group, respectful of one another's skills and experiences. Yet this cohesion did not come without effort. There were conflicts over legislative priorities, media relations, and operating styles.

Conflicts over legislative priorities surfaced because the entrepreneurs had different constituencies and each came with his own personal perspectives and policy preferences. Some were associated with the Minnesota Business Partnership, which advocated greater accountability through the use of statewide tests and measurement of student performance. Others favored policies to promote access and equity, especially for children at risk due to social problems such as poverty, unemployment, and dysfunctional families.

There were major conflicts over what stories the press should be encouraged to cover and how to work with the media. Disagreements also surfaced when one policy entrepreneur wanted to form another group—People for Better Schools—to wage a grassroots campaign supporting the governor. And there was passionate disagreement over the letter that accused the governor, the commissioner, and the legislators of backsliding on public school choice.

Some conflicts could be attributed to differing orientations to large-scale system change. One policy entrepreneur followed Saul Alinsky's community organizing approach so enthusiastically that he would not agree to an interview unless we assured him that we had read *Reveille for Radicals* and *Rules for Radicals* (Alinsky, 1989a, 1989b). The veteran policy entrepreneurs, on the other hand, had developed their own set of rules of thumb for change, which they had honed in their years of working together:

- Know where you want to end up and don't lose sight of where you are headed.
- Don't play the "Washington game" by trading away the fundamental elements of the plan. Compromise may yield bad policy. Say "no" rather than give up the fundamentals of what you really want.
- Wait for the "background conditions" [political context] to change, thus necessitating the kind of change you want.
- Mature bureaucracies like education rarely initiate meaningful change from within, so outside pressure is needed to force them to respond.
- Change never comes through consensus. Get the key leadership to back your idea and the "pack will rush to follow."
- Money is needed to make change. . . . Get the elites involved.
- Stay with issues where you have the advantage.

- Keep the educational establishment talking about change and structural issues, and you'll change some minds.
- Destabilize the opposition by co-opting one of the educational establishment groups.
- Be willing to be bold.

The grassroots organizer had a different view of change from the veterans, and felt ambivalent about the presence of the Minnesota Business Partnership. Its total silence in January, 1985, during the crucial weeks after Perpich's announcement, was to him a stark contrast to its highly visible and expensive campaign to reduce taxes by sending engraved tea boxes to each legislator. He characterized his conflict with the Partnership as a "clash of worldviews, styles, and priorities." Meeting with Perpich, he agreed to form People for Better Schools so there would be a "visible, immediate, and public presence standing up and saying public school choice was a good idea." Meanwhile, other team members viewed the grassroots organizer as an overly independent activist. The veterans were uncomfortable with his style and what they believed to be his lack of judgment in choosing tactics. "He doesn't use good political sense. We lost 'at risk' in the Governor's Discussion Group on the 19th because of him. . . . He's a loose cannon who acts on his own."

Yet despite their frustration with him and his own threats to bolt from the group to launch a more public support of policy initiatives, the group wanted the grassroots organizer to stay aligned with them. Besides recognizing his many talents and contributions, they wanted to minimize any unilateral action on his part, fearful it would dilute their policy goals. "Any crack in the dike of the good guys' side would look bad, like we didn't have our act together. . . . It would be very difficult to maintain momentum," one of the members said. A friend in the group was assigned the job of working to channel his enthusiasm and energy—of which he had a great deal, as the youngest and newest member of the group. "It was my job to keep him in the fold," the friend reported. "In fact, I was told three times last week . . . to 'keep him in the fold.'"

The group worked through its differences and agreed on a set of priorities for their legislative program. The main goal would be redesigning education and the mechanism to achieve it would be public school choice. Testing and measurement would be priorities for the Business Partnership after school choice was in place, although it was free to work on them unilaterally if it so desired. Advocating an intentionally vague and open-ended agenda, which subsumed all their points of view, and paying sequential attention to their goals, the team minimized its conflict. The members put their individual preferences aside and presented a united front on the points they agreed must come first.

Thus, while conflict did divert some attention away from strategic activities, it did not cause major problems. None of the members believed their overall effectiveness or their desire to work together was seriously threatened. Even the grassroots organizer, the source of consternation among the senior members, said that he was reasonably comfortable working with the group, and that it was important for them to work together. Avoiding direct confrontations and showdowns on members' positions, and working to guide and mentor "difficult" members, the group eventually accommodated individual differences. Members described it as having "substantial overlap in terms of many of the objectives and *very strong* overlap in terms of spirit and approach." In addition, it had "a willingness to suspend major egos to work together" and "to agree that there were some things that we would do differently." "Sometimes we agreed to disagree," said one member in summing up their views.

Resource Base

Working on a volunteer basis, the team carried out its tasks with limited resources. Commented one member, "We've just developed a kind of style that doesn't require anything significant in the way of financial resources. . . . We can operate on a shoestring." Another said that their underfunded efforts sometimes felt like "trying to organize D-day out of a phone booth."

Instead, the team relied heavily on sheer hard work. Spending seventy to eighty hours a week on the reform effort during the legislative battle, members seemed to be everywhere at once. Critics attributed their effectiveness to their willingness to work day and night on their issue. One education leader remarked that a particular entrepreneur was so effective because "he works longer and harder than anyone else. . . . He lives and breathes this stuff, even in his spare time."

Group members also relied on their previous experience and policy expertise as a substitute for more tangible resources. As one commented, "our greatest resources are the unique political skills we have developed and the ability to use them. We are focused; other players have too many things that they want." Said another, "Our resources are certainly not money. . . . It's the ability to handle ourselves and manage the press. . . . We know how to strategize about these things. 6M has all the power and we did end runs around them." Another would describe their advantage as their ability to "work the system"—to think on their feet, formulate strategies, and outsmart the opposition.

Experience gained in earlier policy battles, coupled with their long involvement in the policy-making arena, enabled the policy entrepreneurs to build a network of contacts. As we noted in Chapter Three, they drew on these strategically placed people when they needed to get information or arrange a meeting with a key decision maker. They also were successful in developing a network to keep them up-to-date on what was happening on the state and national levels—which had some psychological advantages besides information sharing: "Another resource that we should throw in there is enough knowledge to connect with anything worth getting at elsewhere in the country . . . contacts with people and familiarity with other projects under way," one reported, adding, "and a psychological resource that stemmed from the sense that what we were doing was kind of leading-edge. It wasn't so much our drawing from other people as it was that those people were calling us to see how it was going." Group members also organized information as a service to busy policy makers "who often [did] not have the time to develop and analyze policy alternatives or seek out innovations or novel ideas."

Working and reworking ideas into a coherent package, the group provided "conceptualized, analyzed, and justified policy proposals [for officials] to use because they [were] so busy." In the case of the proposal to the governor, "all that remained . . . to do was to decide which elements were politically feasible and to put the governor's imprimatur on the package—choice only in the public schools."

These intangibles yielded a valuable resource—credibility. Many lawmakers and policy makers were prepared to accept the group's recommendations, ideas, and strategies because of the momentum generated by their past successes, their former elected offices, and their reputations. As an entrepreneur explained, "We have credibility with key people in the Minnesota Department of Education such as Ruth Randall. This was very important in the implementation of [the Postsecondary Enrollment Options Act]. We were able to advise the MDE in that process. Credibility with the governor is number one. Also credibility with some legislators and their aides. We have credibility with the news media and contacts with educators and parents."

Building on this formidable foundation, the group also had access to important tangible resources to sustain the process, as shown in Table 4.1. Most team members received support from their employers (referred to in the table as indirect support) in the form of salaries, benefits, and secretarial services, as well as mail, phone, and copying privileges—and occasionally, money for research assistance. Although allocating no specific budgets for the reform effort, employers did allow the entrepreneurs significant flexibility in their work and let them pursue their personal goals of educational reform.

Group members also had access to important funding sources, and through their network they were able to obtain resources when critical needs arose. For example, policy entrepreneurs affiliated with the Citizens League established Public School Incentives (PSI), a 501(c)(3) nonprofit, to serve as a fiscal agent for foundation grants. The Northwest Foundation then funded PSI to test the idea of school-site management and the initial planning for teachers-in-private-practice. And the McKnight Foundation allocated money to one policy entrepreneur for research on how school choice could help children who had not succeeded in school, and to revise a book on educational reform. Later, some members of PSI would form their own lobby group, People for Better Schools, to push their initiatives in the legislature.

In addition, the group benefited from its association with the Minnesota Business Partnership and its member firms. The Partnership independently funded a $250,000 study to assess Minnesota education and investigate ways to improve student performance. Thanks to several entrepreneurs' hands in the design of the study,

Table 4.1. Support to Entrepreneurs, by Phase of Innovation Process.

	Phase		
Organization	*Creative*	*Design*	*Implementation*
Berman-Weiler	• worked with PE to design education study and set design parameters • conducted research • wrote study recommending choice		
Brainpower Compact	• sent representative to Governor's Discussion Group	• lobbyist went to PE meetings and coordinated lobby efforts with PEs	
Citizens League	• 1980 Report on Public Services Redesign • 1982 Report *Rebuilding Education to Make It Work* • secretarial support • locus of meetings and interaction • sent representatives to Governor's Discussion Group • indirect support	• publicly endorsed governor's education initiative • testified at legislative hearings • wrote articles in support of choice • indirect support	• support to PEs on evaluation task force • secretarial support to evaluation study • wrote articles on evaluation study • indirect support

Table 4.1. (*continued*)

Governor's Discussion Group	• generated ideas and recommended educational policy to governor from 1985 to 1987 • PEs invited to participate as representatives from different organizations	• governor took recommendations and developed legislative initiatives	• monitored implementation on choice laws with PEs
Governor's Office and Staff	• indirect support	• worked with PEs to write governor's initiative on school choice • coordinated lobbying on governor's plan with PEs	• indirect support
Hubert H. Humphrey Institute of Public Affairs	• indirect support	• indirect support	
League of Women Voters		• lobbied for school choice at legislature and coordinated efforts with PEs	

Healthcare Nonprofit	• indirect support	• indirect support	• indirect support
McKnight Foundation	• funded study on school choice		
Law Firm	• indirect support	• indirect support	• indirect support
Minneapolis Business Partnership	• commissioned and funded a $250,000 study of Minnesota education • hired Berman-Weiler to do study • promoted findings throughout state • sent representative to GDG • indirect support	• CEOs help sell governor's plan • funded lobby group Brainpower Compact, PR consultant, and lobbyist • sent out mailings in support of choice • wrote letters to the editor in support of choice • coordinated lobbying efforts with PEs	
Minneapolis Star & Tribune	• editorials supported Citizens League and MBP studies • PEs furnish editorial writers and reporters with ideas on school choice • attended GDG	• editorials supported governor's initiative • editorials critical of lack of progress • PEs provide information on reform efforts	• editorials highlight positive results from choice legislation • PEs provide information on reform efforts

Table 4.1. (continued)

Minnesota Department of Education	• convened and staffed GDG • commissioner advocated educational reform • PEs worked with reformers in department	• helped draft governor's plan • supported governor's plan in legislature • PEs worked with reformers in department	• coordinated and monitored implementation of choice legislation • provided technical assistance to districts for implementation of choice laws • coordinated evaluation task force • PEs served on evaluation task force
Minnesota Department of Finance	• PEs presented choice ideas to select members • members advocated school choice to governor • members worked with PEs to draft proposal on school choice for governor • supported governor's initiative at the legislature		
Minnesota House of Representatives and Senate	• PEs worked with staff and legislators to write and pass choice legislation		• PEs worked with staff and legislators to monitor and evaluate choice legislation

Minnesota State Planning Agency		• helped write governor's education initiative with PEs • advocated governor's plan at legislature	• monitored implementation
Minnesota Public Radio	• covered GDG • PEs invited to discuss education issues	• PEs invited to discuss education issues	• PEs invited to discuss education issues
National Governors' Association		• indirect support	• indirect support
Northwest Area Foundation	• provided $1.5 million to fund school-site management pilot projects, often using PSI as fiscal agent		
PTA		• lobbied for governor's initiative • coordinated activities with PEs during enactment • found parents and students to testify for choice	

Table 4.1. (*continued*)

People for Better Schools		• formed by PEs to lobby for governor's plan • wrote letters to the editors supporting choice throughout state • testified at hearings on choice legislation	• members participated in choice evaluation study • testified at evaluation hearings
Public School Incentives	• established by reformers and PEs • generated new ideas on education • issued position papers • used as a design shop to test creative high-potential ideas • acted as fiscal agent for McKnight and Northwest Area Foundations • sent representatives to the GDG	• mobilized members to testify for choice	• member participated in evaluation task force for choice laws
Public Television	• PE hosted public affairs program • program used as forum to discuss ideas in education	• invited PEs to discuss educational reform and school choice	• invited PEs to discuss educational reform and school choice

St. Paul Pioneer Press	• reported on educational reform issues • PEs furnish reporters with information on educational reform	• reported on educational reform issues • PEs furnish reporters with information on educational reform • PEs sent letter critical of governor on the progress of educational reform	• reported on educational reform issues • PEs furnish reporters with information on educational reform
Spring Hill Conference Center		• indirect support	
U.S. Department of Education			• PEs made contact with department • provided financial and contract support to evaluate choice laws

Note: GDG = Governor's Discussion Group; MBP = Minnesota Business Partnership; PE = Policy Entrepreneur.

the group was able to draw on the report's findings to buttress its arguments for school redesign. The Partnership continued its financial support throughout the innovation process, helping with mailings and letter-writing campaigns during legislative debates over public school choice. The Partnership also started its own lobby group, the Brainpower Compact. The Compact then hired a public relations consultant and a lobbyist to promote its recommendations for educational change at the legislature.

Thus, the Citizens League, Public School Incentives, and the Minnesota Business Partnership promoted the innovation process directly, and their memberships in them gave the policy entrepreneurs the chance to encourage and direct the creation of spin-off organizations to carry out specific activities to support their efforts. This *organizational multiplier effect* had several advantages. Rather than attending functions and activities as a single group of change agents, they could truthfully claim to represent many different groups in the community. That tactic worked especially well for them in the Governor's Discussion Group. The Citizens League, Public School Incentives, People for Better Schools, the Minnesota Business Partnership, and the Brainpower Compact were all invited to send representatives to the GDG meetings. Instead of one small group doing battle against the most powerful interests in the state, the policy entrepreneurs came to the GDG representing several different well-known organizations, which measurably increased their visibility and clout.

Implications of the Network Structure

When we map resource support against the different time periods of the innovation process, we also gain some important insights. Table 4.1 reveals that most organizational activity occurred during the design phase of the innovation process. The increasing number of organizations supporting the group during this period was due primarily to the activity surrounding legislative sessions. Lobby groups and government departments began to align themselves with the entrepreneurs in the push for educational reform. We also find organizational activity during the implementation phase, when lawmakers required the Department of Education to monitor and evaluate the execution of public school choice.

With the exception of the Department of Education, however, it is striking that no governmental organizations were involved with the group during the creative phase of the innovation process. And only three organizations—the Citizens League, Public School Incentives, and the Minnesota Business Partnership—provided resource support during the years prior to 1985 when the innovative ideas were germinating. The creative phase sets the parameters and the terms of the policy debates that follow, and it is significant that so few organizations, compared to the total set of interested parties, contributed resources to support the group during this critical time period.

Idea generation is time consuming and expensive, especially when it involves support for radical ideas that deviate far from the status quo. It is important to note what organizations could afford to provide entrepreneurs with the luxury to think, write, discuss, and analyze social problems and their solutions. Of those providing direct support, three are nonprofits dedicated to public policy reform. The Citizens League functions as a think tank to debate public issues and to generate solutions for them, while Public School Incentives functions as a design shop to test the viability of new educational ideas in practice. The third organization, the Minnesota Business Partnership, is an elite group of chief executives from Minnesota's largest corporations. Like the Citizens League and Public School Incentives, it is devoted to change and improvement in the state.

Of those providing indirect support in the form of employment during the creative phase, again, all were nonprofits: the Citizens League, a health care nonprofit, the Hubert H. Humphrey Institute, the McKnight and Northwest Area Foundations via Public School Incentives, and the Minnesota Business Partnership. These organizations allowed the entrepreneurs a great deal of discretion and latitude to pursue their personal goals as long as they met their official obligations. Thus, nonprofit organizations both directly and indirectly sustained the creative energies of the policy entrepreneurs and provided them "safe havens" from which to launch radical educational reform.

Further examination of Table 4.1 also reveals the close connection between the policy entrepreneurs and the media. The media provided access to the public—an extremely important resource during all phases of the innovation process. By providing coverage of educational events, inviting entrepreneurs to appear on programs to debate the issues, writing favorable editorials and printing letters to the editors, the media not only disseminated the policy entrepreneurs' ideas, but helped cultivate and sway public opinion so much that traditional educational groups were moved to protest their one-sided coverage. The media even became a vehicle to chastise the group's own allies among government officials, when it appeared they were moving too slowly on the reform path. Aside from the policy entrepreneurs' employers, the only two other organizations to provide such a sustained level of support to the group during all phases of the innovation process were the Citizens League and Public School Incentives.

Despite this impressive array of support, group members felt dwarfed when matching their resources to those of their opponents, the established educational groups. As one commented: "In some respects, I suppose you could argue that we have substantial resources in terms of everything from the Partnership's member companies, the influence of the CEOs, some monies that were generously contributed. . . . At the same time, I don't think any of us have ever felt that we had particularly large resources to draw on. It's literally been a handful or a collection of people. . . . I would say our level of resources versus the establishment organizations [is] peanuts. . . . I'm always amazed that the thing didn't fragment and . . . die an early death."

Chapter Five

The Individuals Behind the Ideas

Personal Characteristics of the Policy Entrepreneurs

Cautious, careful people, always casting about to preserve their reputation and social standing, can never bring about a reform. Those who are really in earnest must be willing to be anything or nothing in the world's estimation and, publicly and privately, in season and out, to avow their sympathies with despised and persecuted ideas and their advocates, and to bear the consequences.
—SUSAN B. ANTHONY, *ON THE CAMPAIGN FOR DIVORCE LAW REFORM* (1860)

It is time to introduce the policy entrepreneurs themselves and seek to understand what fueled their insistence on radical policy change and their search for better ways of doing things. By studying their backgrounds, knowledge, and skills, we gain some understanding of them as individuals. It was uncomfortable for them to share some of this information with us, but they acceded to our requests and permitted us to probe into their personal and professional lives. We appreciate their candor and willingness to allow us to share details of their lives and careers.

By necessity, then, we walk a fine line. We want the reader to understand the personal side of entrepreneurship, yet we must protect the privacy of the entrepreneurs in our study. To resolve this dilemma, after the career summaries we discuss the attributes of entrepreneurship without following any set order with regard to comments about individuals, so that the observations will apply to the group as a whole.

As They Describe Themselves

All the policy entrepreneurs on the team are white males. In 1988, two were between forty and forty-five years of age; two were between forty-six and fifty; one between fifty-six and sixty; and one between sixty-one and sixty-five—thus all were in the period that has been called the years of peak productivity. All are highly educated: two have Ph.D degrees in educational administration, two have J.D. degrees, one has a Ph.D. degree in economics, and one has a masters degree in public affairs. Their undergraduate degrees range from political science, education, and economics to English, history, and religion.

Employment histories reveal a diverse range of experience in the public and private sectors. The entrepreneurs have moved back and forth among positions in law firms and corporations, elected public office, and other nonprofit and public sector positions in teaching, administration, and management.

The veteran policy entrepreneur received his law degree and became a state legislator in his twenties. Moving to Washington D.C., he became a top aide to a Minnesota congressman. He returned to Minneapolis to become executive director of the Citizens League. After some years of service, he made what he called a "practical and pragmatic decision" to join a Fortune 500 firm—in part, to put his children through college. (He is proud of his three children, each of whom has an MBA and "a conscience.") As a vice president and director of corporate planning, he oversaw corporate strategy. Throughout this period he remained very active in civic affairs, serving on the boards of directors of two major hospitals (one for nineteen years). Upon his retirement from the private sector, he became the head of a nonprofit health care organization that seeks innovative solutions to the health care problems of the frail elderly.

Another policy entrepreneur began his career as a reporter covering general stories for a major city paper. He began to cover city hall and the police beat. He eventually joined the editorial staff, a job he liked very much because it enabled him to use his generalist skills to advocate ideas and policies. Eventually he became assistant city editor, but found he disliked the management of day-to-day activities. He left journalism to become executive director of the Citizens League, a move that allowed him to spend even more time developing and advocating public policy. Building on his experience at the League, he joined the Hubert H. Humphrey Institute of Public Affairs at the University of Minnesota as a senior fellow, where he taught a graduate seminar on public services redesign and continued to develop new policy ideas. He currently works in a think tank that specializes in health care and education issues, searching for structural and systemic change options in those two policy areas.

A third policy entrepreneur began his professional life as a lawyer. He served on the Minneapolis city council, where (in the late 1960s) he was a catalyst in founding Southeast Alternative Schools, an intradistrict magnet program. He returned to general legal practice for some years, and when this study began, was executive director of the Minnesota Business Partnership. He has since returned to the private practice of law.

Armed with a Ph.D. in economics, the fourth entrepreneur began his career as a Department of Defense policy analyst. In the late 1960s, he assumed a subcabinet position in Health, Education, and Welfare. He left government to form and direct a school of public affairs, which later became the Hubert. H. Humphrey Institute at the University of Minnesota. Later, he successfully ran for office, serving in the Minnesota House of Representatives and later the Minnesota State Senate. He has since returned to academia full time.

A fifth policy entrepreneur began his career as an instructor and guidance director in a private high school, then moved into administration, eventually becoming vice president and then president of three different community colleges. Recruited by the Citizens League, he made an "unplanned career change" when he became its executive director, where he remained during the course of this study. Calling it the "hardest job I ever tried to do," he found the work stimulating. After spending his career "launching policy grenades over the wall," he decided to become an insider, first as a governor's chief policy advisor, then deputy chief of staff, and eventually as chief of staff. He reports that it is a lot harder than it looks on the inside—and that he is rethinking his earlier statement about the hardest job he ever tried to do.

The sixth policy entrepreneur, who at the time of this study was a consultant and researcher, began his career as a public school teacher and administrator. He left K-12 education after a number of years to play a more active role in promoting change. He received financial support for his research from the McKnight Foundation through Public School Incentives. After revising an earlier book on school reform, he was hired as a consultant and staff person to coordinate a project for the National Governors' Association. He eventually returned to Minnesota to become a fellow at the Spring Hill think tank and conference center, to work on rural development issues. He subsequently joined the Hubert H. Humphrey Institute at the University of Minnesota as a senior fellow responsible for directing a school reform project.

Values and Motivation

It is difficult to say exactly what shaped the entrepreneurs' dedication to the public service and their desire to change public policy. However, they did identify certain factors that they believed helped develop their values and build a commitment to the commonweal.

All the entrepreneurs credited their parents with teaching them to do useful things with their lives and talents. One policy entrepreneur believed that public service was a "calling to be of service and to help. I believe my calling is to bring useful, new ideas into government. . . . I believe that one justifies one's life through service." His educators, a religious order of Catholic monks, also provided a "quiet and pervasive" influence on his life. "Their stability was particularly important and their commitment to service was key," he said. "The instinctive and natural and life-long sense of service [had] a great effect on me. . . . They live a life of service." He reports major influences from "Catholic social thought . . . the encyclicals of the church, and . . . upbringing in a Catholic family." This early experience was reinforced by his first job, where he got "hooked on the public sector and public service" working in Washington when Kennedy was in the White House. "This changed my life tremendously. . . . I gained a sense of being needed as well as important. . . . Going to Washington taught me that public service is exhilarating and tempting."

Another policy entrepreneur credited his father with inculcating in him the desire to help people by public service. "I'm sure in childhood the fact that my father was a minister put some kind of stamp on me about the responsibility to be involved in society and not simply taking from it. . . . I've flirted with and prudently retreated from imitating his career, but I'm sure there must have been some shaping there that guided me toward trying to be into some things that serve people."

A third entrepreneur also emphasized the importance of public service. "It is my value to give more than I take out . . . and to do something important . . . worth doing. . . . [My] motives are civic interest and the welfare of the community . . . to see decisions made well and right and not dominated by vested interests." This entrepreneur spoke of his deep and personal relationship with God, which he described as a driving force in his life. For him, the spirituality of a deeply held religious conviction was his source of personal motivation and provided guidelines for living. His religion helped him put others first. He needed only two things to satisfy him and enable him to feel good about himself: God and his own conscience. He felt his faith helped him keep things in perspective and remain clear about what was important in life, such as his family, work, and longstanding friendships.

Two policy entrepreneurs credited the civil rights movement of the 1960s with whetting their appetites for public service. Soon after the Civil Rights Act was passed in 1964, one of them became a legal advocate on a civil rights project in North Carolina. He relished using his talents creatively and was energized by "working on the outer edge of public policy, right at the cutting edge of the most radical things society was going through." From that experience, he learned that systemic change is possible, especially when mounted by committed outsiders laboring beyond the boundaries of the formal power structure.

The other policy entrepreneur who worked in the civil rights movement had been a college activist involved in student government. Attending Saul Alinsky's Community Organizing School in Chicago, he grounded his model of change on Alinsky's populist principles. Alinsky's egalitarian ideas held intuitive appeal for him given his preference for change strategies that depend on the local community and the empowerment of grassroots constituencies.

The sixth policy entrepreneur, described by one of his fellows as "a public affairs institution in this town for which there should be an endowment," derived pleasure from influencing other policy actors. He learned his values from his father, whom he held in high regard for his entrepreneurial nature, risk taking, and tenacity. Crediting his father for teaching him the value of hard work, making your own luck, and aggressive pursuit of goals, he took his father's lessons to the public arena and made the search for better public policies his cause.

All of the policy entrepreneurs felt rewarded when they were able to influence the direction of public policy. As one said, it was evidence of progress that sustained him. "I am not dependent on passing a particular piece of legislation to feel good. . . . I see an inevitability to the general direction of policy and I am helping to form that direction." Another commented that he cared about how society worked, and liked to make an impact and see the results of his efforts.

While being key players in the educational reform movement motivated all of them, public recognition was not a consistent factor. Three found it motivating and named it as one of the reasons they did what they did. One acknowledged he got "ego reinforcement from being involved" and liked to have people seek him out for his opinions. Another called it a great day when Governor Perpich introduced him to a legislative audience saying: "[Name's] got a view of the way the state ought to go and here's what it is. Now I hope you do it."

Others disliked public recognition, believing that taking credit or seeking recognition limited their effectiveness. "Attention is counterproductive if you want to do something," one said. He saw himself as unlike other corporate managers, "not motivated by the individual achievement system." He added, "Monetary rewards don't do much for me. . . . I don't have to be a big shot on the team. . . . I don't need to build myself up. I don't really get concerned with what happens to me personally. It's how you play the game that counts . . . that you give more than you take out." An organization in which he was involved had recently won a prestigious award for its activities, and he was uncomfortable with the credit he was receiving for the honor. Warning of the trap of self-aggrandizement, he advised, "You don't build anything when you mention certain people, you need to say that the company won the award and deserves the recognition. . . . If you talk about it as an organizational victory, then you can replicate it through other organizations. This is the way to get things done . . . not to focus on me."

Policy Expertise and Knowledge

The policy entrepreneurs' education, experience in government (three had held elective office at some point), and career progression in public and private sector organizations helped them build a knowledge base in seventeen policy areas from education to municipal services. All identified themselves as experts in educational policy and at least one other policy domain. Here is a summary of their reported expertise:

Substantive Area	Number of Experts
K-12 Educational Policy	6
Health Care Policy	3
Agricultural Policy	2
Economic Development	2
Governmental Structures	2
Land Use and Development	2
Tax and/or Public Finance	2
Transportation and Transit	2
Higher Education	1
Economics Education	1
Defense Policy	1
Electric Power Supply	1
Public Service Delivery	1
Philanthropy	1
Social Services Funding	1
Solid Waste	1
Welfare	1

This breadth of experience was reinforced at the Citizens League, where all had participated on study committees. Three had served as executive director of the League, a job that required them to be policy generalists and speak for the organization on a variety of topics.

One policy entrepreneur reported feeling disappointed early in his career, because his knowledge was scattered across many topics rather than concentrated in one specialty. As a reporter, he said, "you've got to cover politics and farm programs, the upper Mississippi Basin Development Program, the electric power supply, state budgets and school reorganization, all this kind of stuff." He added, "I was feeling really kind of down because everybody else was moving along and getting to be an expert in something. After a couple of years of work, I was still dinging around and doing a little bit of everything." He began to see the advantage of broad-based knowledge when a legislative researcher pointed out that he "got the benefit of being able to move around and talk to all kinds of different people in all kinds of different positions." Furthermore, this work enabled him to "see patterns from system to system," and to translate and transpose solutions from one situation to another.

Skills and Personal Attributes

Values, motivation, and policy knowledge were important factors in their self-assessment, yet the entrepreneurs underscored the importance of two other elements—the acquisition of particular skills and the development of certain personal attributes.

Problem-Solving and Systems-Thinking Skills

All the policy entrepreneurs noted the importance of critical thinking and problem-solving skills. For one it meant the ability to "cut through extraneous detail to the essence of a problem." For another, it meant "finding and understanding the essence" of an issue. Another described his problem solving process in action. After devoting some time to a problem, he said, "Pretty quick you think . . . it's pretty simple. And then if you stay with it a little while, it seems very complicated. And you get really kind of depressed about it. But if you stay with it long enough then it becomes simple again. The heart of things, they are simple. There is a simplicity in the heart of even the most complicated things if you can just get to it."

Getting to the heart of things meant "pricking the assumptions," and "challenging the givens" of acceptable practice. It meant never assuming that the standard ways of doing things were the best ways of doing things. It meant searching for the core of the problem rather than getting lost in the details, distracted by the problem's symptoms rather than its causes. It meant searching for fundamental causes rather than settling for cosmetic, short-run solutions that might easily conceal serious conceptual flaws. It meant freeing oneself from the constraints of current practice to be open to new and innovative ideas. It meant not giving up in the face of complexity.

Central to problem-solving skills was the ability to think in systems terms. Defining this as the capacity to see the whole picture and its interrelated parts, the policy entrepreneurs often reiterated the idea that educational problems were systemic problems. Poor student performance was not due to failure of just one part of the system. If funding was the problem, for example, then spending more money on the schools would be a simple (though not easy) solution. However, the entrepreneurs saw the real problem as the inability of an educational system designed for the early industrial age to meet the needs of information-age society. Rather than addressing any one element, the solution required the invention and design of a new educational system for a new time, a new type of student, in a new environment. This systems-thinking capacity, which they believed was developed through their liberal arts and generalist education and honed through their work experience, enabled them to see patterns and relationships as they moved from one system to another—from governance to health care, from health care to education. It led, said one entrepreneur, to an agenda for change.

Communication Skills

Communicating the critical elements of a message to policy makers and interested publics were important skills for the policy entrepreneurs. For two of them, the message was best delivered through public speaking. One said he developed his oratorical skills at the church where his father was a minister, then went on to make enough money doing after-dinner speeches to get through the first two years of college ("talking about everything from truly philosophical things to a knock-off Sam Spade routine"). Two other policy entrepreneurs communicated best through print media. Both were prolific in writing reports, articles, books, speeches, and copy for the press. One credited his high school newspaper for giving him the technical training to be a reporter on a local newspaper when he finished graduate school. His close association with the media alarmed many among the traditional educational groups, who accused the entrepreneurs of media manipulation and taking unfair advantage in getting ideas publicized by their friends and contacts. Dismissing these charges as unfounded, the policy entrepreneurs nonetheless regarded publicity as an important part of their repertoire of skills. Speaking and writing were not simple intellectual exercises, but opportunities to enable people to see the accuracy of their problem definitions and the viability of their policy solutions. As one said, the ability to promote ideas through persuasion was considered to be even more important than quantitative skills. This entrepreneur also cautioned that they had to be careful to avoid going too far with salesmanship and losing track of the substance. He continued with an example: "Somebody once said of [name]—'you know, he's a very persuasive man. The problem is he's just as persuasive when he's wrong as when he's right.' So you've got to be right too." He described getting policy makers to accept public school choice as "very similar to a salesman overcoming a buyer's sales resistance." In this regard, he admitted, it "wouldn't have hurt to come from a salesman's family," which, of course, he did.

Willingness to Be Bold and Take Risks

Adopting the maxim "It is easier to ask for forgiveness than permission," the policy entrepreneurs were risk takers. They focused on getting the job done and attended to consequences later. More concerned with "what ought to be, not what was politically attainable in the short run," they saw themselves as different from insiders, whose perspective usually seems to run only from election to election.

Politicians, they believed, analyzed a problem and developed a policy that was not the best policy but the most feasible and politically palatable policy. One entrepreneur who had held elective office himself described how most politicians think: "The first question most politicians ask is 'Can this bill get enacted' . . . not 'is the bill sound public policy?'" Elected officials "listen to somebody describe a new problem or new challenge and first of all think about why they can't do it. . . . How it is you can't get there. . . . Who doesn't want to go there . . . and so forth. You end up being overwhelmed and overburdened by the list of why you can't do something."

In contrast, this policy entrepreneur saw himself as a "most outspoken, aggressive supporter of some fairly radical bills which are now respectable policies." He described his approach as pulling—"you pull your fellow politicians to the place you want them to be. . . . I would move the debate out to the purest form where I wanted the policy to be and stick to it. . . . I'd say 'that's what we should do.' This was based on taking the most extreme position of what I would like to see happen, and analyze the problem not so much on what could be done, but what ought to be done."

The *inside game* (as he called the politics of elected office) rarely yielded innovation. A reformer had to use outside pressure to pull politicians away from business as usual. "The presence of the *outside game*—the pressure from change agents and interest groups—is essential to public policy innovation. . . . Outsiders provide new ideas and fresh views and are needed if dramatic change is to occur. . . . Sometimes policy innovation and large-scale system change involve a new paradigm of thought. . . . This won't happen from the inside."

Another policy entrepreneur explained how he learned very early that it is necessary to take risks and go beyond self-imposed barriers for change. On his first job as a reporter, the city editor took him around the office desk by desk, naming the writers and describing who they were and what they did. "And when he got all done with that he said: 'You can divide them all into two groups. There are some of them that can do only what they have been told they can do and some of them who think they can do anything they haven't been told they can't do.' And then he pointed to my desk and said: 'This is your desk'." The future entrepreneur saw it as a challenge to decide with which group he would identify.

Comfort in Being Different

To pursue risky courses of action, the policy entrepreneurs needed to feel comfortable when out of step with the majority. One, for example, described himself as "not a typical politician" because he placed greater importance on ideas than interests. "I have the vision," he said, "not the folks." "That's what I was elected to do." Disliking day-to-day politics-as-usual, he preferred to see himself as a "Burkean legislator who is not particularly good at politics." In contrast to that consummate politician, Hubert H. Humphrey, who was "buoyed by strangers . . . and inspired by the political process," his own antipathy for "bean feeds and handshaking" made him unique among his peers. "I wish I were more political, but I'm not. I need the quiet of home and time with my family. . . . I am ambitious, but I insist on defining myself. . . . I won't be pegged."

Another policy entrepreneur also expressed a lack of concern for accepted authority and a willingness to take on the majority if need be. He drew on his Citizens League experience to make the point. "There were all kinds of times at the Citizens League when you end up doing things that are really unpopular and just make the established political or business supporters real angry. And if you think that is the test of being right you'd be in terrible trouble. You'd just be swinging around in the wind all the time. *And so the willingness to try to be unpopular makes it kind of psychologically possible for you to be innovative without being overly concerned what others think"* (emphasis added). He said he had learned early in his personal life that being popular wasn't his strong suit, so he would not permit it to be a factor in his professional life, either.

This policy entrepreneur saw many people confusing being right with being in the majority. Quoting a famous line, he said, "You're not wrong because people disagree with you." He added, "All kinds of times you find that some things that were unpopular when you first said them turned out . . . to be right." Taking the long-term view and being proven right "teaches you a certain amount of confidence, which I think you have to have in this kind of work, and not [to] get too concerned about conventional wisdom or the daily majority."

Self-confidence developed in youth also helped other entrepreneurs accept their uniqueness. One fondly remembered how his father had instilled in him the belief that "you have what it takes," that "you could do anything you set your mind to do." Another remembers his father's concern when he was growing up. "I was not automatically a leader when I was young. . . . I had a C average in school and scored in the 49th percentile on the

SATs. . . . There was no evidence in high school that I would be more than an average person. At this time, my dad was frustrated with me. . . . He thought I could do better, and he was right." Ultimately, his father's faith helped him develop his confidence in himself. He added that his "deeply held religious convictions" also played a part. His relationship with God was a "source of strength, meaning and direction in day-to-day life." His life was simple, he said. "I . . . don't care what others think of me or what I do. . . . I'm proud of my life and accomplishments."

Being Focused and Tenacious

The policy entrepreneurs underscored the importance of being focused and persistent in their work. They knew that immediate acceptance of their ideas was unlikely, especially those that were furthest from routine practice. Hence, one advised, it was important to take the long-haul perspective, focus on areas that were strategically important—and stay with them no matter what happened.

Another entrepreneur added that you have to have infinite patience and be willing to wait a long, long time for what you want. "When you are trying to change things, you've got to be prepared to be rebuffed and keep moving forward . . . and you never give up." He learned that lesson well from his salesman father. "In my family," he said, "you grew up hearing 'you just don't take no for an answer.' Anybody who takes no for an answer, just isn't going to make it as a salesman." Nor, by implication, as a policy entrepreneur.

Other entrepreneurs admitted that this ability to focus and work long hours had taken a toll on their lives. "Working too much" had affected their marriages and their families. "My spouse did not like me working this hard," said one. Two others cited their hours and their commitment to work as factors in their divorces, one for a second time. In reflecting on his career, the veteran policy entrepreneur (nearing retirement age) said he was cutting back on his work week—often eighty hours—to spend more time with his family, who had been very understanding of his schedule over the years.

As Others Saw Them

Educators and other observers of the innovation process expressed strong opinions on the policy entrepreneurs and their activities.

Comments ran the gamut from highly critical to highly favorable, with negative views predominating at first and more moderate views emerging after interaction increased between entrepreneurs and educators in the Governor's Discussion Group. Criticism tended to focus on several themes: lack of understanding of education issues, lack of a meaningful political constituency, unfair tactics and media manipulation, and intellectual arrogance and abrasive interpersonal style.

Educators criticized the policy entrepreneurs for lack of professional experience in education and for superficial and uninformed views about how education worked. The entrepreneurs "are not educators and just do not understand education," one insisted. "This leads them to suggest things that won't work or be in the best interest of kids," commented another. They were accused of making proposals that weren't based in cognitive development. "The reforms are not geared toward the right things to help kids learn more. [The entrepreneurs] know little about the learning process in designing the machine to teach. [Name] believes that if you just do this to the machine, you'll get the right output. Yet he comes up with fixes that are unworkable."

Some educators and lawmakers also criticized the policy entrepreneurs for lack of appreciation of the effects of open enrollment on rural school districts. Fearing the reforms were part of a hidden agenda to force consolidation of small rural school districts, some charged that the entrepreneurs "didn't understand rural America" and only cared about metro area issues. Thus, as one observer commented, their lack of knowledge of the educational process hampered them strategically, because they did not know "the nuts and bolts of education to recommend changes."

Although all the entrepreneurs saw themselves as having K-12 policy expertise, educators credited only the one who had been a teacher and assistant principal with first-hand experience in education. And he was criticized for leaving the classroom, which was said to suggest that he was not really committed to education after all—despite his thirteen years in the field and the awards he earned from local and national parent and professional groups. Educators were also unwilling to accept the relevance of another entrepreneur's background in higher education. Although he did a "pretty good job of research and developing his positions, [he

had a] credibility problem," said one critic. "Some of his perceptions were off and inaccurate [because] change is different in
higher education."

Educators did regard one policy entrepreneur, a veteran of
thirty-five years of public policy change, as educable. They saw him
"soften his hard line on education after learning and really understanding the issues as a result of the Governor's Discussion Group."
Said one educator, "He realized that he didn't have the background
and needed more indoctrination into schools." Another noted that
he "Should have stayed in retirement . . . because at the Governor's
Discussion Group, he asked a lot of dumb questions"—but went on
to say that the entrepreneur's questions "led to new answers for him
and he changed his point of view . . . so the questions helped a lot."

Educators targeted much of their animosity on one man they
described as a policy gadfly. Identified as the most influential
among the policy entrepreneurs, he served as the lightning rod for
educators' frustrations and anger. His ideas were challenged and
disputed, sometimes with a very personal tone. Said one educator:
"He puts out the shammiest of stuff. . . . I don't have a lot of respect for [him]." "His mind is cluttered," commented another. "He
can't single out the issues. But maybe he is just so brilliant that
he can't communicate to the rest of us. He has problems in an
intense situation." "No one understands him at the Governor's Discussion Group," added still another. "He can't convince anyone of
things."

Criticism also focused on the policy entrepreneurs' lack of constituency. Leaders of educational groups, who represented large
numbers of teachers, school board members, principals, and
administrators, were fond of asking rhetorically who the policy
entrepreneurs represented. They saw the policy entrepreneurs as
loose cannons and free agents, with phantom constituencies giving
them little credibility. Legislators and educators were warned that
the entrepreneurs should not be taken seriously because they could
muster no votes and represented no power bloc. Curiously, though,
on other occasions critics expressed the view that they were out-
numbered by the policy entrepreneurs. At the GDG, for example,
some felt on the defensive. "Together we represented thousands of
people and grassroots positions. Some others just represented themselves," one complained. From some educators' perspective, it was

inappropriate for the policy entrepreneurs to represent so few people and yet have an equal voice in the deliberations.

Educators also charged the policy entrepreneurs of violating the rules of the game and creating chaos by circumventing the Department of Education instead of working with the department to develop their proposals. Knowing how to get to the governor (whom educators identified as the most important change agent) gave them an unfair advantage, according to some. "The outside groups have some impact primarily because the governor listens to them and they got to the governor early with a number of ideas." One policy entrepreneur, singled out for his access and ability to get Perpich's attention, was called "the Ghermazian Brother of public policy." (This was a reference to the Canadian businessmen who had persuaded the governor to support the very controversial "mega-mall" project. The success of that project didn't affect the intended insult.) Noting this entrepreneur's extensive national contacts, another educator voiced concern about his "access to governors, both inside and outside the state of Minnesota . . . He is a consultant type and therefore gets called in for his ideas."

Educational leaders also criticized the policy entrepreneurs for their special power to shape and define issues in the media. Gradually unraveling the entrepreneurs' media connections, some educators expressed the opinion that the team "had the advantage" because "the media likes to focus on change and controversy." In the Twin Cities, the "print media was controlled and used" by the policy entrepreneurs, they asserted. In fact, the policy entrepreneurs had "the media in their pockets." Another added that the *Minneapolis Star and Tribune* had lost "its perspective in its news coverage" of educational issues and "made the issue more visible than it needed to be." A 6M representative warned of outsider influence: "I feel that organizations like the Minnesota Business Partnership, largely because of access and control of media, have great power in determining educational policy. . . . It's incredible how their recommendations, ideas, and proposals that are favored will get paper and editorial page attention. . . . It's very well organized and intertwined."

Some educators deeply resented the way local media, with the encouragement of the policy entrepreneurs, depicted educational groups as obstructionists who opposed change and wanted to preserve the status quo. "The local press created the ideas of the big, bad educational establishment blocking progress . . . and not being willing to change." "We are not opposed to change," said one, "just the radical change being proposed here." "We prefer orderly change that occurs in sequential fashion, not bold change without study and research."

While some educators blamed the policy entrepreneurs for creating an unfair perception of them in the press, others admitted that infighting between teachers' unions and school boards was partly responsible for the perception that education was opposed to change. "Some of that is our own fault," said one. "We haven't done a good job talking up our achievements. . . . The time was right in Minnesota, the governor was listening, there were the national reports, educational policy making was in the spotlight nationally . . . but we [the teachers' unions, superintendents and school boards] were too busy fighting with each other. The public did not like . . . all the adversarial things. . . . I'm not blaming but we may have gone too far."

A lobbyist for one of the educational groups concurred that there was some truth in the perception that educators were change averse. The Minnesota School Boards Association, for example, had not been very proactive in initiating and enacting change-oriented legislation—but was very good at defeating it, he said.

In an attempt to explain their perspective on the change process, one educational consultant noted: "Any changes that are brought into a current structure are dependent on the hierarchy to implement. Therefore, when leadership changes, which happens regularly, the new leader wants to put his/her stamp of identity on things. A new agenda and a new set of priorities supersede the old. This leads to an attitude in the schools that can be summarized as 'this too shall pass.' If we just wait long enough, the thing will go away. They are right. It almost always becomes irrelevant whether you agree or disagree with the policy because 'this too shall pass.'" The consultant felt it was understandable why educators had adopted a reluctant attitude about change. She also believed that the outsiders were no more reflective than the educators, and needed to develop "a healthy respect for the equally intelligent, well-intentioned people within the system."

The policy entrepreneurs also came under attack for their interpersonal style. Observers maintained that the entrepreneurs always thought they were right and refused to listen to other points of view. They were said to want change for the sake of change and options for the sake of options, without respect for the experience and knowledge of the professionals. Some educators viewed them as arrogant and patronizing, referring to them as single-issue zealots who were rigid and unwilling to compromise. Commenting on the convergence of their opinions, positions, language, and examples, some participants in the GDG saw them not as independent thinkers, but as parrots of an accepted party line who acted and sounded as if they were on a mission or crusade. One policy entrepreneur was considered particularly intransigent, making it difficult for educators to work with him. Another was criticized for being too much of a radical, having "a fuzzy-haired Einstein look," and engaging in name-calling. His ideas were good, commented one educator, but his PR was bad. Said one exasperated educator, "In the minds of most players, he is a pain in the butt!"

According to a state official, two entrepreneurs were not well liked at the legislature. Several legislators on key committees considered them antagonistic. One legislator said he was so angry at them he wouldn't listen to them. A member of the governor's executive team added that the lawmakers were fed up with the recognition and credit going to the policy entrepreneurs, saying a "powder keg situation" had developed between the two groups.

The policy entrepreneurs did get some positive commentary from observers. Even some of their strongest critics described them as brilliant, and educators singled out one for his "great mind," referring to him as the best pure intellect of the group, and very well organized. Educators also acknowledged the policy entrepreneurs' keen strategic sense, identifying several as creative and visionary. "Way beyond me," said one educator. Noting their ability to challenge underlying assumptions, opponents and supporters alike saw them as prime movers and key sources of innovative ideas. An observer described one entrepreneur as follows: "He is just phenomenal. He is very creative. . . . He comes up with a comparison or critical question that jars your sense of the givens. . . . Most of us assume the presence of boxes without even seeing the walls. . . . He pushes the walls down and looks beyond."

Observers also remarked about the policy entrepreneurs' work ethic. Many declared them to be effective because they outworked everyone else, putting in as much as eighty hours a week during the legislative session. One entrepreneur's dedication to reform was so renowned that an observer described him as a "policy junkie" who never stopped working because "it's his cause."

Both critics and supporters of the policy entrepreneurs also singled out several for their integrity and dedication to public service. One, who had worked with educators on previous projects, was described as a person "who really puts his principles into practice. In fact, he won't schedule breakfast meetings because each morning he gets up at 6:30 to fix breakfast for his family, and then they have family devotions. . . . I really admire the man, he lives his convictions." This same individual earned the respect of a journalist, who often saw him supporting issues "that everybody else runs away from, holding their noses." He received high marks for his "rock-bottom integrity" from others as well. He and two other entrepreneurs were frequently described as "persons of high integrity who respect others and their views, although we don't always agree."

Observers also acknowledged the entrepreneurs' skills in the change process. Singling out one for his exceptional ability in public speaking, a principal called him "the E. F. Hutton of the reformers. When he talks, people listen." Another educator on the GDG identified a second entrepreneur as "the best pure speaker with lots of passion and heart. He is the mobilizer. . . . I would call him the Lech Walesa of the group . . . verbal, passionate and good at brinkmanship. . . . I really admire him." A third entrepreneur was called the linchpin of the Governor's Discussion Group. His compassion, commitment, tenacity, and passion were cited as his strengths. "He is very strong and very vocal. . . . He spent lots of time. . . . and was extra tenacious [about] the issues he wanted," said one participant. "He made a tremendous contribution and he is wise enough to realize the middle group where [another entrepreneur] could not," commented another. A Department of Education member was especially impressed with his effectiveness in using anger as a tactic to make his points.

Summary

Our policy entrepreneurs shared a background including liberal arts and generalist education complemented with graduate degrees. They had diverse employment histories in the public, private, and nonprofit sectors, but all placed value on public service and were committed to a search for better public policies. They had all had broad exposure to many policy areas and were experts in at least two policy domains. All were critical thinkers and creative problem solvers, especially skilled in systems thinking and strategic analysis. They had highly developed skills of communication and persuasion enabling them to disseminate their message in various media from public speaking to writing books, speeches, and copy for the press. They also shared a willingness to be bold and take risks, exhibiting a high degree of comfort and self-confidence in being different and taking unpopular stands. They were focused, tenacious, and patient in pursuing their ideas, which enabled them to take a long-term perspective.

Part Two

Lessons Learned

Chapter Six

Entrepreneurial Identity
Personality, Values, Motivation, Knowledge, and Skills

> *We're like the spokes on a wheel, all radiating out from the*
> *same center. If you define us according to our position on*
> *the rim, we seem separate and distinct from one another.*
> *But if you define us according to our starting point, our*
> *source—the center of the wheel—we're a shared identity.*
> —MARIANNE WILLIAMSON, *A RETURN TO LOVE*

In search of a deeper understanding of the policy entrepreneurs and their behavior, we sought their cooperation to probe even further. Several questions guided our efforts. Was there a unique entrepreneurial identity? Did that identity rely on learned behavior or on the individual's innate characteristics? Could anyone be a policy entrepreneur by acquiring certain skills or knowledge, or did policy entrepreneurship call for a particular personality? If entrepreneurship could be learned, then what aspects would we recommend others develop, especially for radical change?

To begin this process, we asked the policy entrepreneurs to complete three standardized personality assessment instruments. The first part of this chapter presents results from these instruments, describing attributes the policy entrepreneurs have in common as

Note: The psychometric data in this chapter are drawn from King (1988) and King and Roberts (1992).

well as those that make them different from each other. Three of the six policy entrepreneurs refused to take the test battery, giving reasons such as "I don't believe in tests" or "I'm too busy." Although data from all six would have been ideal, those who did not participate were characterized in terms similar to the others. For example, educational leaders viewed two of the three as "sources of innovative ideas" and "key players" in mobilizing support for enactment of the ideas. The third policy entrepreneur was described as a "passionate" spokesperson and a "key strategist" for change.

In the second part of the chapter, we construct a composite picture of the policy entrepreneurs, based on assessment results, observations of behavior, self-reports, and views of others. The composite pulls together our understanding of their values, skills, knowledge, motivation, and personalities and describes how these elements interact to forge a unique identity.

The third section explores the variation in personality between the policy entrepreneurs in this study and other public entrepreneurs. In particular, we draw from developmental theory to account for personality differences between policy and executive entrepreneurs. As a result of the variation, we believe that public entrepreneurship entails more than innate personality characteristics. Much of what constitutes public entrepreneurship can be learned and passed on from one entrepreneur to another.

The fourth section introduces a developmental model of change agentry. The model enables us to view the policy entrepreneurs as master change agents who operate at the systems level of analysis in pursuit of large-scale change. As seasoned experts, they are role models for other change agents to emulate in the future.

The chapter concludes with an answer to the question of whether anyone can be a policy entrepreneur, and a summary of this chapter's lessons learned.

Standardized Instruments

The three standardized instruments we used were the California Psychological Inventory (CPI), the Myers-Briggs Type Indicator (MBTI), and the Loevinger Sentence Completion Test (SCT). All three are widely used instruments with well-established measures of validity and reliability, and all provide comparative data on the responses of various groups. Table 6.1 summarizes the results we obtained with each of the three instruments, and the remainder of the section discusses our interpretation of them.

California Psychological Inventory

The CPI (1988) provides a standardized assessment of many facets of personality, including self-acceptance, independence, responsibility, self-control, flexibility, and empathy. It also examines other aspects we thought would be pertinent to the entrepreneurial process—leadership potential, managerial potential, and creative potential.

Responses to the CPI items classify individuals into one of four types: Alphas ("enterprising, dependable, and outgoing"); Betas ("reserved, responsible, and moderate"); Gammas ("adventurous, restless, and pleasure-seeking"); and Deltas ("withdrawn, private, and to some extent disaffected") (Gough, 1987, p. 25). Within each type, scores range from Level 1, "poor integration and little or no realization of positive potential of the type," to Level 7, "superior integration and realization of the positive potential of the type" (p. 23).

Table 6.1 shows that the three policy entrepreneurs all scored as Alphas—those who "invest their values in the shared, interpersonal world, and in adherence to norms. Alphas are doers, people who carry out the sanctioned mandates of the culture. At their best, they can be charismatic leaders and instigators of constructive social action. At their worst, they can be self-centered, opportunistic and manipulative" (Gough, 1987, p. 27). Within the Alpha personality type, all three policy entrepreneurs scored at Level 7, the highest possible.

On the specialized scales, all three policy entrepreneurs are assessed as having clear leadership talent. Two of them have superior managerial talent, while the third is above average. One shows above-average creative potential, while the two others have somewhat above-average and average creative potential.

The creativity scores puzzled us at first. We expected the policy entrepreneurs to be higher on this scale. However, we know from our field data that the three who did not complete the test battery were key players in the innovation process, especially in the

Table 6.1. Results from Standardized Instruments.

Results	Person 1	Person 2	Person 3
California Personality Inventory			
Type	Alpha	Alpha	Alpha
Level	7	7	7
Leadership potential	Distinct talent	Distinct talent	Distinct talent
Managerial potential	Well above average	Distinctly superior	Distinctly superior
Creative potential	Average	Above average	Somewhat above average
Myers-Briggs Type Indicator			
Extroversion/ introversion	Extroversion	Introversion	Extroversion
Sensing/ intuition	Intuition	Intuition	Intuition
Thinking/ feeling	Thinking	Thinking	Thinking
Judgment/ perception	Judgment	Judgment	Perception
Type	ENTJ	INTJ	ENTP
Loevinger Sentence Completion			
Level	I-5	I-4/5	I-4/5
Stage	Autonomous	Individualistic	Individualistic

initial formulation of the innovative ideas. The scores on hand may underrepresent the policy entrepreneurs' range on this dimension. Alternatively, the anomaly may have to do with the CPI itself—the CPI creativity scale is under development, and may not adequately capture the complexity of creativity. If so, the scores may not be a valid indicator of the policy entrepreneurs' creative potential.

Myers-Briggs Type Indicator

The MBTI offers insights into the way people perceive and the way they make judgments. Since perception—by definition—determines what people see in a situation and judgment determines what they decide to do about it, it is reasonable to conclude that basic differences in perception and judgment result in corresponding differences in behavior (Myers, 1980).

The major objective of the MBTI is to capture and identify four basic preferences that are believed to direct the use of perception and judgment: extroversion versus introversion, sensing versus intuition, thinking versus feeling, and judgment versus perception. Each preference is measured by a separate index in the instrument—identified by initial letter, except for intuition, which uses N to distinguish it from introversion (I). The respondent's preferences form the four-letter type code that gives the instrument its name. The theory assumes that all types are necessary and valuable, each with its own strengths and vulnerabilities.

Table 6.1 shows that the MBTI identified two of the policy entrepreneurs as extroverts and one as an introvert. All three are assessed as intuitives and all three prefer thinking to feeling in decision making, indicating that they value logic over sentiment. Two of the policy entrepreneurs prefer judgment over perception while one prefers perception over judgment.

Combining their choices on the four preference indices, each of the policy entrepreneurs represents a different type. Person 1 is scored as an ENTJ, referred to as the "standard executive type" (Myers, 1980, p. 86). Persons of this type are interested in the "possibilities of a given situation" especially those that are "beyond what is present or obvious or known." Intuition sparks their intellectual pursuits, interest in complex problems, and concern for long-range consequences. ENTJs tolerate theory, exhibit insight and vision, and are able to see the broad picture. Needing problems to solve, they are expert at finding new and innovative solutions (Myers and McCaulley, 1985, p. 22).

Person 2 is scored as an INTJ, an "introverted intuitive." Identified as the "most independent of all the sixteen types," their greatest gifts come directly from their intuition—the flashes of inspiration, the insight into relationships of ideas and meaning of symbols, the imagination, the originality, the access to resources of the unconscious, the ingenuity, and the visions of what could be" (Myers, 1980, p. 113). Whatever their field, INTJs are "likely to be innovators" since "intuition gives them an iconoclastic view of the possibilities" (Myers, 1980, p. 115). They trust their insights and vision, regardless of popular beliefs, established authority, or universal skepticism. Wanting to see their ideas worked out in practice, they have a tendency to ignore the views and feelings of those who don't agree with them. They are "logical, critical, decisive, determined, often stubborn" and they "tend to drive others almost as hard as they drive themselves." They also are "apt to be effective, relentless reorganizers," also "efficient executives, rich in ideas" (Myers and McCaulley, 1985, p. 29).

Person 3 is scored as an ENTP, an "extroverted intuitive." ENTPs are described as "enthusiastic innovators" always open and alert to new possibilities and new ways of doing things (Myers and McCaulley, 1985, p. 28). They are independent and creative with an "intuitive vision" of some possibility in the external world. As ingenious problem solvers, they are "stimulated by difficulties" and will work tirelessly at what interests them. They hate uninspired routine and avoid humdrum detail. Being perceptive, they are able to understand people rather than judge them and in so doing win support for projects. At their best, ENTPs are "gifted with insight amounting to wisdom and the power to inspire" (Myers, 1980, pp. 108–109).

Loevinger Sentence Completion Test

The SCT is designed to measure *ego development,* which combines four facets of personality—impulse control, character development, interpersonal style and conscious preoccupation, and cognitive complexity (Loevinger, 1976, p. 26). The underlying assumption is that human development involves a series of definite and irreversible stages, ranging from I-1, Symbiotic, to I-5, Autonomous. Each stage represents an integrated, internally consistent perspective on the world and the individual's place in it. With each transformation from one stage to the next, the individual's former worldview becomes part of a more inclusive worldview.

Table 6.1 shows that SCT results indicate that Persons 2 and 3 are at the Individualistic level (I-4/5) and Person 1 is at the Autonomous stage (I-5). According to Loevinger (1976), people at the Individualistic level of development have a heightened sense of individuality and a concern for making a unique contribution to society as a whole. Believing that what one sees depends on one's worldview, individuals at this level are comfortable in creating a unique frame of reference and using it not only to frame their reality but also in structuring the reality of others. Individuals at this level attend as much to process issues as to outcomes—and process involves not just rules and customs but also judgment, theory, intuition, and the ability to be creative in the moment. Such individuals show a marked increase in toleration of ambiguity and a comfort with paradox and contradiction, using all of these elements to solve problems, make decisions, and manage conflict. Resolution of conflict, however, is seen as mostly external—if only society (or one's spouse) would be more accommodating, there would be no conflict. Conflict is not recognized as part of the human condition until the Autonomous stage.

The defining characteristic of the Autonomous (I-5) stage of development is the acknowledgment of dual needs for autonomy and interdependence in oneself and others. For some I-5 individuals, a shift in emphasis or priorities may occur in which seeking fulfillment becomes an important life goal, at times supplanting achievement as a primary motivation (Loevinger, 1976, p. 23). A person at this stage respects autonomy, individuality, and uniqueness in self and in others, while recognizing the need for emotional interdependence and close ties and bonds with others. Individuals at this stage exhibit a deepened conceptual complexity, a tolerance for ambiguity, and an ability to integrate what appear to those at a lower stage of development to be incompatible alternatives and solutions. Instead of ignoring conflict or projecting it onto the environment, the Autonomous person acknowledges and deals with it. Conflict becomes the natural consequence of competing perspectives, roles, and demands, to be managed but never completely resolved—a fundamental part of the human condition. Autonomous individuals take a broad view of life, and generally adopt abstract social goals such as justice and fairness as ideals. In addition, they recognize that one can function differently in different roles and that different roles have different requirements.

Shared Characteristics in the Test Results

Commonalities among the policy entrepreneurs emerge from the battery of tests. All share the following characteristics:

- *All are highly intuitive* (MBTI N preference). Generally rest-less, they have no taste for life as it is nor do they have much capac-ity for living in or enjoying the present. They dislike occupations that require them to pay close attention to immediate events. Indifferent to other people and their physical surroundings, they are imagina-tive, inventive, and original, primarily interested in future opportu-nities and possibilities. They contribute to the public welfare by their enterprise, achievement, initiative, and inspirational leadership in every direction of human interest (Myers, 1980, p. 63).

- *All are critical, analytical thinkers* (MBTI T preference). Thinkers "value logic above sentiment." If pressed to choose be-tween truth and tact, they usually prefer truth. They are stronger in executive ability than in social arts and are likely to question other people on principle—assuming them to be wrong. They are brief and businesslike, and often appear to "lack friendliness and sociability without knowing or intending it." Their tendency is to suppress, undervalue, and ignore feelings that are incompatible with thinking. "They contribute to the welfare of society by the intellectual criticism of its habits, customs, and beliefs, by the expo-sure of wrongs, the solution of problems" (Myers, 1980, p. 68).

- *All are instigators of constructive social action* (CPI Alpha). They are action-oriented and have the potential to be agents working for positive social change (California Psychological Inventory, 1988; Gough, 1987).

- *All have well-integrated personalities* (CPI Level 7). "For persons at this level one can expect exceptional initiative, self-confidence, constructive ambition, effective decision making skills, and a talent for leadership" (California Psychological Inventory, 1988, p. 1; Gough, 1987).

- *All have highly evolved, developed egos* (SCT Scores of I-5 and I-4/5 compared to U.S. modal level of I-3/4)). Individuals at these stages are concerned about making a contribution to society as a whole. They are comfortable with paradox, contradictions, and conflict, appreciate uniqueness in self and others, and are con-cerned with both outcomes and processes, including creativity, used to achieve goals (Loevinger, 1976, pp. 22–23).

- *All have a high level of leadership potential* (CPI Special Scale). They "like the role of leader, and [have] a distinct talent for lead-ership" (California Psychological Inventory, 1988, p. 2).

- *All have a high level of managerial potential* (CPI Special Scale). One is "well above average in managerial potential" and two are "distinctly superior in managerial potential" (California Psychological Inventory, 1988, p. 2).
- *All have average or above average creative potential* (California Psychological Inventory, 1988). As noted earlier, these scores may be skewed either by the limited number participating in the test or by the nature of the test itself.

Compared to others who have completed these assessments, the policy entrepreneurs are distinctive on many dimensions. Studies using the MBTI, for example, estimate the frequency of intuitive types in the population as about 25 percent (Myers and McCaulley, 1985, p. 45). Yet *all* of the policy entrepreneurs who took this test are intuitives. Comparing college graduates to the policy entrepreneurs' results on the Myers-Briggs, we find 9.5 percent are rated as INTJs; 5.65 percent rated as ENTPs; and 11.43 percent rated as ENTJs (p. 46). The mode for the CPI is at Level 4; these policy entrepreneurs scored at Level 7. The normal distribution of individuals scoring at Level 7 on the CPI is approximately 8.6 percent of the population (Gough, 1987, p. 21). The modal level for adults in the United States on the SCT is I-3/4, Self-Aware, while the policy entrepreneurs are estimated to be at I-4/5, Individualistic, and I-5, Autonomous (Loevinger and Wessler, 1970). Thus, the policy entrepreneurs score well above the mode on all three personality assessments.

Identity of Policy Entrepreneurs

Combining the results from the standardized tests, our own observations, the self-report data, and the reports of others, we found a reasonably consistent identity emerging for the policy entrepreneurs. Individualistic, intuitive, innovative, and analytical, they excel at critical thinking and problem solving. They appear to be change agents, alert to new possibilities and solutions, and constantly searching for ways to convert their visions of the future into reality. Such an orientation often requires them to assume leadership positions, for which they seem to have distinct talent.

This identity closely resembles descriptions of both public and private-sector entrepreneurs in the literature (Kingdon, 1984;

Lewis, 1980; Ramamurti, 1986a, 1986b; Doig and Hargrove, 1987). Entrepreneurs have been found to be more energetic, autonomous, with less need for social support and more need for independence than nonentrepreneurs. Self-confident and action-oriented, they tend to be more thick-skinned, ambitious, and articulate than those less inclined to entrepreneurship, and to have a high need for achievement, tolerance for ambiguity, and propensity for risk taking (Bird, 1989).

In addition, we saw the policy entrepreneurs as confrontational when necessary, and skillful at managing the conflict that ensued. They are tough enough to handle the frustration of being misunderstood and cope with their own anger when facing setbacks and defeats. They have developed patience, endurance, and courage in the pursuit of radical innovation, which is often a long-term process that tests them physically, mentally, and emotionally. Less affiliative than most people, they pursue ideals and visions rather than popularity. Although they may enjoy praise, they do not rely on recognition to keep them moving forward. They take a degree of comfort in being marginal.

We believe that marginality is important to their identity and that it has emotional, cognitive, and physical aspects. Emotionally and cognitively, policy entrepreneurs establish clear boundaries between themselves and others and are able to maintain their distance. In pursuit of radical change, they are comfortable espousing ideas beyond acceptable practice. In fact, they seem to enjoy their uniqueness and separateness from others. Physically, policy entrepreneurs are marginal in the sense that they tend to seek nonmainstream positions. Rather than assume visible offices of power and influence, they are more comfortable with positions on the sidelines or in the background. Kanter (1988) reminds us of the advantages of such positions, noting that creativity springs up at the boundaries of specialties and disciplines rather than in the middle. Since innovation is often a matter of combining two separate ideas, marginality is likely to increase the ability to innovate. Research on scientists supports this view. Those who had more contacts outside their field were more creative and productive; outsiders were more likely to innovate than those who rose by more orthodox means within their organizations (Peltz and Andrews, 1966).

Given their single-minded pursuit of an innovative vision, it is understandable how the policy entrepreneurs in this study see themselves as dedicated, tenacious, and serving the public interest. At the same time, it is equally understandable how those who find their ideas threatening see them as stubborn, unwilling to listen, and grandstanding for personal gain. "Where one stands depends on where one sits" often came to mind as we listened to comments about the entrepreneurs and their behavior. Reactions are just as likely to reflect the observer's own goals as they are to reflect on the policy entrepreneurs. Those who oppose the innovative idea and resist radical change tend to condemn the policy entrepreneurs and their actions, while those who share their ideas and approach to change are likely to be more complimentary in their descriptions and characterizations.

One way to capture the entrepreneurial profile in all its complexity is to envision it as a wheel (see Figure 6.1). The hub or center of the wheel represents the individual's identity (I), or sense of self. The structure of an individual's profile depends on the dynamic interplay among five elements represented by spokes in the wheel: personality, values, motivation, knowledge, and skills.

Personality is defined as "the collection of attributes, dispositions, and tendencies that make up a single individual" (Smith, Sarason, and Sarason, 1982, p. 672). It is an important part of identity because it captures the more enduring aspects of a person, or as some define it, the genetic predisposition that distinguishes one individual from another. As measured by the three standardized instruments described earlier, we believe the policy entrepreneurs in this study can be characterized as having action-oriented, autonomous, and individualistic personalities. Ready to be bold, different, focused, and tenacious, they are doers and leaders, constantly searching for new solutions and new possibilities.

Values on the Identity Wheel are defined as the individual's ideals. As beacons to guide behavior, values serve to mold expectations for self and others. In this instance, we understand how the policy entrepreneurs were nurtured and encouraged by their families and educators to make a difference, to search for ways to improve society, and give back more than they received. The results from the SCT are consistent with these self-reports. At levels I-5 and I-4/5, they show a concern with higher-order values such as justice,

Figure 6.1. Entrepreneurial Identity Wheel.

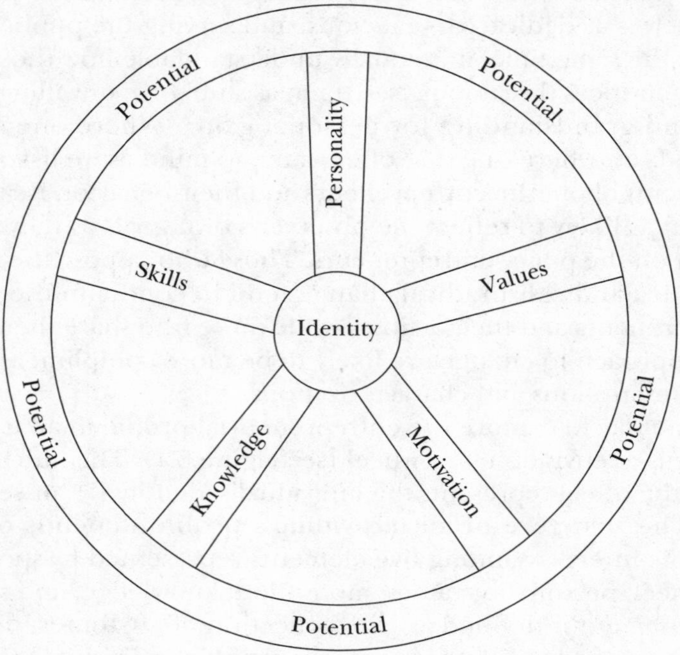

equity, and the common good. The policy entrepreneurs pursued changes in education because they wanted children to have a more equitable, efficient, effective, flexible, humane, individualized education—the adjective depended on the entrepreneur's values. Thus, values provided them with a *raison d'être* and a way to explain to themselves and others why they were doing what they were doing. Without ideals, actions lack purpose and meaning. It is difficult to make a long-term commitment to radical change, to attract others, and to endure the inevitable disappointments, without the grounding and sustenance that values give.

Motivation, defined as inducements and incentives for action, is the third component of the Identity Wheel. This component provides the impetus for action by stimulating and reinforcing certain behaviors while extinguishing others. In this case, the policy entrepreneurs learned, through effort and application, that they would be rewarded for their actions. For some entrepreneurs the rewards were extrinsic, in the form of recognition and acknowledgment from others. For others, the rewards were intrinsic, in the form of self-satisfaction for a job well done. Whatever the particular motivational pattern, by continuing to press for change in different policy domains, the policy entrepreneurs apparently find that the incentives for action outweigh the risk of failure and the comfort of inaction.

Motivation also can be defined in terms of internal needs or drives. From this perspective, the focus is on what is inside the person, as opposed to those rewards or incentives that are the mechanisms of motivated behavior (Angle, 1989). This aspect of motivation is difficult to assess for anyone, including the policy entrepreneurs, because it delves into motives beneath the level of awareness. True, we can infer a high achievement motivation to the entrepreneurs from their life accomplishments, and we have CPI results revealing above-modal scores on two scales measuring achievement motivation—Achievement Via Conformance and Achievement Via Independence. But experts such as McClelland (1987) doubt the validity of self-report measures to capture the unconscious. He advocates the Thematic Apperception Test (TAT) instead, a projective test that assesses the strength of a person's unconscious needs for achievement, power, and affiliation. Since we did not administer the TAT, we are unable to speculate on internal motivations. However, we can draw on research on other entrepreneurs to speculate on what the motivational pattern of these entrepreneurs might be.

Knowledge, defined as specific information and understanding in a policy area, is another element of the policy entrepreneurs' identity. Having the personality of an entrepreneur, and the values and motivation to support it, may be sufficient to become an apprentice in change agentry, but without the *content knowledge* of a particular domain (what the problems are and what the solutions might be) and the *process knowledge* (how to intervene to affect that domain), little may be accomplished in complex political and interorganizational settings.

All the policy entrepreneurs did see themselves as *process experts* in large-scale system change. Having what they described as the ability to think wholistically about education policy issues, they expressed confidence in defining the system as a whole and understanding the interrelationship among its parts. They also were able to conceptualize interventions in education that were intended to effect large-scale change. They championed choice in the schools, not because it was their favorite idea, but because they believed it gave them greatest leverage for changing the entire system. Their previous experiences had taught them to look for the lever of change—the point of intervention most likely to have important direct consequences (first-order effects), and also to release a floodgate of other innovative ideas and changes (second-order effects). In combination, these first and second-order effects would be apt to produce system-wide transformation. This process knowledge, more than any other factor, distinguished them from their adversaries, who defined domain expertise only in terms of content knowledge. While it is unlikely that such extensive knowledge is required to launch an entrepreneur's career, we believe that ultimate success in radical policy change depends on the ability to develop this process and system knowledge.

Skills provide another important spoke in the entrepreneurs' Identity Wheel. The policy entrepreneurs exhibited skills in public speaking, writing, persuasion, networking and coalition building, organizing, bargaining, and negotiating, as described in Chapters Three and Four. Honed over many years of education and work, these skills enabled them to connect with a wide audience—from grassroots activists and citizens to reporters, administrators, legislators, and executives at Fortune 100 firms. By all accounts, they excelled at using these political skills and the tools of communication and information dissemination. It is difficult to imagine how an entrepreneur could be successful without them. As we saw in Chapter Four, though, not all were equally proficient in every skill area. This was one of the advantages of working as a group. While some were the wordsmiths or writers of the group, others were called on to be the speakers, negotiators, or organizers. Whatever the tasks, the sum total of these skills enabled the group as a whole to walk in the corridors of power and to exert a great deal of influence.

In summary, we suggest treating each of the five components as essential parts of identity. Just as the strength of a wheel depends on the sturdiness of each spoke, so skills, knowledge, values, motivation, and personality undergird the entrepreneurial identity.

Remove one element and the identity is diminished, perhaps changed completely. Individuals without the skills of entrepreneurship lack the wherewithal to make their vision a reality. Those without drive and ambition are easily distracted by roadblocks along the innovation path.

Entrepreneurial Personality Variations

Certain aspects of the identity outlined here, although reasonably consistent among the six entrepreneurs in our study, are not shared by all public entrepreneurs. Two well-known figures, J. Edgar Hoover and Robert Moses, serve as examples. They have been characterized as "conventionally neurotic . . . not 'well-adjusted' or even 'well-rounded'" (Lewis, 1980, p. 236). "Willing to use people as though they were objects" (Lewis, 1980, pp. 235–236), they employed "nearly any means at all" to reach their ends, including bending the rules (Lewis, 1980, p. 243), and outright illegality (Ramamurti, 1986b, p. 154). They are "crafty . . . snake-oil salesmen of the first order," according to Lewis (1980, p. 243). These public entrepreneurs used ethically questionable strategies to reach their organizational and personal ends. They attained high levels of autonomy and freedom and rearranged the allocation of both public and private resources to build their empires. Their flagrant abuse of authority enabled them to gain undisputed control over their domains (Lewis, 1980). For example, Caro (1975) described Moses as having many New York City officials living in fear. He "hired skilled investigators he called 'bloodhounds' who were kept busy filling dossiers. Every city official knew about those dossiers, and they knew what use Moses was capable of making of them" (pp. 14–15).

The contrast between Moses and Hoover and the six policy entrepreneurs in this study is stark. What do these differences mean for the entrepreneurial identity? We can view each spoke on the Identity Wheel as representing a range of potentials. An individual entrepreneur can register different scores on each spoke. For example, we have seen variation among the six policy entrepreneurs in terms of their motivation and skills. And there is even greater variation in personality among Hoover, Moses, and the six entrepreneurs in this study. In the aggregate, different scores on each spoke can produce different profiles for each entrepreneur, although all share the overall entrepreneurial identity. What would be useful to know, and we lack the data at this point in time to predict, is how great the variation is among entrepreneurs. Not all combinations of scores on the five spokes are expected to result in an entrepreneurial identity. But just what is the range of possibilities before one stops being an entrepreneur and takes on another kind of identity has not been determined. These are questions to guide future research.

Differences in entrepreneurial profiles lead us to speculate on why these differences occur and what they may mean in practice. One explanation comes to mind, suggested by the examples of Hoover and Moses. Note that both were executive entrepreneurs, in charge of public agencies. Both launched ambitious programs of agency expansion, and exercised great reward and coercive power as a result of their positions (French and Raven, 1959). Scholars have speculated that people in such positions have a high *need for power*—a concern about having "impact, control, or influence over another person, group, or the world at large" (Winter, 1973). More than likely, these two executive entrepreneurs chose to build and lead government agencies precisely because public bureaus are "power instruments of great significance" (Lewis, 1980, p. 250). They would have held onto their positions—enjoying long tenure—because the positions permitted them to act in ways they found rewarding.

In contrast, the six policy entrepreneurs occupied positions outside government. Their power came from their innovative ideas and their ability to attract a following among those inside and outside government. Without the means to control others, their power was collective rather than competitive or coercive. They worked with others rather than exerting power over them (Roberts, 1986, 1991). Although the entrepreneurs needed power to move their ideas beyond initiation to implementation, that power was manifested in ways decidedly different from the executive entrepreneurs.

McClelland (1987) appears to support this interpretation. He postulates that stage of psychosocial development "modulates the expression of the power motive" (p. 302), meaning that the way a person pursues power changes with the person's level of maturity.

Finding differences in personality profiles among entrepreneurs (Lewis, 1980; Ramamurti, 1986a, 1986b), and following McClelland's reasoning and evidence (1987, pp. 302–311), we speculate that the policy entrepreneurs in our study are at a higher stage of socioemotional maturity than the executive entrepreneurs we have described. Although we did not use McClelland's typology or scoring system, we do have evidence from the SCT to gauge the policy entrepreneurs' development. As we noted above, all had achieved a highly evolved stage of ego development. Based on the spiritual, altruistic, and service reasons they used to explain their involvement in policy change, we would judge them to be at McClelland's Stage IIIb or Stage IV.

Stage IIIb is characterized by socialized power—an individual high in power needs and impulse control, and low in affiliation needs. An individual with this motivational pattern demonstrates respect for institutional authority, discipline and self-control, liking for work, caring for others, and concern for justice and just reward (McClelland, 1987, p. 315). He is a "socially responsible person who manages things well and often assumes a leadership role in organizations or the community" (McClelland, 1987, p. 315). Stage IV individuals express power in a generative and mutual manner. They are moved to serve because they value "understanding of others, tolerance, serving the common good," and compassion (McClelland, 1987, p. 304).

The critical difference between Stage IIIb and Stage IV is the reasons *why* such people serve others. McClelland poses the following questions to differentiate the two stages: "Are they doing it on behalf of themselves or truly out of a commitment to a higher good?" (McClelland, 1987, p. 315). He answers the question by describing the inner motives of Stage IV individuals as characterized by selflessness and a lack of a need for recognition. "Those in Stage IIIb see the power and authority coming from themselves and they are serving others to extend their own influence. Thus, they have not achieved the highest levels of maturity in which they have become true selfless instruments of higher authority. . . . People in Stage IV would not care whether what they had done was recognized or not" (McClelland, 1987, p. 315).

In contrast to the policy entrepreneurs, the executive entrepreneurs appear to be at Stage IIIa, referred to as the *assertion modality.* Characterized as the conquistador pattern (high in power motive, low in affiliation motive, and low in impulse control), Stage IIIa people exhibit impulsiveness-aggressiveness, sexual promiscuity, display, and anti-institutional activities (McClelland, 1987, p. 327). They may lie more, drink more, collect valuable objects symbolic of their importance, and be driven to obtain and express power, without submitting that power to any higher authority. Building up their bureaus to extend their personal control, and manifesting their power in coercive, manipulative ways, the executive entrepreneurs in Lewis (1980) and Ramamurti (1986a, 1986b) appear to us to be good examples of individuals operating at this stage of development.

If these findings hold for larger samples, they will bear out what we believe is an important implication of this study. The executive entrepreneurs described earlier do not reflect the motivation and personality of all public entrepreneurs, who can and do have differing profiles. Concerns about the darker side of public entrepreneurship may be misplaced (Reich, 1990; Terry, 1993). We do not deny the existence of expedient manipulators who play fast and loose with the public interest. Lacking accountability, some free-wheeling public entrepreneurs flagrantly abuse their power, misuse resources, and behave in unethical ways. *But it is not the public entrepreneur in general we should be concerned about; it is the public entrepreneur who lacks socioemotional maturity who warrants our concern.*

We should remember too that the entrepreneurial profile is shaped by and interacts with its environment. The environment is like the road over which the identity wheel travels. As the wheel turns, the rim activates potentials on each spoke in response to road conditions. Certain profiles will match the conditions, and others will not. It is difficult to imagine how a profile like that of Hoover or Moses would fit today's terrain of intense media coverage and high expectations for accountability and ethical conduct. On the other hand, the policy entrepreneurs' profile, based on higher-order values, mutuality, and collective power, appears to be a better match with current reality. Thus, we believe that it is not the profile alone that is important in understanding entrepreneurship, but how that profile interacts with its environment. Perhaps humorist Garrison Keillor is right, and there is something special about the terrain in Minnesota ("where all the women are strong, all the men are good looking, and all the children are above average") that produces the particular profile of these policy entrepreneurs.

Developmental Model of Change Agentry

The developmental perspective is useful in identifying differences among public entrepreneurs in terms of their ability to pursue complex, long-term, system-wide policy changes. Permit us to briefly turn to the leadership literature to put these accomplishments into a larger context.

Jaques (1986, 1989) and Hunt (1991) have been developing what they call the *stratified-systems theory* of leadership. The basic idea is that leaders face increasingly complex, critical tasks at each level of a system. Increasing task complexity is considered to be a function of the uncertainties in dealing with a more encompassing and turbulent environment.

According to Jaques (1986, 1989), seven levels are needed to deal with task complexity. These levels can be grouped into three domains—systems, organizational, and direct leadership. The systems domain describes leadership at the corporate and group levels; the organizational domain describes leadership at the company and division (general management) levels; and the direct domain describes leadership at the department, section, and shop floor levels. The three domains are based on Jaques's measure of task complexity for each level.

The measure of task complexity, described as the *time span of discretion,* is calculated in terms of the longest of the maximum target completion times of the critical tasks performed at each level of leadership. The time span of discretion for someone engaged in direct leadership will be less than a year, and probably nearer three months. The time span of discretion of someone involved in organizational leadership will be five to ten years. And the time span of discretion of leaders at the systems level will be twenty years and up. Jaques maintains that it is only at the top three levels (organizational and higher) that individuals operate in an *open system,* one that is not contained within the boundary conditions established by the organization. Here, at this strategic level, leaders function in what almost amounts to an unbounded, world environment.

It is Jaques' systems level that provides a parallel with the policy entrepreneurs. Their domain, open and unbounded, is beyond the limitations of any single organization. They span organizations and develop their own ideas on which to build a consensus for the future. Effective at developing a resource base to support their work, they are capable of influencing their environment to be receptive to them and their ideas. All these traits are characteristic of system-level leaders.

We also see the policy entrepreneurs as having the conceptual complexity required to match the task complexity they face at this strategic level, which is also a requirement of the stratified-systems approach to leadership (Jaques, 1989). *Conceptual complexity* is defined as the raw mental power that enables a person to absorb information, play with it, analyze it, combine and recombine it, judge and reason with it, draw conclusions, make plans and decisions, and take action with it (Hunt, 1991, p. 17). It describes the maximum scale and complexity of the world that one is able to pattern and interpret, including the amount and complexity of information that one is capable of processing (Jaques, 1989, p. 33). Well above the norm of the general population in terms of their profile, it appears that these policy entrepreneurs also are well above the norm in terms of their cognitive complexity and time-span of discretion as conceptualized by Jaques.

Assuming their tasks, environments, and cognitive powers are similar, it is not too difficult to understand how the profiles of leaders of private businesses operating at the strategic level (as found in Hunt and Jaques) and of policy entrepreneurs operating at the systems level (as found in this study) would be similar. In fact, it may account for the apparent ease with which the policy entrepreneurs moved so freely among positions in government, business, and nonprofit organizations. Developmental models, whether they are based on leadership or ego development, all tap into at least one similar, underlying dimension—cognitive complexity (Loevinger, 1976; Hunt, 1991; Jaques, 1986, 1989).

If our assessment is correct, it implies the existence of a *developmental model of change agentry* comparable to the developmental model of leadership. And like the leadership model, it may be based, among other things, on an individual's cognitive complexity, as manifested in the time span of discretion. Our sample of mature policy entrepreneurs may well illustrate the upper bounds of such a model for public sector change agents.

Summary

Our study of the change process in Minnesota has led us to conclude that individuals matter, especially when the issue is large-scale, radical change. People with an entrepreneurial identity make a difference because they create the frames of reference that structure reality into particular problems and their attendant solutions. As instigators of social action, they remind us to look beyond our individual concerns to find ways to contribute to society as a whole. We rely on their flashes of insight and inspiration to develop new ideas that begin the policy innovation process. Drawing on their cognitive complexity to map out the broad contours of the change process, we are invited to think wholistically and strategically. We appreciate their comfort in dealing with paradox and contradiction, which helps us integrate what at first glance appear to be incompatible alternatives and solutions. We welcome their tenacity in teaching us how to overcome resistance, and their patience in teaching us how to endure the disappointments and setbacks when we fail. Second-order change requires a long time horizon; it is not the province of those easily discouraged. Nor is it an attractive arena for those who lack the ego strength to endure the criticism that comes from challenging popular authority. "If you are going to be durable," said the veteran policy entrepreneur, "you can't be personal. If you do, you will lose your perspective."

Can Anyone Be a Policy Entrepreneur?

Can anyone be a policy entrepreneur? If the developmental model of change agentry is supported, the straightforward answer is no. Not everyone can be a system-level change agent who has the cognitive complexity to work in open systems that require an extended time span of discretion. These policy entrepreneurs also appear to have a unique identity with certain innate personality characteristics. Furthermore, as in business, it is likely that "only some potential entrepreneurs become entrepreneurs, and only some entrepreneurs can succeed (survive and grow)" (Bird, 1989, p. 137).

What, then, are the alternatives for individuals without this entrepreneurial identity who nevertheless wish to participate in changing public policy in innovative, radical ways? We suggest two alternatives. The first requires focusing on those components of the Identity Wheel that can be learned: skills and knowledge. Although policy entrepreneurship springs from certain innate characteristics of personality and motivational makeup, much of public entrepreneurship is *learned behavior.* Evidence from research on human creativity provides a good point of comparison.

Not everyone possesses the same creative abilities. Some are better than others in the ability to make associations between ideas, to see divergent uses for a single idea, to access the subconscious, or to visualize potential solutions (Barron and Harrington, 1981). Yet despite these differences in potential, there are those who believe and have demonstrated that it is useful to teach people how to enhance creativity through techniques designed to stimulate creative behaviors. (See, for example, Burnside, 1990; Farr, 1990).

We believe that a person can learn to behave more entrepreneurially even without an entrepreneurial identity, just as one can learn to behave more creatively even without strong natural abilities. We find no reason why the behavior exemplified in the policy entrepreneurs' communication and political skills (Chapter Five) and their complex set of activities (Chapters Three and Four) cannot be learned by others. The fact that the policy entrepreneurs were able to learn some of this behavior by observation (as we describe in the next chapter) and teach it to others suggests that there is a repertoire of activity that can be learned, modeled, and passed on from one generation of policy entrepreneurs to another.

We also should point out that this behavioral pattern was not learned overnight but over a period of years. The policy entrepreneurs' backgrounds (Chapter Five) indicate that they chose work experiences enabling them to develop skills and mature as policy entrepreneurs, but that this was not necessarily their original, conscious intention in making earlier career choices. Over time, they learned how public policy is made; they developed their communication and political skills to work in that arena; they developed networks of contacts necessary for information gathering and coalition building; and most importantly, they became system-level change agents who could apply their systems knowledge creatively to solve problems in different policy domains. As the development model of leadership suggests, it is possible to build a repertoire of skills by practicing on a more constrained set at lower organizational levels. Despite having a shorter time span of discretion, a narrower scope of issues to consider, and a range of actions more constrained by organizations or procedures, one can practice the behaviors of entrepreneurship just as one can practice the behaviors of leadership. Recall that public entrepreneurship is manifested at all levels—bureaucratic, executive, and political—as well as at the policy level.

To the extent that we want to pattern our actions after experts rather than novices, these policy entrepreneurs appear to be excellent role models. They possess domain-specific and adaptive knowledge, or what we referred to in Chapter Five as content and process knowledge. They share these traits with other experts, and they likewise tend to make appropriate responses to unpredictable situations (Holyoak, 1991; Mayer, 1991). Also, like other experts, they are adept at applying routine solutions to problems as well as inventing new procedures based on their expertise, and even reframing problems they encounter (Scribner, 1984). In these qualities, they provide a sharp contrast to novices, who tend to have less domain-specific knowledge, to be more rule bound because they assume that the same principles apply in all situations, and to be more likely to treat problems very literally (Dreyfus, Dreyfus, and Athansian, 1986; Ericsson and Smith, 1991; Salthouse, 1991). From our perspective, the entrepreneurs are system-level change agents who model skills and behaviors that others would find useful, no matter what their location in the policy system. They offer us a rare glimpse of master change agents in action.

Although systems-level change agentry may be beyond the skill level of the novice entrepreneur, this developmental model implies that a person could practice some of the entrepreneurial skills by choosing mentors and assignments that build mastery over time. For those who suspect that their profiles may be somewhat different from this set of policy entrepreneurs, we advise less concern about the profile and more focus on learning how to behave entrepreneurially. Until researchers can sort out the reasons and implications for the variation among personality attributes, it makes greater sense to concentrate on learned behavior rather than innate factors. Furthermore, the evidence on entrepreneurial behavior at all levels is very consistent with the activities and behavior of the policy entrepreneurs, despite their system-level perspective.

You have a second alternative if your profile does not match the one described here. As noted in Chapter Four, successful entrepreneurship is often a group effort rather than an individual one. By drawing people into a group and leveraging talents and resources, many can participate in the policy innovation process: policy intellectuals during the creative phase, policy champions during the design phase, and policy implementers and evaluators during the implementation phase. Team entrepreneurship has many advantages over individual entrepreneurship. Not only can participants complement one another's expertise and skills, but they can share the enormous burden of the effort. We observed how the group we studied provided support, served as mentors and colleagues, and substituted for one another when occasion warranted. An additional advantage from the practitioner's point of view is that you can be less concerned with your personal attributes and more concerned with how your skills and abilities map against those of your team members. Perhaps the better question is not whether anyone can be a policy entrepreneur, but what is the profile of the entrepreneurial team and how well do the members fit together as a whole? That is the question we turn to in the next chapter.

Lessons Learned

There is a unique entrepreneurial identity that distinguishes entrepreneurs from nonentrepreneurs. Public entrepreneurs are intuitive, individualistic, and analytical change agents who excel at critical thinking and problem solving.

The entrepreneurial identity derives from skills, knowledge, values, motivation, and personality. It depends both on innate characteristics such as personality and motivation and on learned behavior such as skills, knowledge, and values. There is variation in innate characteristics and learned behavior among entrepreneurs, and the full range of personalities and behaviors has not been established.

A developmental model of change agentry seems to distinguish experts at the systems level from novices working at the group level. We believe the policy entrepreneurs in this study are models of mature change agents. We further speculate that to be successful, radical change requires change agents expert at the systems level who have both process knowledge and content knowledge of a policy domain.

Potential change agents without the personality profile described here should focus on qualities that can be acquired. These include the behaviors, skills, and process and content knowledge of public entrepreneurship. Team entrepreneurship can also allow individuals to combine their own parts of the profile into an effective whole, allowing groups to serve as change agents even when none of the individuals involved have all of the qualities needed.

Chapter Seven

Collective Entrepreneurship
The Role of Teams in Policy Innovation

We must all hang together, or assuredly we shall all hang separately.
—BENJAMIN FRANKLIN (1776)

The cooperative nature of the entrepreneurial process is central to the lessons learned from this study. We recognize the importance of individuals, but note that individuals who join forces to work for a common purpose greatly enhance their impact. As issues grow more complex, constituencies more diverse, and change more discontinuous and radical, we expect groups to supplant individuals as the primary unit of analysis. What follows is a series of lessons distilled from our glimpse into the operations of the entrepreneurial team. For us, they signal the close of the age of the heroic entrepreneur and the beginning of the age of collective entrepreneurship.

Characteristics of an Effective Entrepreneurial Team

An effective team can be defined as "a small number of people with complementary skills who are committed to a common purpose, performance goals, and approach for which they hold themselves mutually accountable" (Katzenbach and Smith, 1994, p. 45). To flesh out the definition, think in terms of between two and twenty-five people with a good mix of skills: technical or functional expertise, problem-solving and decision-making skills, and interpersonal skills including such things as risk taking, helpful criticism, and active listening. A common purpose gives direction and commitment to team activities and performance goals help a team keep focused on getting results. A common approach clarifies how work is to get done, specifying such things as who will do particular jobs, how the group will make decisions, what roles the members will assume. Mutual accountability ensures that members are committed to the team's goals and trust one another to be responsible for the team's performance (pp. 43–64).

The entrepreneurial team featured in this study fits this profile well, as outlined in Chapter Four. The core group was small enough to convene and communicate easily and frequently. Although some members possessed more technical information about K-12 education than others, all knew the change process well, and all were expert at problem solving and decision making. Their highly developed interpersonal skills enabled them to manage their differences and learn from one another. All shared and vigorously supported the common purpose of redesigning education. Their goals were specific and well articulated—choice in the public schools to be followed by statewide testing of student performance. Members established a clear working approach that enabled them to develop strategies for action, share work, assign tasks, and capitalize on all members' skills. Rather than maintain a strict hierarchy, the team's structure was kept organic and fluid (Burns and Stalker, 1961). The political environment demanded quick and adaptive responses, so this flexibility was essential to their success. Roles of leaders and group members were blurred without apparent ill effects, and influence was based on expertise rather than position or authority. In addition, all felt a sense of accountability to the team and its purpose. To diminish the team would have been to diminish them as individuals. They were, by all these measures, an excellent example of a high-performance team. (See Katzenbach and Smith, 1994, for an extended discussion of high-performance teams and their profiles.)

Team membership was intentionally diverse, drawing in people who at first glance would not be expected to work well together: one grassroots activist and two top business executives, for example. However, many reports link the quality of team performance with the diversity of team membership. Diversity turns out to help avoid the pitfalls of *groupthink*—the tendency of people to avoid conflict and rush to consensus—and to promote creativity by allowing a team to draw on the differing backgrounds, problem-solving approaches, skills, and styles of its members. (See Bird, 1989; Janis, 1989; King and Anderson, 1990; and Kanter, 1977, for discussions of group diversity.)

We believe that this diversity is particularly important in public settings, because policy is made and implemented in a diverse rather than a homogeneous world. Look-alikes can develop an "us versus them" mentality and drive off potential supporters. If a team is unable to gather a diverse group of people who share the same purpose, it seems likely that it will also be unable to attract a diverse coalition of external supporters. And a diverse coalition of external supporters is very useful. Not only will it add to entrepreneurs' functional knowledge and expertise, other idea generators attracted to the group can provide a sounding board to test the entrepreneurs' ideas as well as contributing ideas of their own. Policy champions in positions of power can provide bases of support as well as opening doors to important contacts and resources. Midlevel bureaucrats can share knowledge about the system and how it works. Administrators, with the skills of implementation and evaluation, can help overcome resistance by anticipating it in advance. All have valuable contributions to make, as we saw in this study.

Time is also an important factor for high-performing teams. "Creating change requires stability" (Kanter, 1988, p. 195), especially the stability that comes from continuity of personnel (Katz, 1982). It takes time to learn to work as a team, as it takes time to push an idea over the threshold of public awareness. Before an entrepreneurial team can manage the attention of others who must be convinced of the innovative idea's merit (Schön, 1971; Van de Ven, 1986), the team must first learn to manage its own attention and stay focused on its goals.

Decision making and deliberation can be fluid and informal as long as team members and their extended network share an innovative idea or purpose. Ideas rally people and can substitute for more formal means of control. If an idea sparks a common vision of what could be, there is little need to adopt a formal structure of authority to constrain behavior. On the other hand, a team chosen for diversity is likely to experience conflict over means and methods, and perhaps even over ideas. A team's success depends on its ability to become a *learning system* (Senge, 1990)—a group able to monitor its environment, gather information to evaluate its performance, make changes in line with feedback, and manage the conflict this process engenders. This is certainly a challenging prospect for a team that has no formal mechanism to restrict individual behavior, and no way to appeal to higher authority to resolve differences. What holds an informal team together is members' trust and respect for each other, their ability to work through differences, and their belief that they are a more potent force as a team than as individuals.

Virtual Organization

Unlike many innovative teams in the private sector (Bushe and Shani, 1991; Kanter, 1988; Kidder, 1981; Stewart, 1989; West and Farr, 1990; Katzenbach and Smith, 1994), no one organization or individual had direct authority over the entrepreneurs' ideas, strategies, or day-to-day activities. While the team relied on resources from supporting organizations, such contributions did not support the overall entrepreneurial venture. Instead, they were for specific tasks of interest to the granting organization, such as writing a book, funding a study, or experimenting with a new program. It was the team's collective mission and vision that molded the many activities into an integrated and coherent whole, not any centralized authority or outside group.

Thus, this team was not concerned with protecting itself from interference and control. It had little need for the boundary management and gatekeeping roles so characteristic of private sector innovation teams (Gladstein and Caldwell, 1985). Without the need to establish physical separation in a "skunkworks" (Lockheed's term for innovative project teams) or a "reservation" (Galbraith, 1982) or to protect itself by limiting outside interference, the team constantly sought to exchange information and resources with the community of organizations around it.

This independence freed the team to create its own virtual organization. Although not (as far as we know) formalized on paper, the team developed an ad hoc arrangement that had the characteristics of a formal organization: broadly defined purpose and goals (redesigned education via public school choice); specialization (some members developed innovative ideas, others mapped long-range strategies, while others provided leadership for legislative battles); funding sources (money from foundations and interest groups); coordination and control of tasks (organizing member and nonmember activities); and mentoring (guiding newer members and keeping their actions within the parameters of the team's normative structure). Drawing together a constellation of like-minded individuals and groups, these entrepreneurs put together a virtual organization independent from any other agency to support their venture.

The mentoring process was a particularly interesting feature of the virtual organization. Members consciously thought about how to orient and socialize new people. For example, one seasoned entrepreneur sent a new member to talk with Dr. Paul Ellwood, nationally recognized as the policy entrepreneur behind health maintenance organization legislation. The intent of the meeting was to provide tutoring in change agentry and help broaden the newcomer's repertoire of skills and strategies, and it worked. The newcomer described the experience as "very helpful."

Other team members commented that their participation in the Citizens League had taught them "how you get things done around here." It helped them increase their content knowledge in different policy domains and broaden their understanding of large-scale systems change. Several mentioned the learning experience involved in developing the Metropolitan Council, a Twin Cities area regional governance body—another protracted battle (1959–1968) resulting in widely heralded, innovative legislation. Summing up his mentoring and training experiences, one policy entrepreneur said, "We are what we are because we worked for the Citizens League."

The contours of this ad hoc, virtual organization were barely visible prior to 1985. Few knew of it, though actions of individual entrepreneurs were certainly visible to those in the education policy community. Normally, a shadow structure of this type would open up questions of accountability, but in this case there was a great deal of oversight in one form or another. The team worked openly with government officials and legislators. In addition, after its debut in 1985, school choice drew constant media attention that kept its merits and limitations in the public eye. Opposition groups also scrutinized and debated bills that carried the entrepreneurs' ideas through the legislative process. Thus, while the team lacked direct *organizational oversight*, it did work in an *authorizing environment*—a community of organizations that endorsed or opposed team activities, an informed public opinion, and a group of public officials who debated enabling legislation and programs to implement the innovative ideas.

The team's virtual organization has its counterparts inside business and government. Described as collateral organization (Zand, 1974, 1981), parallel organization (Stein and Kanter, 1980), dualistic structures (Goldstein, 1985), shadow structures (Schein and Greiner, 1977), and parallel learning structures (Bushe and Shani, 1991), these entities are created to operate beside a formal structure. Their purpose is to facilitate change and increase a system's learning capacity (Bushe and Shani, 1991, p. 9). Although not completely comparable, since employees and officials belong both to their formal structure and to its parallel learning system, there is still a great deal of similarity with the policy entrepreneurs' team. The policy entrepreneurs established a learning system that worked beside the formal apparatus of government to facilitate innovation and change. Although most of the team members were not participants in government, and did not work for the benefit of any one organization, their intent was to increase the policy system's capacity for learning and innovation in the ultimate hope of implementing radical change.

Self-Organizing System

The entrepreneurial team also exhibited the basic features of what Morgan (1986) calls a *self-organizing system*. According to Morgan, such systems have a "capacity to be flexible, resilient, and inventive" (p. 78). They are based on four principles of design: redundant functions, requisite variety, minimal critical specification, and learning to learn.

The principle of *redundant functions* holds that "capacities relevant for the functioning of the whole are built into the parts" (Morgan, 1986, p. 99). The principle of *requisite variety* holds that "all elements of an organization should embody critical dimensions of the environment with which they have to deal, so that they can self-organize to cope with the demand they are likely to face" (p. 100). The principle of *minimal critical specification* directs managers and designers to "specify no more than is absolutely necessary for a particular activity to occur" since a system should "find its own form" (p. 101). And the principle of *learning to learn*, or *double-loop learning*, holds that systems can "sense, monitor, and scan significant aspects of their environment," "relate this information to the operating norms," "detect significant deviations from these norms," and "initiate corrective action when discrepancies are detected" including changing operating norms when necessary (pp. 86–87).

The team modified its strategy and tactics to follow swings in the political mood, making adjustments in response to its successes as well as its setbacks. We believe this activity demonstrated a self-organizing capacity and the ability to apply principles learned in private sector innovation projects. (Smaller project teams in business are preferable because they eliminate bureaucracy, allow faster and unfettered communication, rapid turnaround time, and instill group identity and commitment; Quinn, 1985.) And like their private sector counterparts, the small entrepreneurial team was able to operate without the constraints of formal plans, board approval, and committee oversight. In fashioning a loose, ad hoc structure, sharing leadership, rotating task assignments, setting few standard operating procedures, and forging a culture based on a shared purpose and vision, the team minimized its design requirements and responded to problems as they surfaced.

Although each member preferred certain activities, all were both willing and able to substitute for one another as needed to lobby, give a speech, write, strategize, attend a meeting, or network with other groups. This redundancy of function enabled the team to respond to almost any contingency, especially when facing competing claims on members' time.

The team's network ties broadened its connection and base of support within the larger community. Coupled with members' wide-ranging policy knowledge, expertise and skills, and collective experiences in government, nonprofits, and private enterprises, the team had the requisite variety to match the complex environment of educational policy making. And finally, the team's ability to question educational givens and advocate radical alternatives demonstrated an ability to engage in double-loop learning, and even more significantly, to teach others the process as well. Decried as a radical idea, public school choice eventually became acceptable practice, endorsed by the governor, legislature, and public, and even by many educators who had originally rejected it, thanks in large measure to the team's efforts.

Locus of Extended Network

Moving beyond the team's internal operations, we must underscore an important implication about its larger network and its success in the innovation process. Although representing an energetic force for change, the team owed its survival to the resources and support it drew from the political, economic, and social infrastructure around it. The team did not operate in a vacuum. The linkages that bound the team to the larger community sustained the entrepreneurs' momentum throughout the innovation process. While resources were constrained by what the team could convince other organizations to provide, we found no evidence that the team curbed its activities or restricted its movement because it lacked sufficient resources to pursue its preferred course of action. True, more people would have helped share the burden at the legislature; more media coverage would have spread the word faster; more secure employment for all team members throughout the innovation process would have made life more comfortable. But the team benefited greatly from working in an environment that was relatively rich in resources.

The importance of a community resource base is clear in the literature on the diffusion of innovation. Researchers have found that some states and regions offer fields more conducive to change, experimentation, and innovation than others (Walker, 1969; Downs, 1976; Gray, 1973). They attribute these differences to size, wealth, industrialization, or development. In comparison to other states and regions, Minnesota typically ranks in the top quadrant in terms of the diffusion of innovations and among those rich in community resources. While these studies do not explain the mechanisms or processes responsible for the "strong statistical relationships between industrial output and innovation" (Walker, 1969, p. 887), we believe that innovation occurs in Minnesota because it

has the community resources and the capacity to support entrepreneurs and their endeavors.

A recent research study sponsored by the Ford Foundation and
the Aspen Institute supports this view. The report, *Pioneers of Progress: Policy Entrepreneurs and Community Development* (Bollier, 1991),
identified a "new breed of sophisticated, influential organizations"
that have become "catalysts for innovative economic development
agendas" (p. 5). Forging a link between state policy elites and grassroots groups, these nongovernmental organizations facilitate collaboration between the public and private sectors to "expedite the
process of experimentation and inquiry" (p. 17). According to the
study, "They can speed the state along the 'learning curve' of new
developmental approaches. . . . They can risk experimentation and
failure in a way that is difficult for state governments to do" (p. 17).
The Citizens League of Minneapolis features prominently as one
of the "pioneers of progress" and the Minnesota Business Partnership also receives special mention.

The Citizens League is a nonpartisan group that provides
research on current issues confronting state policy makers. In its
forty-year history, it has sponsored studies on such issues as early
childhood education, public school choice, and taxation of nonprofit organizations. Avoiding any ideological or political position,
it has maintained an open-minded approach to issues on a case-by-
case basis and has earned credibility among the public at large. As
a citizens organization, its goal is to be fair-minded and pursue the
common good. It accepts corporate contributions for projects as
long as there is no conflict of interest involved, but it seeks an
extended membership base to support its annual budget of
$560,000 (1989). "Apart from the Chamber of Commerce and the
Minnesota Business Partnership, the Citizens League is one of the
few non-governmental bodies in the state equipped to make
sophisticated analysis of issues" (Bollier, 1991, p. 53).

The Minnesota Business Partnership is also an important community resource (Ouchi, 1984). Indeed, we share the assessment
that it is one of the reasons why Minneapolis works. Founded in
1977, the Partnership attracts the top officers of companies such
as General Mills, Dayton-Hudson, Northwest Airlines, 3M, Control
Data, Honeywell, Pillsbury, Burlington Northern, and Land
O'Lakes. It was patterned on the Business Roundtable, an associa-

tion of executives from the 160 biggest companies in the United States. Its goal is to involve Minnesota corporate chief executives and their senior managers in public matters that affect not only their own business interests, but also the interests of Minnesota and its citizens, rather than to lobby on specific issues. To this end, it funds studies and promotes policies that enable the state to make the changes necessary to support a healthy economic and social environment.

In our view, the Minnesota Business Partnership, the Citizens League, and Public School Incentives (the design shop described in Chapter Three) provided a rich resource base for the entrepreneurs. Depending on the specific task or need and the stage of the innovation process, the team could count on these "incubators of entrepreneurship" (Bird, 1989, p. 157) to enhance its internal capacity. As pioneers of progress, these organizations provided *venture capital*—both direct and indirect support—to the team throughout the innovation process, making the whole time-consuming and labor-intensive effort feasible.

The link between the team and its resource community has important implications for change agents wishing to pursue innovation by entrepreneurial design in other settings. Skill in self-design and self-learning is necessary but not sufficient for a successful team; we believe any team needs support from the community to survive battles with traditional and entrenched interests. It is our contention that policy innovation flourishes to the extent that there is an *ecology of organizations* willing to provide seed money to support issue analysis and experimentation with new policy solutions. Without this underlying ecology, we believe it will be difficult to sustain policy entrepreneurship over the long haul, especially in pursuit of radical change. The entrepreneurial team benefited from a variety of public and private organizations willing to support social experimentation, a network of leaders in close proximity to one another, and a group of people with a durable habit of interaction on issues of major importance. "Launching D-day out of a phone booth" may have worked in this case because the phone booth was in downtown Minneapolis and there was plenty of organizational support at the other end of the line. It is not clear who answers the phone when entrepreneurs call in other, less resource-rich communities.

Resources are critically important to innovation (Kanter, 1983; King, 1990; Angle and Van de Ven, 1989). The broader the rami- fications and greater the uncertainty of an innovative idea, the larger the coalition of supporters it will need (Kanter, 1988), and since radical change usually entails a great deal of uncertainty, entrepreneurs need to think in terms of very large coalitions. Building such coalitions requires extensive resources.

There is another reason to be concerned about community capacity. By definition, idea generators and entrepreneurs initiate the innovation process. Their creativity sparks system renewal and learning. Yet how can creative people work to mold innovative ideas into something viable if routine responsibilities demand their full attention or if they must worry about supporting themselves and their families?

As we saw in Chapter Five, five of the six entrepreneurs had fairly stable employment, but the sixth relied on consulting assign- ments, grants, and research projects. Although safe havens such as the Hubert H. Humphrey Institute, the Citizens League, and other nonprofits provided indirect support by giving the entrepreneurs employment and some financial stability, protection for indepen- dent policy thinkers and analysts is not a luxury that all communi- ties can afford. This issue is becoming even more acute during a period of retrenchment, when universities and institutes face declining budgets. In the press for fiscal accountability, will there be any slack left to support the entrepreneurial ventures of the future? What or who will sustain the policy entrepreneur if com- munity resources dry up? Although policy entrepreneurs are dri- ven by deep-seated values and strong motivations, sole reliance on their enterprising spirits would neglect important contributions that the community structure and its resources can and should make. Indeed, an important question to ask is whether a commu- nity has sufficient resources to support the policy entrepreneur and her team.

State communities like Minnesota do have unique properties. In the tradition of "do something" government that has paid off, Minnesota has been called a model of success (Peirce and Hag- strom, 1984). "Search America from sea to sea . . . and you will not find a state that has offered as close a model to the ideal of the suc- cessful society as Minnesota" (p. 539). Success is attributed to several factors. Minnesotans "appear to control their own destiny" thanks in large part to their open political structure, which is "issue-oriented" and "responsive." Questioning "how things are done—up to a very high level—is not only tolerated but encouraged" (p. 539).

Citizen participation has become institutionalized through organizations whose *raison d'etre* is to sponsor such inquiry. A partial list includes the Citizens League, the Hubert H. Humphrey Institute, the Minnesota Center on Corporate Responsibility, Spring Hill, Interstudy, the Metropolitan Council, the Downtown Council, and numerous foundations—the McKnight Foundation, the Northwest Area Foundation, the General Mills Foundation, the Dayton Hudson Foundation, the Bush Foundation, the First Bank System Foundation, the Bremer Foundation, the Pillsbury/Grand Metropolitan Foundation, and the Minneapolis Foundation.

This web of socially responsive organizations establishes processes and mechanisms that enable people to interact. For example, according to one policy entrepreneur, "There is a climate unique to the Twin Cities, a habit of interaction between public and private sectors that makes it possible to recognize opportunities and seize them. It is this climate that ultimately explains the frequency, variety, and success of public-private partnerships." The habit of interaction also depends on an overriding premise of *constrained self-interest* (Ouchi, 1984), which creates conditions wherein members of organizations consider the greater good for the whole community as well as their own narrow self-interests. Communities need entities that care about the commonweal.

One way to determine if your community has the capacity to sponsor and sustain entrepreneurial activity is to arrange an audit of all community organizations likely to engage in policy advocacy and development. Resources for each can range from a willingness to fund demonstration projects, contribute office space, print newsletters and literature, and distribute and disseminate information, to the offer of safe havens to those who wish to work on their own entrepreneurial projects. A stakeholder audit can be modified for the purpose (Roberts and King, 1989b). Of course, it helps if these organizations have a venue for deliberations with one another and have developed a norm of supporting inquiry and problem solving similar to the one that exists in Minnesota.

For those whose assessment indicates a paucity of organizational support for entrepreneurial activity, there are other solutions. One alternative is to begin building community capacity yourself along with other like-minded people. While this is not a short-run solution, it may be the best alternative in communities with a limited resource base. One place to start would be by establishing a Citizens League, modeled on the institution behind many Minnesota innovations (Ouchi, 1984; Peirce and Hagstrom, 1984; Wilhelm, 1984; Bollier, 1991). This advice has been anticipated in some areas—groups based on the Citizens League are already active in St. Louis and Kansas City (Bollier, 1991). The Ford Foundation and the Aspen Institute credit the Citizens League and similar organizations with articulating a new vision of community and discovering new ways to stimulate community renewal. "They are an important force for regenerating the often-frayed fabric of community and civic culture. Pioneers help ascertain community sentiment, formulate new policy directions, and build new consensus for change" (Bollier, 1991, p. 10). They have become "key players in the reinvention of state development policy. . . . and architects of far-sighted state economic development agendas that help people better compete in the changing world economy" (Bollier, 1991, p. 11).

Another example of capacity building is the nonprofit Public School Incentives, developed by the policy entrepreneurs. Even in their relatively rich resource environment, the team found no place to test high-potential ideas. They had to build their own design shop and support it with grants from foundations. Nothing prevents other policy entrepreneurs from adopting this strategy and attracting money from state or even national foundations.

Alternatively, you may wish to consider developing a formal approach to innovation and entrepreneurship by establishing an Office of Innovation in your government. Such an office operates as a conduit for ideas and employs facilitators to link the principals in the innovation process. These facilitators ensure that ideas circulate freely from idea generators to gatekeepers, champions, and sponsors, all of whom are necessary for innovation. Companies such as Eastman Kodak and Union Carbide have had success with this approach (Rosenfeld and Servo, 1990). While such an undertaking might be difficult to sustain given the constraints of public bureaus (Wilson, 1989; Roberts, 1993b), our current reinvention and reengineering context might provide some measure of support (Osborne and Gaebler, 1992).

Another option is to establish deliberative bodies such as the Governor's Discussion Group to assist public officials in formulating public policy. Stakeholder collaboration, separated from the partisan politics of the legislative process, may enable people to think more creatively and engage in real dialogue about important issues. Such undertakings, however, require very careful consideration of group process—the wide diversity of opinion among participants means that they need expert facilitation and leadership. Questions about membership, decision making, and conflict management have to be addressed before such groups are convened. Success (defined as an outcome that all can live with) is never guaranteed, but experiments in dialogues of this type are being recommended as alternatives to deadlock and adversarial legalism (Roberts, 1993a; Roberts and Bradley, 1991; Gray, 1989).

Developing greater proficiency as a change agent also can be considered a form of capacity building. Entrepreneurs are not made overnight. They need time and practice to hone their skills. Starting out with small, limited projects enables a person to develop experience and gain a reputation for getting innovative things done. Success can build on itself and help attract a network of supporters for the future. Needless to say, working with another, more experienced entrepreneur willing to share experiences can expedite the learning process.

Team Advantage in Radical Change

The discussion of the entrepreneurial process in Chapters Three and Four showed the range of the policy entrepreneurs' behavior, from the intellectual pursuits of problem framing and problem definition to the administrative concerns of program evaluation. Working outside the formal system, they engaged in a wide variety of activities to push their ideas into practice. They could not rely on positions of power in government to press for funding or to guarantee media coverage for their ideas. Instead, they had to search out funding sources and create their own demonstration projects, and to learn how to attract and hold media attention. They were outside the work-related networks among people with jobs or offices in the educational system, and had to forge their own contacts both in and out of government. This was particularly important because they could not count on invitations to official meetings where key policy discussions took place, and therefore needed to cultivate bureaucratic insiders to keep them abreast of the latest developments.

We believe the extent of these activities is due to the radical change the policy entrepreneurs espoused. One of them summed up the problem by quoting Jean Monnet, architect and master builder of the European Economic Community: "Resistance is proportional to the scale of the change being attempted."

Research indicates that people tend to be relatively willing to try innovations when they see them as offering a clear advantage over the status quo, and as having characteristics best described as compatibility, trialability, observability, and simplicity (Rogers and Kim, 1985, p. 88). Although these are not the only qualities that affect adoption, they emerge as the most important in explaining adoption rates (p. 89). School choice started out at a disadvantage in all these areas. When the idea was first introduced, most educators perceived it as logistically impractical, disruptive to school routines, more complex than the practices it was to supersede, and certainly not based on sound pedagogy. It seemed to be incompatible with their values, past experience, and needs. There were no experimental results to assess the potential impact, and most educators strongly resisted the whole idea. From their perspective, there was no crisis to warrant such dramatic and discontinuous change.

Responding to the wide resistance to public school choice, the entrepreneurs were compelled to engage in a variety of creative, strategic, and administrative activities to maintain momentum for their idea through the policy innovation process. Given the scope of these activities and the time they required, it is unlikely that any one individual could find the resources or energy to do everything. Under such circumstances, it is reasonable to conclude that radical change will require team effort to be successful. Thus we speculate that the more radical the idea, the greater the resistance, and the greater the resistance, the more extensive the innovators' activity structure has to be to overcome that resistance. The more extensive the activity structure, the more likely it is that policy entrepreneurs will benefit by joining forces with others.

Collective Versus Individual Entrepreneurship

The policy entrepreneurs could not have accomplished what they did without significant help from government officials. In this case, the governor and legislators, the commissioner, and the bureaucratic insiders all made critical contributions to the innovation process. In fact, we postulate that policy innovation will be successful to the extent it brings together people involved in the various parts of the policy process: *policy intellectuals* who launch the process as idea generators and problem framers, *policy champions* who lead the political debates during enactment, *policy administrators* who nurture and protect the innovation during implementation, and *policy evaluators* who monitor the innovation during the critical implementation period. The close contact among the various individuals who performed these wide-ranging activities in our study suggests that coordination and integration of these efforts promotes an idea's acceptance over time. Indeed, we believe the more these individuals work in tandem, the greater the potential for successful implementation.

The importance of this collectivity underscores a point Polsby (1984) makes about the *symbiotic* relationship between entrepreneurs and politicians. Politicians need to be identified with issues and programs and often have little time to frame problems or generate solutions, and entrepreneurs need allies to move their ideas forward to enactment, so the two can join forces in a mutually beneficial relationship. The politicians get the public credit they "need to survive in an election-dependent world" (p. 172) and policy entrepreneurs get the help they need to enact their ideas into practice. Extending this analysis, we believe the symbiotic relationship applies to others. Policy entrepreneurs also need sympathetic administrators to implement and monitor their ideas just as administrators need help in operationalizing legislation important to their careers. By joining forces, they derive mutual benefits.

Building on Polsby's insight, we came to understand why it is difficult for one person, especially one inside the government, to take on all the activities of entrepreneurship. Originally, we expected the commissioner to be an executive entrepreneur, because she was appointed as the governor's change agent in the Department of Education. Given her mandate for change, we were puzzled when she struck an impasse with the governor's executive committee, and others became the vanguard for change. However, we eventually realized that the commissioner had a very complex stakeholder map (Roberts and King, 1989b), spanning multiple groups at the local, state, and national levels. She had to administer a large state agency, prepare and defend the state's biggest single budget item, and at the same time tend to the needs of her educational constituents in 435 state districts. The competition for her time and attention was enormous, exacting eighteen-hour days in her first years in office (Roberts and King, 1989b). The demands of redesigning education while administering the department, which by most accounts was very traditional and conservative, placed her in the difficult and challenging role of defending an institution and its constituents while trying to change them. The commissioner worked these competing priorities out over time by becoming more and more concerned with administrative issues. For example, in preparation for the legislative session, she formed a task force to consider how the governor's proposal could be implemented in the schools. Her concern focused on the question of how to implement the innovative ideas rather than how to initiate or enact them.

What we learn from the examples of the governor and the commissioner is that the constraints of elected and appointed office make it difficult for an incumbent to be a single-minded change agent. Other obligations get in the way of inventing and developing radical policy ideas. To initiate second-order change, one generally needs to be relatively free of organizational constraints and able to think creatively, independent of organizational maintenance activities. The marginality of the policy entrepreneurs—that is, their position outside government—worked to their advantage in this regard, allowing them to keep their ideas alive. As one observer said, "It is too easy for ideas to die on the inside."

Although they did not enjoy a symbiotic relationship with the policy entrepreneurs, we would be remiss if we did not underscore the contributions bureaucratic insiders made toward the collective effort in the innovation process. The Department of Education staff member whose comments about access to the governor's policy team helped get the innovation process moving in late 1984 gave us some useful observations. He said that idea people often talk to the wrong officials, partly because decision points change over time, so he recommended the use of insiders to pinpoint where the key decision points are. Insiders also have institutional memory, he says. They keep a score card of those who have similar interests and concerns—which can be very useful, as it was when this insider pointed out that Representative Levi had once sponsored similar school legislation and would be insulted if the governor's staff failed to talk to her.

Unfortunately for the policy entrepreneur, this information source was cut off when the official moved from the Department of Education to Perpich's staff. As the governor's advisor, the insider could only say "trust us" and hope that would be enough. Additionally, since the governor's strategy now involved very quiet background negotiations, there was little information to share. But these changes left the policy entrepreneurs feeling out of the loop. No longer kept abreast of the strategy and the governor's current thinking, and lacking trust in the governor's leadership, they embarked on their own independent action. Their confrontation in the press with the governor, commissioner, and legislators shows what happens when important information sources and ties with strategically placed insiders are changed or eliminated. Without this insider's knowledge, it is difficult to imagine how the collective efforts would have begun in the first place.

Entrepreneurship Without Entrepreneurs

Building on this discussion of collective entrepreneurship, our final point is perhaps the most important of all. *We believe it is entirely possible to have public entrepreneurship without public entrepreneurs, so long as there is a collectivity to support the innovative venture.* Let us explain how this can happen. Recall that public entrepreneurs initiate and develop innovative ideas, translate them into proposals, bills, and laws, and oversee their implementation. By definition, they are public entrepreneurs because they see their ideas through the whole innovation process, from creation through implementation.

But instead of individual entrepreneurs, suppose that *policy intellectuals* initiate an idea. They are joined in a dialogue with *policy advocates* who decide to push the idea forward. The policy advocates make the idea more explicit and tangible by drafting a proposal, and work the proposal into a bill without direct assistance from the originators of the idea. The advocates ultimately win the endorsement and support of *policy champions,* who help write the bill and support its enactment into law. Also, in anticipation of the problems and challenges of implementation, the advocates or champions build additional support by joining forces with *policy administrators* sympathetic to the new idea. Policy administrators then carry the idea through the testing and experimentation and oversee its eventual implementation into practice.

In this scenario, the collective talents, abilities, and resources of policy intellectuals, advocates, champions, and administrators create entrepreneurship in the policy system—a new idea has been designed and implemented into public practice. No individual entrepreneur as defined here is visible, but other actors in the innovation drama fulfilled the functions necessary for innovation to occur. Thus, we can say that entrepreneurship is built into this system by social actors who are engaged in different functions of the innovation process.

One of the difficulties in the literature and research has been the inability to separate innovative functions from the individual entrepreneur. If we are going to understand public entrepreneurship, it is important to recognize its collective possibilities. There can be entrepreneurship without individual entrepreneurs to the extent that policy intellectuals, advocates, champions, and administrators integrate their efforts. Although each may specialize in one or two aspects of the innovation process, their joint action can produce an innovation over time.

We do not yet know to what extent innovations are driven by individual entrepreneurs or emerge from the collective efforts of large numbers of people. Given the complexity of innovation in government, we suspect that collective entrepreneurship is a more common phenomenon than individual entrepreneurship. This will be an important area for future research.

Summary: Lessons Learned

Public entrepreneurship can be an individual or group phenomenon. As policy issues become more complex, constituencies more diverse, and change more discontinuous, we believe that team entrepreneurship will replace individual entrepreneurship.

The more radical the innovative idea, the greater the probable resistance (especially if no consensus on a crisis exists). The greater the resistance, the more comprehensive the activity structure of policy entrepreneurs needs to be to overcome the resistance. The more comprehensive the activity structure, the more likely policy entrepreneurs will find benefit in working with others to effect radical change.

For a community, an entrepreneurial team functions as a parallel learning structure outside government to facilitate innovation and change in a policy domain. Within the team, members operate as a self-organizing system.

Policy entrepreneurship prospers in the public sector when an ecology of community organizations lend it support. Organizations like the Citizens League, the Minnesota Business Partnership, and Public School Incentives are excellent examples of this support structure.

Team entrepreneurship can involve individual entrepreneurs, but need not do so. Public entrepreneurs who engage in the three active phases of the innovation process can work together as a group. Alternatively, a collection of specialists, representing different functional areas of the policy process (policy intellectuals, policy advocates, policy champions, policy administrators, policy evaluators) can combine their efforts and work together to produce an innovation. In the first case, there are individual entrepreneurs who guide the whole process. In the second case, no individual entrepreneur exists; functional expertise is applied serially at different points in the policy system to push an idea through the hurdles of the innovation process.

Chapter Eight

Keys to Managing the Policy Innovation Process

We haven't got the money, so we've got to think.
—LORD RUTHERFORD

To recap the Introduction, the policy innovation process can be viewed as a set of phases: creation, design, implementation, and institutionalization, each with its own product. Proposals emerge from initiation, bills and laws from design, programs from implementation, and accepted practice from institutionalization. We see these phases as hurdles that policy actors must pass before an innovative idea can become an accepted part of its culture. Close observation of the phases allows us to derive four lessons from the process:

- Innovation can be radical and phased in by steps.
- Management of meaning and attention is vital.
- Political dynamics can promote acceptance of radical policy change by those who continue to disagree.
- It is important to differentiate between what policy entrepreneurs do and the policy innovation process itself.

Radicalism in Steps

The paradox of this radical innovation by entrepreneurial design is that it happened in stages over a four-year period. The policy entrepreneurs would have preferred immediate acceptance of the governor's entire package, but opposition strength, public skepticism, and lack of support among lawmakers forced them to take a step-by-step approach. Some members of the team believe that open enrollment could have been signed into law in 1985 had the momentum not been slowed by the commissioner's task force on implementation, but we disagree. Little was known about the effects of cross-district choice in 1985. There had been some metropolitan experiments in Minnesota and some out-of-state experiments in local districts, but the consequences of widespread open enrollment were unknown and unpredictable. Given Minnesota's reputation for educational excellence, and the lack of consensus about a crisis in education, it was unlikely that Minnesotans and their lawmakers would opt for radical change without some trial or experimentation to guide the way. There was just too much at stake.

To cope with the initial setback, redesign advocates crafted a successful strategy to expand choice to certain subgroups in the school population rather than renew efforts for an all-or-nothing battle. When results of the initial choice program for high school juniors and seniors proved to be positive in 1986, advocates built on the successful experiment and argued for extension of open enrollment to other segments—to all at-risk students and to all school districts on a voluntary basis in 1987, to large school districts in 1988, and eventually to smaller districts in 1990. Successful experiments with subgroups of the school population showed the skeptics that open enrollment had sufficient merit to risk expansion to other groups.

It was fortunate for the proponents of open enrollment that the idea lent itself to such segmentation and experimentation. We speculate that radical innovations without a similar advantage falter when they face all-or-nothing confrontations with entrenched interests and wary lawmakers. Dividing the innovation into components that logically built on one another made it easier and less threatening to deal with each part on its own. As Perpich is reported to have said, "If I can get one aspect of public school choice, then I can get the rest." The end result was a recombination of the parts to form the radical whole that was originally envisioned. Thus, radical innovation was successful by moving in smaller legislative steps.

Change agents will do well to note that as long as they maintain the integrity of an idea, they can reduce its scope and apply it to a subset of the system and still succeed. Although it is reasonable to be concerned that additional time will dissipate energy, divert attention, and slow momentum, the trade-off may be worthwhile. There is a difference between compromising on the basic premises of an innovative idea and compromising on its scope. In the absence of a clear crisis, the only alternatives may be complete rejection or limited experimentation. Change agents can be strategic about their choice of a radical idea as well as about its application. This advice is in line with cognitive theory, which warns that radical change risks overloading people's capacity for change, resulting in *cognitive inertia*—a tendency to keep the status quo and resist changes that counter the fundamental orientation of the society. A cognitive perspective on organization change recommends a middle-ground or moderate degree of change—sufficiently large to overcome cognitive inertia, but not so great that it is likely to be misunderstood and fail (Reger, Gustafson, Demarie, and Mullane, 1994).

The social-psychological literature also offers theories to explain the advantages of a step-by-step approach. A successful innovation, no matter how small, can offer vivid rather than pallid information to observers (Nisbett and Ross, 1980). *Vivid information* is "emotionally interesting, concrete and imagery provoking, and personally more meaningful to the individual" (Farr, 1990, p. 214). *Pallid information*—dry statistical reports or abstract descriptions—can not sell an innovative idea nearly as well as a concrete example that demonstrates how the innovation works. It is especially useful to have participants describe their own experiences and tell how the innovation helped them. Vivid information like this is likely to change observers' beliefs and judgments and to make them more receptive to similar changes. Moreover, the more concrete the descriptions, and the better tailored they are to the intended audience, the more likely they will have a positive effect (Rogers, Kuiper, and Kirker, 1977). Accounts of real-life experiences help observers perceive the need for change, identify personal payoffs from pursuing the innovation, and believe in their own ability to make similar changes (Farr, 1990, pp. 224–225).

Thus, we see the logic in providing tangible proof of benefits. The more radical the idea, the more distant it is from people's experience—and the harder entrepreneurs will have to work to forge a link between innovation and experience. People need time to get adjusted to radical ideas. Over time, exposure makes the radical seem less threatening and more achievable. With positive outcomes, it is easier to understand how the innovation can be an attractive alternative to the existing situation.

Along these lines, workshops and guided programs introducing the innovative idea also have merit because they can increase its salience. Through such contact, people can be helped to imagine how situations or outcomes are improved with successful implementation of the idea, and in the long run, to form positive judgments about the innovation (Farr, 1990, p. 215).

Our policy entrepreneurs gave a special twist to these principles by providing news stories that illustrated the danger of maintaining the status quo. The media, hungry to find ways to explain complex issues, were captivated by vivid descriptions of flaws in the current educational system. One policy entrepreneur recalled the case of a working mother as an excellent example. She wanted to place her five-year-old, who needed special education, in a kindergarten in the district where she worked. This would let the mother have lunch with the child, and a unique day-care provider could pick up the child after school and administer physiotherapy. Reporters—all working mothers themselves—kept the story alive for weeks, provoking calls from hundreds of outraged parents who wanted to know why the request to change districts was denied. The superintendent played the perfect villain, explaining that schools were not set up for the convenience of parents.

We also would recommend that entrepreneurs follow the advice of social psychologists who study minority group influence on majority attitudes. (See Farr, 1990, pp. 216–217, and West, 1990, pp. 327–328.) Minorities can change the perceptions, attitudes, and behavior of the majority population if they express their views in a confident, consistent, and persistent manner. The process, labeled *conversion,* has been used to explain how groups like the Greens and feminists change public opinion when they are in conflict with the majority and those in power (West, 1990).

Management of Attention and Meaning

A radical idea, by definition, is very different from existing practice. When we consider that radical ideas are apt to be perceived as less attractive than familiar solutions closer to the status quo, we can begin to appreciate how difficult the policy entrepreneur's task is, especially if the radical idea is a complex one and difficult to demonstrate on a trial basis. Somehow, the entrepreneur has to increase people's comfort level with the radical idea and make it fit with their experience.

Making it fit involves at least two efforts: *managing attention* and *managing meaning*. The first is to keep people focused on a policy area long enough for them to gain some familiarity with the major issues. The second is to define the problem so that the once-radical idea becomes preferred over competing solutions, originally perceived as less radical and thus more acceptable.

There are always hundreds of issues competing for public and lawmaker attention. With limited resources and time to devote to policy questions, people tend to focus on those of immediate concern. That is why a crisis is so useful—it gets attention. Of the many prompts to innovation, such as disruptive events, scarcity, court rulings, cross-pollination of ideas, and serendipity (Kanter, 1988; Kingdon, 1984; Rogers, 1983; Schön, 1971; Schroeder, Van de Ven, Scudder, and Polley, 1989; Walker, 1981), it is easiest to capture interest when crisis has prepared the way. Crises can "trigger the action thresholds of individuals to appreciate and pay attention to new ideas, needs, and opportunities" (Van de Ven, 1986, p. 594). Without a crisis, advocates of radical ideas have to work much harder to overcome people's built-in reluctance to focus on nonroutine issues, and society's built-in reluctance to move beyond inertia, conformity, and conflict-minimizing strategies (Van de Ven, 1986).

Fortunately for the policy entrepreneurs, *A Nation at Risk* and the reports from the Citizens League and Minnesota Business Partnership helped focus attention on education. Debates on what to do about education became commonplace. Public dialogue opened a window of opportunity through which the team could push their previously untested innovative ideas onto center stage.

Yet attracting attention was only the beginning. Managing the interpretation of events was the real challenge. Although national and state reports warned of performance declines and many policy intellectuals viewed education as being in serious trouble, there was no consensus on what the problem was. Experts disagreed—especially in Minnesota, a state with a reputation for educational excellence. Some questioned whether standardized test scores were a valid measure of what students had or had not learned, arguing that if test scores were a poor indicator of learning, the declines might not be significant. Others differed about how long test scores had to drop, and to what level, before a serious problem existed. Still others believed it was the family that was in crisis, not education. Viewed in this light, public education was not the problem, it was an important part of the solution. The debate went on and on.

The difficulty of finding a consensus on the problem was only the beginning. Even if one came to see the educational system and its underlying principles as the problem, there was scant evidence to suggest educational redesign as the preferred solution. Although reports from prestigious groups like the Citizens League and the Minnesota Business Partnership did advocate educational choice and redesign, these reports did not prove that their policy solution was better than others. The reports provided reasoned arguments but not hard evidence in support of the solution they favored.

In all fairness, finding hard evidence for radical solutions is never easy. The incompatibility between radical ideas and current practice reduces the opportunity for testing and evaluation and increases the probability of opposition. Radical ideas lose out on all the factors that promote acceptance for nonradical ideas: the amount of learning needed to understand and use them is high rather than low; their relative advantage is generally obscure rather than easy to see; they are difficult rather than easy to apply and observe on a restricted basis; and they are perceived as inconsistent rather than consistent with users' values, experiences, and needs. As a result, their acceptance will depend on the entrepreneur's ability to interpret and manage the connection between the policy problem and its solution rather than on mountains of data attempting to prove a point. (See Rogers and Shoemaker, 1971, for a discussion of idea acceptability.)

This is where rationales justifying a radical solution come in. They provide a logic of appropriateness (March and Olsen, 1989) and can substitute for data in arguments over possible solutions. Four rationales—public service redesign, expanded opportunity, community perspective, and accountability—were employed quite effectively in this case. Market efficiency and accountability attracted the business community. Freedom, choice, and a belief in community appealed to conservatives. Expanding opportunities and promoting equity drew in liberals. These had been conflicting ideologies in other policy debates, but the policy entrepreneurs were able to weave them together to broaden their base of appeal and build credibility for their ideas.

These rationales also helped connect public school choice to larger political, social, and economic forces, and to further establish its credibility. Arguments for school redesign and choice were associated with the movement toward New Federalism, deregulation of certain sectors of the economy, and a return to the market as a regulator of services. Linking school choice with the public mood, prevailing political forces, and changes in administration, the rationales enhanced the idea's appeal while lessening the attractiveness of alternative solutions in the improvement mode. Eventually endorsed by President Bush, the President's Commission on Privatization (Linowes, 1988, pp. 85–99), the National Governors' Association (Lieberman, 1989, p. 234), and presidential candidate Clinton, public school choice succeeded in breaking up traditional alignments to forge a new consensus on the problems of education and their solutions. It reflected, said one observer, "the capacity of Americans to accommodate what first appears to be conflicting ideas."

Watching the policy entrepreneurs convince others to connect the problem with their preferred solution, we understand how the definition of social problems depends on the management of meaning, especially when data are unavailable, sketchy, or based on fleeting impressions. We conclude, as others have before us, that policy problems are socially constructed. They depend not so much on whether a problem and a solution really exist, but whether people believe they do. Multiple problem definitions and solutions are feasible. The question becomes identifying what is "most credible and politically acceptable at any particular time" (Cobb and Elder, 1983, p. 173). The challenge for policy intellectuals and entrepreneurs is to manage the meaning and shape the problem definition so that their interpretation becomes acceptable and appropriate in the existing context, and a clear link is established between the problem as they define it and the solution they recommend. As demonstrated in Chapter Three, the policy entrepreneurs were very effective in using various forums, media, and channels of communication to do just that. (For an expanded description of other "sense makers" and "sense givers," see Gioia and Chittipeddi, 1991.)

This brings us to a final point about the management of meaning. The term *radical* is threatening in itself. It radiates displeasure with the current way of doing things and casts doubt about those in charge. By implication, if people had been doing their jobs all along, drastic measures might not have been needed now. When we openly espouse radical innovations, we should not be surprised to encounter defensive reactions from those responsible for system maintenance. The initial response from traditional education groups and some lawmakers over choice in the public schools illustrates the point well. In 1985, they were angry, defensive, and ready to do battle to protect their interests.

Yet there are advantages to open pursuit of radical innovation. Radical ideas most often engender debate as well as resistance; debate attracts and keeps media attention; media attention focuses and directs public interest. Sustained over time, public interest can evolve into familiarity with the issues, and ultimately build support. We watched this process and charted it through public opinion surveys on school choice. When first queried in 1985, only 18 percent of Minnesotans supported open enrollment for all grade levels. By 1990, the figure was up to 51 percent (Corson, 1990). And by 1992, 76 percent of those surveyed favored public school choice (Hotakinen, 1992, p. 1B).

Announcing support for radical innovation also has the advantage of staking out new conceptual territory and making others respond. As we heard in our interviews on the Governor's Discussion Group, traditional educators were kept so busy on redesign issues that they had little time to develop initiatives of their own. They were forced into a reactive mode as redesign proponents took the initiative, framed the issues, and eventually convinced many educators that public school choice had merit. We were not surprised, then, to hear some of the original opponents of choice say in 1988 that open enrollment was really incremental change, and not the radical idea it was first thought to be. In fact, it was said to be "no big deal." The initial threat had become familiar with time, and experience made it acceptable practice—a conclusion the policy entrepreneurs did not attempt to dispel. Having won acceptance of open enrollment, they saw the advantage of promoting continuity between the past, the present, and what they hoped for the future.

Political Dynamics of Radical Policy Change

If change agents expect to advance radical ideas, they must think through ways to cope with the inevitable politics of resistance and build a power base strong enough to overcome it in each phase. For the policy entrepreneurs in our study, those calculations began very early on.

Policy Initiation

By the time the governor signed on to champion public school choice, the policy entrepreneurs were well entrenched. They had garnered intellectual and analytical support from very credible organizations and people, and secured financing to experiment with new ideas. An extensive network of bureaucratic insiders and external backers stood ready to provide information and assistance. They had prepared a complete package of ideas linking problems to solutions. Trial legislation had been introduced. Taken in concert, these activities established a solid power base before the beginning of the design phase.

We concur with Polsby (1984) that the first phase of the innovation process deserves much more attention. Long neglected in favor of enactment and implementation—due to the difficulties of tracking innovative ideas before they reach the more visible phases—the creative phase sets the tone and establishes the potential on which the later phases can draw. Without a solid power base on which to launch the design phase, such as the one the policy entrepreneurs built in Minnesota, we suspect that a radical idea's chances of survival will be very low.

But selecting which radical ideas to promote is challenging. From the policy entrepreneurs and from other evidence on innovation (Schroeder, Van de Ven, Scudder, and Polley, 1989), we learn that many ideas surface during the creative phase, not just one obviously good one. There tends to be a proliferation of ideas and modifications to the original ideas. The team we studied evaluated many options before choosing the idea of public school choice. They eventually bet on it because they saw it as a way to break the existing paradigm of education. If it succeeded, it would unlock doors for follow-on innovations and build the momentum for transformative change. We conclude that radical change requires people adept at systems thinking who can identify ideas at the key leverage points for change, that is, the ones that are most likely to shift the system to a new order. This is a very sophisticated level of social and political analysis—hence our emphasis on the unique attributes of individual entrepreneurs that made them capable of this type of thought.

Idea selection is also important to the policy process because it embodies core values. Some looked at public school choice and saw freedom, equity, accountability, expanding opportunity, and public service redesign. Others saw violation of administrative order and routine, growing chaos in the schools, and the end of public education. Since ideas gain influence on the basis of their resonance with life experiences, frustrations, dreams, and deep-seated values (Moore, 1988), we can expect the heart of radical change to be a political debate over values. One is forced to ask and answer the question: What are my values and how will this innovative idea move me closer to them? And how will I deal with ideas that embody values different from mine?

Design and Implementation

Radical ideas intensify political dynamics during design and implementation. Although we agree that political scientists are sometimes preoccupied with power and politics to the neglect of ideas in assessing what moves people to action (Reich, 1988; Kingdon, 1984), power and politics are at the heart of radical change. Compared to the relative calm of policy initiation, with politics obscured by detached theorizing and rational analysis, the design phase can be explosive. As we saw in the case of public school choice, the process was confrontational and noisy. The front-page battle with opponents of public school choice began with *Access to Excellence*—a warning blast to signal the new legislative agenda. The shock from that explosion did not subside until the governor took public school choice off the decision agenda. Even then, politics did not disappear. It went underground for others to carry until he got what he wanted. And politics continued unabated through the implementation process, as opponents fought (and continue to fight) a rearguard action in the schools. By moving the idea beyond the entrepreneurs' original terms and into a more formal legislative proposal, Perpich framed the political debate that would last through four legislative sessions, as the idea cycled and recycled through enactment, implementation, and evaluation.

Policy Champions

As policy champion, Perpich played a central role in the politics of the design and implementation phases. Without his advocacy, open enrollment would probably have continued to languish at the periphery of policy debate. His willingness to put controversial ideas on the legislative agenda and to take on powerful vested interests in their defense points to the importance of political courage in the innovation process. Policy champions do not play safe politics. They seem to delight in being provocative and stirring up interest in new and visionary ideas. Although public support for choice was initially so low that advisers warned against taking on the educators, Perpich relied on his own beliefs and instincts. He was willing to expend political capital to do what he thought was right. When asked why he supported educational choice, he drew in part on his personal belief that it was unfair to deprive poor children of the chance children from wealthy families had to choose their schools.

The policy champions in the legislature who joined Perpich seemed to be cut from the same cloth. One lobbyist described Senator Peterson as having "no buy-in for traditional ways of doing things, no commitment for the way things are done. As a high achiever himself, he would always ask, 'Is there a better way of doing this?'" Being indifferent to criticism also helps, according to Peterson, and so does "being willing to be perceived as crazy for a while." Both can provide tremendous influence, he points out, adding that the legislature "needs someone to stand up and say this doesn't make sense" and to recognize a new idea when it comes along. Legislative champions are particularly important in this regard, because it is very difficult to push ideas through the com-

plex committee structure to enactment without their active involvement and influence. Someone central to the legislative process has
to be willing to carry the torch and "be perceived as crazy," at least
for a little while.

Political Cost-Benefit Analysis

The case study also reveals another important political dynamic.
Radical change occurred, not because those in opposition modified their views or became convinced of its merit (although some
did alter their positions), but because some of the most vocal opponents realized they had more to lose than gain by their stand. It
was awkward and difficult for teachers to be viewed as more concerned about the educational system than about kids and learning.
Said a teachers' union lobbyist, "strenuous opposition would have
won us the title of 'opposition to education,' opposing reform,
unfriendly to change, so we muted our opposition. . . . It was dangerous to oppose the governor and dangerous to always be in the
opposition to choice. . . . It was not good for us to generate bad
feelings." And to underscore the risk of taking on the powerful
interests that advocated school choice, one lobbyist candidly
acknowledged the clout of the Minnesota Business Partnership by
saying, "We are not so dumb to think that we can beat up on the
fifty largest corporations in Minnesota. We don't need them upset.
They are good upstanding citizens in Minnesota; they have an 'in'
with editorial writers; and they pay taxes. We want them to feel that
they have accomplished something and open enrollment makes
them happy."

Living with an objectionable idea may be less of a problem
than alienating powerful interests whose support is important if
you hope to reach more important political goals in the future.
Thus, we can understand, as one legislator put it, why public school
choice passed in 1988. "No one opposed it."

New Forums

The Governor's Discussion Group, created to help hammer out
educational policy prior to its introduction to the legislature, was
an important element in the innovative process in 1987 and 1988.
Shrill confrontations in the legislature gave way to more reasoned
debate in the GDG, enabling politics to take a different form. We

draw from the participants' comments about the GDG to underscore the advantages of constituting a broad-based group of this
type to deal with the politics of radical policy innovation.

Participants viewed the GDG as having the potential for building better understanding and communication among the stakeholders and permitting the formation of new coalitions. New
channels of communication could offer the opportunity to begin
a dialogue about differences free from the normally divisive and
combative politics of the legislature. Maximizing debate prior to
the legislative session could help minimize conflict during the session, and at the same time, enhance participants' knowledge and
background on proposals prior to their formal introduction. Politicians also could benefit from having a safe place to try out and test
new ideas. This type of forum could provide a buffer for them to
assess the merits of serious reforms and to determine who else was
interested and whether agreements were possible. As one participant commented, "It is better to fight out the issues at the policy
development level than at the political level, for example, the legislature. It is the only experience where groups small and large
[have] the opportunity to be heard and their issues discussed
openly. Otherwise the policies are determined solely by the groups
that have the most political clout—and PAC money—in the legislative setting."

GDG participants believed that if consensus were established
on certain policy initiatives, enactment would be easier to achieve.
They saw direct evidence of this in the passage of the 1987 educational package. A majority of GDG participants believed that their
proposal was directly linked to the legislation. Participants also credited the GDG with having a positive impact on the legislative
process, and believed their initiatives were able to get legislative priority and support. Said one participant, "The agreed-upon planks
were very instrumental in greasing the skids for passage."

While some GDG participants saw disadvantages in the forum
(too much time; too much divergence of opinion causing problems in agenda setting; too little legislator involvement) they did
acknowledge its benefits. "While at times frustrating, it was also satisfying to see that experts in the field of education could come
from so many different polarized positions and reach a consensus
on [a] visionary plan for education," said one. Another described

it as "a wonderful idea. . . . It allowed people to get to know one another personally and learn about one another's positions in a nonthreatening environment. It shows how people of good will can change attitudes and behaviors."

We will return to the importance of creating community forums for discussion and debate on policy initiatives in the next chapter. At this point, suffice it to say that we concur with the participants' assessment of the GDG and regard it as an important element in the enactment of public school choice. It was especially important in validating the participation of outsiders who normally do not get to the table for discussions like these. Although the GDG did not invent the radical idea of choice, we believe it gave legislators the chance to espouse and endorse it. Others apparently agreed. Observers credited the meetings with helping to resolve differences that threatened the governor's ambitious agenda. One called it "the most important intervention into educational policy making in Minnesota."

Planning Versus Groping

Policy innovation has been characterized either as planning or as groping along (Golden, 1990; Sanger and Levin, 1992; Levin and Sanger, 1994). *Planning* implies a neat and orderly process: finding the right innovative idea through the systematic and rational analysis of policy alternatives, then carefully refining and implementing it with careful thought for problems that might arise along the way. By contrast, *groping along* implies a messy process: jumping from a general impression of a problem to a rough approximation of a solution without framing an idea as a policy statement. People try something, make mistakes and learn from them, and go on to refine their course of action on the basis of operational data.

There is a major difficulty in applying either of these labels to policy innovation. The dichotomy confounds the trajectory of the innovative idea over time with the activities of the entrepreneurs who support it. These are two very different dynamics. Ideas do not plan or grope along. Entrepreneurs do. Groping and planning may well describe the entrepreneurial process; they do not describe the innovation process. It is important to keep the two distinct.

The trajectory of the innovative idea can be orderly or disorderly, sequential or iterative, convergent or divergent, follow one well-developed idea through the entire process or track relatively vague and sketchy notions that proliferate and feed back on one another creating a map that looks like a fireworks display (Schroeder, Van de Ven, Scudder, and Polley, 1989). While some ideas can lead to dead ends, others can move all the way through the innovation process.

In the case of public school choice, the idea was very well formulated by the end of the policy initiation phase. Its trajectory was easily discernible as it was translated into more formal and specific statements—proposal, initiative, bill, law, program—markers that established the phases of the innovation process. While subsets of the idea recycled through the design and implementation phases over a four-year period, overall we would characterize the trajectory as reasonably orderly, and sequential within each legislative cycle. We observed minimal variation and modification to the original idea as it moved from initiation through implementation.

On the other hand, the major players' behavior did not coincide with the idea's trajectory through the phases of the innovation process. Their actions did not follow a sequential logic nor did they move on any predetermined path. For example, the commissioner, in charge of the implementation of educational policy, participated in the deliberations on *Access to Excellence* during the design phase. Even before the governor submitted his initiative to the legislature, she publicly raised questions on implementation issues, to the consternation of the policy entrepreneurs. Department of Education staff members, who would later oversee the implementation and evaluation of the law, testified on behalf of open enrollment legislation during the design phase. Legislators and administrators concerned with evaluation issues sought to secure dollars and expertise to assess the fledgling innovation even before the law was enacted.

In supporting the innovative idea, the key participants acted out of concern for their functional areas of expertise rather than moving in lockstep with the phases of the innovation process. They anticipated what would be required to translate the idea into action and behaved accordingly, independent of the innovation stage. We suggest, in fact, that the complementary activities of those who formulate public policy and those who implement and evaluate it, whenever they occur, are important for the successful completion of the innovation cycle. To the extent that idea generators, designers, implementers, and evaluators work together throughout all phases of the innovation process, they increase the probability that a radical idea will survive and become a full-blown innovation.

We will return to the issue of how to characterize entrepreneurial behavior in the next chapter. The important point here is to think of the innovation process not in terms of what people do (planning or groping along), but in terms of the idea's integrity and trajectory over time. To what extent is the idea well formed? Does it require further elaboration? How likely is it to have a smooth trajectory if it is launched in its present state? How much support does it have now and how much will it need to survive the innovation process? Can the idea be piloted or do we have to accept it without testing? Are we willing to risk multiple iterations of the process (initiation, design, implementation) to give shape to the idea or would this approach give the opposition too much time to compromise the idea's integrity and water it down? Is the time right for an introduction or would it be wiser to wait for a more propitious moment to push the idea onto the decision agenda? Should we delay the introduction to gain time to perfect our idea, or should we go forward and take our chances before the opposition has time to mount its counterattack? These are the questions of the policy innovation process—the care and development of innovative ideas and the timing of their introduction to the policy arena.

We believe the answers to these questions lie in the type of change inherent in the innovative idea. Radical change is not an evolutionary process. Tinkering around the edges and moving in slow increments does not produce a fundamental reordering of a system. Although we have shown in the case of public school choice that it was possible to move step-by-step over four years, that strategy was effective only because the principle of public school choice had been established as policy in the first place. Once an idea is initiated, it is important to move it through the policy process as quickly as possible.

A well-articulated idea helps maintain momentum; it avoids the need for honing and shaping during design and implementation. Once the design phase starts, delay helps the opposition, not the entrepreneur. Better to introduce a coherent, consistent, and logical idea that links solutions to problem definitions than one that is incomplete or logically flawed. Policy initiation is the time for testing and modifying radical ideas; by the later stages of the innovation process they should be ready for action.

Summary: Lessons Learned

It is advisable to press as quickly as possible for radical policy change. Movement through the legislative process can be engineered in steps to the extent that the radical idea, as a principle, has first been established in law. Its scope can be extended in later legislative cycles.

Policy entrepreneurs in the innovation process need to manage the attention and meaning surrounding the innovative idea. Policy problems are social constructions. The challenge is to manage the meaning and shape the problem definition so as to make the interpretation acceptable and appropriate in the existing context and then to establish a link between the problem as defined and the recommended solution.

Power and politics are at the heart of radical change. They intensify the dynamics of the change process. The expression of power and politics varies depending on the stage of the innovation. Creation of new forums, such as stakeholder groups, has the potential to change the face of politics and reduce the level of conflict if the process is well managed.

Innovation and entrepreneurship are complementary processes of radical policy change. The innovation process marks the trajectory of the idea (characterized as either orderly or disorderly, sequential or iterative, convergent or divergent). Public entrepreneurs develop the idea and build support for it; their activities characterize the entrepreneurial process.

Coordination among idea generators, designers, implementers, and evaluators increases the probability that a radical idea will survive to be a full-blown innovation. Rather than moving in lockstep with the phases of the innovation process, functional experts should work in concert, anticipate what is required to move the idea forward, and act accordingly.

It is better to test an innovative idea during the policy initiation phase than to spend time honing and shaping it during the design and implementation phases. Delay in the innovation process works to the benefit of the opposition, not the entrepreneur.

Chapter Nine

Remaining Lessons for Pursuing Radical Change

Chance favors only the prepared mind.
—LOUIS PASTEUR (1854)

A wise man turns chance into good fortune.
—THOMAS FULLER, *GNOMOLOGIA* (1732)

Throughout this book, we have offered numerous lessons to guide future change agents: explanations about the policy entrepreneurs' identity, summaries of their heuristics and comprehensive activities for radical policy change, advice on how to build an entrepreneurial team to support collective entrepreneurship, and suggestions on managing the movement of ideas through the innovation process. Yet we still have a number of questions to consider about policy entrepreneurship and radical change:

- Is it best to plan or grope along through the entrepreneurial process?
- What are the costs of radical change? Do the benefits outweigh the costs?
- What is the best vantage point to pursue radical change?
- Must strategies for radical change be confrontational and politically charged?
- How do we keep entrepreneurs accountable to the public?
- How do policy entrepreneurs sustain themselves through the radical change process?

We frame the remaining lessons learned as answers to these questions and offer them as a guide to others who may wish to embark on their own entrepreneurial ventures. Then we offer some advice from the policy entrepreneurs themselves, who take this opportunity to comment on the process and distill their experience for the reader.

Questions and Discussion

We believe potential entrepreneurs should consider these questions and the answers we propose very carefully as they map out their path to radical change.

- *Is it best to plan or grope along through the entrepreneurial process?*

As discussed earlier, *planning* is meant to convey a systematic process using rational-analytic techniques to sort through competing ideas and select one idea to champion. Planning also anticipates resistance and builds incentives into design and implementation, making acceptance more likely (Golden, 1990). In contrast, *groping along* is a disorderly process of exploration and experimentation, based on a general sense of a problem or a general mission to create change rather than a specific idea. The point is to try something, learn from that experience, and be ready to correct errors as the experimentation produces results (Behn, 1988; Golden, 1990).

We have a somewhat different view of planning and groping along from that often expressed in the literature. We consider both to be valuable strategies, with the choice of one or the other depending on the level of uncertainty experienced by participants in the change process.

Planning is appropriate for an innovator with a well-defined problem and a well-developed idea of a solution. Planning also makes sense when you have enough information to make rational-analytic comparisons among competing solutions. If you know the outcome you want to achieve and have a fair idea of what behavior to reinforce to achieve that outcome, you can plan your way through the process.

Short of this level of certainty, it is necessary to rely on various degrees of groping along. Specific ideas can be hard to find, leaving only a general direction to follow. This poses a high degree of uncertainty, and we end up groping along to define a problem.

And many specific ideas are hard to test, leaving us without data on whether they work or compare favorably to other alternatives. Having an idea reduces the level of uncertainty to some extent, but it is still necessary to grope along until there is more information on its application in practice. A trial run to gather some data can reduce the level of uncertainty—if the results are interpretable and they can help potential users understand the idea and how it might be applied. It can be tempting to try to convince people that data do exist (even if they don't) to support the idea against competing alternatives. If that political tactic works, it reduces the general level of uncertainty even more. And because an idea that has been used elsewhere with demonstrable results reduces the level of uncertainty even further, it is easier to introduce a borrowed or adapted idea than an original one. At each step of the problem-solving path, reducing the level of uncertainty for the innovator and for potential users reduces the need to grope along.

Think of groping along as useful when the situation has unclear boundaries or lacks gates to constrain action. Without constraints, we have a wide set of options to consider. We are free to aim in any direction and experiment. But to the extent we believe there is an answer to some problem, and we have definite ideas on what the new behavior around the solution should be, and how to reinforce it, we then begin to set up constraints for ourselves and others. The more certainty we have, or think we have, the more constraints we impose. At some point, when the parameters of action are narrow enough, we move into the planning mode.

So it was with public school choice in Minnesota. The policy entrepreneurs groped along to formulate their view of the problem and its solution. This reduced their own uncertainty, but they still had to deal with the uncertainty others experienced. Meanwhile, operating under a different set of constraints, traditional educators were planning within well-established frameworks that did not include public school choice. To open up educators' parameters of action, the policy entrepreneurs began to craft grand strategies of change. Their goal was to establish a new set of parameters for educators and they resorted to more directive, strategic, and political action to make it happen.

But the entrepreneurs had chosen a unique and novel idea, with little data behind it. They could not use rational-analytic techniques because there were no statewide performance results to evaluate. The best the team could do was to provide rationales to explain why the idea was a good one, and to supplement logic with other political strategies that came to hand. When powerful groups and allies began to support the idea, that reduced public uncertainty to some extent. But until the idea was tested in the schools on a limited basis, most people were still very uncertain about it. As the idea crossed each hurdle of the innovation process, the uncertainty surrounding it gradually decreased, making groping along less and less necessary.

To the extent that uncertainty diminished, planning became more of an option. However, maintaining stability and consensus needed for planning is difficult under the best of circumstances. Note what happened when the policy entrepreneurs' access to the governor and information about his strategy was cut off. This unanticipated event made them return to groping along. Returning to a higher level of uncertainty, they reacted by exploring a range of alternatives to find a solution.

The policy entrepreneurs differ in their descriptions of the change process and their group's participation in it. Some characterize their efforts as ad hoc and reactive, certainly in line with groping along, although they did not use the term. Others see themselves as much more strategic and deliberate; they set out on a course of action and pursued it no matter what surprises came their way. From our perspective, we saw both groping along and planning occurring at different times, depending on the level of uncertainty the team and others experienced. It was not just a matter of employing one strategy or the other, but learning under what conditions each might apply. The best advice we have at this point is to develop both strategies. Be prepared to grope along when planning fails. And be prepared to plan when groping along has narrowed the options enough to make planning a viable option.

   • *What are the costs of radical change? Do the benefits of radical change outweigh the costs?*
Radical change, like dynamite, can blow in any direction. It is very difficult to tell how things will turn out. Analyses can be wrong; innovative ideas can fail to deliver as promised. An innovative idea can even have consequences worse than the initial conditions (Morris, 1980). It is hard to predict the costs, let alone the benefits, but we are inclined to believe that those who take a sys-

tems perspective and anticipate first and second-order effects may have a better chance than most.

Even making a retrospective assessment is not all that easy. As we read the journals and listen to experts debate the pros and cons of educational choice and its outcomes in the Minnesota experiment, we still hear no consensus, although from our vantage point, endorsement of school choice appears to be growing. Polls show support ranging from 65 to 75 percent nationally among parents and the general public. Perhaps the question can be answered only when enough time has passed enabling us to gather more data on the consequences of this social experiment.

- *What is the best vantage point for radical change?*

The answer was clear to the policy entrepreneurs. Radical change had to come from outside the target system. Insiders had the advantage of system knowledge, but it was too easy for them to be captured by organizational responsibilities and roles. Change agents needed detachment and distance; their allegiance had to be to the radical idea and not to an institution or its structure. It was far more advantageous to cultivate ties with well-placed and well-informed insiders than it was to be on the inside, laboring under the restrictions imposed by bureaucratic procedures. As outsiders with close ties to insiders, the entrepreneurs gained important system knowledge, yet suffered few disadvantages in acquiring it.

Recent studies support their preference for outsider status. Bureaucratic and executive entrepreneurs tend to be incrementalists (Levin and Sanger, 1994; Sanger and Levin, 1992). Their approach has been described as evolutionary tinkering. They combine old and familiar things in new ways, but do not offer fundamental, radical breakthroughs. Most often, their innovative ideas develop through trial and error and evolve as adaptations to existing practice.

These findings are in line with other studies of appointed executives (Aberbach, Putnam, and Rockman, 1981; Zegans, 1992). Such executives tend to view their role as limited by the legislature, which sets broad directions and makes choices about fundamental issues, new expenditures, and major policy changes. As one said, "For what it's worth, I think major new policy initiatives have to come from elected officials. I mean staff can have ideas, maybe bounce and buzz off of them. But, ultimately, if you're going to affect segments of your public, either in offering a new service or taking something away that's been there before . . . that's their [the legislature's] call" (Zegans, 1992, p. 149).

This conservative role limits executives' degrees of freedom and makes it difficult for radical ideas to surface in their bureaus. In their eyes, tinkering around the edges is preferable to seizing opportunities for fundamental change. Institutional constraints, self-imposed or system imposed, make radical change by management or bureau design an improbable option.

For those who worry about bureaucratic tendencies to do the wrong things right, incremental inside change offers little solace. They can turn to one of two lawful alternatives open to outsiders who wish to shift a system's course: radical change by legislative design, which we document in this book, and radical change by judicial design. Briefly, radical change by judicial design considers appellate justices and the litigants who bring them cases as a shared enterprise of policy entrepreneurship (Pacelle, 1990, p. 2). Through their collective efforts, justices and litigants form a union to fundamentally alter the laws of the land and through them public practice. A review of this approach is beyond the scope of this book, but readers can explore it further in Caldeira and Wright (1988), Cortner (1968), Cowan (1976), Greenberg (1977), Kellogg (1967), Kluger (1976), O'Connor (1980), O'Connor and Epstein (1984), Pacelle (1990), and Vose (1959, 1972).

- *Must change strategies for radical change be confrontational and politically motivated? To what extent are consensus and collaboration possible?*

From the entrepreneurial heuristics outlined in Chapter Four and the urgent recommendation to study Alinsky, we see a marked preference among the entrepreneurs for political and confrontational strategies. Yet many of our colleagues, especially those whose expertise is in the field of conflict management and negotiation, argue that it is possible to achieve radical change through collaboration rather than conflict.

To address this question, let us begin by examining the premises underlying radical change. Advocacy of radical change presupposes a belief that conditions are bad enough to warrant immediate attention and that sweeping action is preferable to limited adjustment of the status quo. Advocacy of radical change also assumes that compromise is unlikely. For example, educational

redesign challenges the fundamental beliefs of traditional school-
ing, and it would be unlikely that the two perspectives could coex-
ist within the same school system beyond a transition period.
Compromise leads to co-optation, the policy entrepreneurs warn,
and co-optation leads to failure. Living in a world of limited
resources, we are expected to make hard choices on what new
ideas to support, especially if those ideas are in fundamental conflict. Scarcity provokes a zero-sum orientation and forces us to
choose one type of system over another.

Radical change inevitably provokes resistance, as some people
will perceive much to lose and little to gain from the process.
Power thus becomes an important variable in the equation.
Resisters may have to be mandated into compliance to protect the
best interests of society as a whole. This assumes, of course, that
the power holders agree with the idea and choose to exercise their
power in this way, and can convince people what is in the best
interest of the whole. Given resource constraints, competition, and
fundamental disagreements over ideas, power can make the difference between an idea's rejection or acceptance.

If these observations are accurate, it appears that power and
confrontational politics are integral to radical change. Whether
one describes the dynamics of innovation in terms of *pluralism*
(where representatives of competing interests bargain with one
another to achieve their goals) or *elitism* (where one group controls the decision process, through access or agenda control or
manipulation of the beliefs and awareness of the less powerful)
(Gray, 1989), power is central to getting things done. No matter
who wields it and how it is applied, it will be an important element
of the change process.

Even collaboration is not devoid of political dynamics, although
it is based on a different model of political behavior (Gray, 1989).
Collaboration assumes power is shared among stakeholders who
collectively define problems and search for solutions. As a group,
participants seek ways to satisfy their self-interests while at same time
searching for solutions to advance the commonweal. Collaboration
can be associated with innovation to the extent that stakeholders
can find new and mutually beneficial solutions to their problems.
To the extent that they are unable to do so without compromising
their ideas, collaboration is a limited strategy for innovation.

The Governor's Discussion Group did use collaboration to reach an incremental innovation—public school choice for at-risk students. However, for collaboration to produce radical innovation, certain conditions must be met (Roberts and Bradley, 1991). Participants must be free agents, able to engage in conceptual blockbusting and explore alternative ways of thinking—requisites for creativity and idea generation (Adams, 1974, 1986; Brookfield, 1987). Group representatives find this almost impossible, as concern about possible repercussions gets in the way. If maintaining a group's position and protecting its views are more important than challenging current practice, people deny themselves the opportunity to explore unthinkable options. In contrast, outsiders such as the policy entrepreneurs are freer to explore beyond existing givens. Limited only in their conceptual ability to envision a new order, they can question tradition and pursue a radical course of action. Thus, we concur that radical innovation is likely to start with small, unconstrained, close-knit groups working outside the institutional order (Roberts and Bradley, 1991). And we believe these groups are likely to use competitive and confrontational change strategies, rather than cooperative and consensual ones.

To underscore this point, one of the policy entrepreneurs gave us a favorite quote from Frederick Douglass to share with our readers: "The whole history of the progress of human liberty shows that all concessions yet made to her august claims have been born of earnest struggle. . . . If there is no struggle, there is no progress. Those who profess to favor freedom, and yet deprecate agitation, are men who want crops without plowing up the ground, they want rain without thunder and lightning. They want the ocean without the awful roar of its many waters."

• *How do we keep public entrepreneurs accountable to the public?* If power and politics are important elements of the innovation process, and radical innovation is more likely to be spawned in small, unconstrained, close-knit groups, what keeps these groups accountable and working in the public interest?

We come to a major issue concerning public innovation and entrepreneurship (Bellone and Goerl, 1992; Terry, 1993). Public policy is concerned with public welfare—the protection, health, education, and economic viability of the citizenry. Innovative changes in policy can alter the delivery of essential services and the conditions of doing business. By the very nature of the function of government, policy changes can have a fundamental impact on the quality of people's lives. How do we know that changes are for the better, that public interest will be served? Launching public entrepreneurship and innovation is risky, not only in terms of return on investment, but in terms of the potential consequences for society. It is one thing for entrepreneurs to assume risks inherent in a business venture in the hopes of a greater return; they calculate the odds of success and are willing to accept the outcome and consequences. But who assumes the risks in a public venture? The children receiving an innovative program, the teachers and schools supporting change, the state legislature and administration allocating dollars and administering the program—or the public entrepreneurs who initiate, design, and implement the innovation? The risks are diffused and borne by a number of people, and those who suffer most directly if the program does not deliver as anticipated are those with the least amount of say in the decision—the children. We need to consider how the best interests of the public can be protected and not disadvantaged by entrepreneurial action.

What certainty do we have that entrepreneurial efforts will be directed in socially meaningful ways? (See Ramamurti, 1986a.) Research on public entrepreneurs has raised just this concern (Lewis, 1980). One can behave entrepreneurially for private interests as well as for public interests. To the extent that self-interest and public interest coincide, the question provokes less debate. To the extent that self-interested behavior displaces or substitutes for public interest, some limits or constraints on entrepreneurial behavior are needed. But it is not always clear where the limits are or what is involved in keeping public entrepreneurs accountable (Ferman and Levin, 1987).

These questions are easier to answer for change agents who pursue radical change by legislative or judicial design. Introducing innovative ideas to the legislature is constrained by lawmaking procedures, just as introducing innovative ideas to the courts is constrained by judicial procedures. We hold people accountable by holding them to the rules of due process. Accountability through legislative design is also maintained through the media, the opposition, and other groups who join in a public discussion about innovative ideas. Reporters asked, on more than one occasion, what the policy entrepreneurs were getting out of their advocacy of public school choice. Several prominent groups in Minnesota kept the debate open to the general public. Thus, we find various checkpoints to ensure additional accountability for the innovative idea. The policy entrepreneurs in our study never broke the law, operated in secret, or derived financial or professional gain from their activities.

Questions of accountability are much more difficult to deal with in the case of executive and bureaucratic entrepreneurship. We know, for example, that a certain amount of rule breaking, bootlegging, or creative bypassing of organizational constraints is not only a natural part of entrepreneurial activity, but is actively and openly encouraged in the business literature (Peters and Waterman, 1982; Peters and Austin, 1985; Peters, 1989). But if rule breaking is a natural part of entrepreneurial experience, the issue is how much are we willing to tolerate and countenance in government bureaus? More important, how are we going to distinguish rule breaking for the public interest from rule breaking in pursuit of self-interest?

We have noted in several places throughout the book that innovation requires openness in the search for new ideas, flexibility in testing alternatives, latitude to experiment and learn from mistakes, and resources to fund new ventures, many of which will not be successful. These degrees of freedom are rarely available within bureaus. For example, it is against the law to bootleg resources from one funding line to another to support a start-up venture. Government auditors and program evaluators frown on such activity and can hold managers liable for deviations, no matter how well intended their actions. Furthermore, the press and public can be harsh judges of would-be entrepreneurs who violate procedures, or spend tax dollars on projects that fail or do not deliver the anticipated returns. Under these constraints, public actors are less inclined to stray too far from what is considered standard practice.

These constraints not only make executive and bureaucratic entrepreneurship harder, they force tenacious entrepreneurs to search for even more sophisticated ways to evade the system. If caught, they can be charged with malfeasance in office—and the event encourages overseers to plug the loopholes with additional rules and regulations. Thus a vicious circle is drawn. Executive and bureaucratic entrepreneurs get caught evading the system to break out of the constraints. The press and public clamor for additional constraints. New constraints limit the freedom to explore, experiment, and innovate in the future. Eventually we wind up with deadened public bureaus and systems that lack any capacity for renewal and change. Many believe this describes the current state of affairs—hence the growing interest in redesigning and reengineering our public bureaus.

Acting out of fear of bureaucrats out of control, we lose on two counts. One the one hand, we set up rules and procedures so tight that dreaming up evasions becomes a pastime for people caught in them, leading the less mature to act against the public interest. On the other hand, we deny the public sector important entrepreneurial talent, thus undermining the government's ability to adapt and change. Constraints can be so restrictive that we either drive out potential entrepreneurs or discourage them from entering government service in the first place, because alternatives elsewhere are more attractive. Clearly, accountability is important in our public systems—but too much accountability may be just as bad as too little.

Frustrated as we are with the reluctance of public systems to innovate and change, we should remember that accountability and oversight protect us from entrepreneurial teams like Oliver North's, who set up shadow structures to pursue their own ends. Accountability, while it may slow down entrepreneurship and innovation, also protects the public from stupidity, malice, and mendacity. There can be a dark side to entrepreneurship, particularly bureaucratic and executive entrepreneurship (Caro, 1975; Lewis, 1980). Containing its force and channeling it in legal directions is an important consideration.

Fundamental questions of the innovative idea always must be asked: For whom and to what end is this idea being pursued? Does the process conform to the ethical and moral standards we expect of our public officials? Would the public endorse the idea and the entrepreneurial team if it knew what was going on? What personal (financial and professional) gains do the idea's advocates stand to make? As we seek to reinvent and reengineer government, we believe concerns should focus on the dangers of the socially and emotionally immature individual, not on the entrepreneur in general. We need bureaucratic and executive entrepreneurs, but we do not need entrepreneurs at lower levels of maturity who endanger our public institutions and run rough-shod over our democratic ideals.

Keeping individual bureau and executive entrepreneurs accountable is even more difficult when we recognize that measuring and assessing performance is problematic, even for goals that are in the public interest. It is difficult enough even for private sector entrepreneurs, who theoretically have measures of profit and loss to maintain accountability. Yet growing evidence points to a much more complicated picture. It seems to be the rule rather than the exception that criteria shift over time and differ among participants (Dornblaser, Lin, and Van de Ven, 1989). "As different types and degrees of criteria were used and emphasized at different points in time, innovation outcome evaluations became increasingly difficult to judge" (p. 200). In view of the problem of deciding what basis to use for evaluating an innovative idea or innovation, the researchers suggest that "it may be more productive to view innovation outcome assessment as 'remnants of a journey,' rather than as objective benchmarks of developmental success" (p. 200).

So if private entrepreneurship—known for bottom-line orientation and market feedback—has difficulty in assessing entrepreneurial outcomes, what chance is there for executive and bureaucratic entrepreneurship? "The public sector has no such built-in process for selecting and encouraging the most efficient or forward-looking agencies. The goals of public agencies are highly diffuse or vague and their technologies are unclear. There is no simple measure of profit and loss to indicate success or failure" (Walker, 1981, p. 84). The difficulty of measuring performance makes it difficult to maintain public attention, and difficult to hold executive and bureaucratic entrepreneurs accountable and find out if the expenditures of resources, time, and energy are worth the effort.

We see another risk in flexibility and experimentation. These values and the institutional arrangements that support them compete with ideals of equity, justice, fairness, and safety, and certain trade-offs may be required. For example, experimentation may increase health and safety risks for personnel. Increasing creativity and flexibility may force us to relax the constraints imposed by personnel systems intended to ensure fair treatment for all employees. It is not clear to what extent the public is willing to substitute the notion of an entrepreneurial government for the notion of a fair and equitable one in pursuit of justice for all. It may not be necessary to look upon executive or bureaucratic entrepreneurship as an either-or proposition that displaces a more conservative interpretation of government's role. Perhaps there is a role for government that endorses and supports both entrepreneurship and accountability, flexibility and safety, experimentation and justice. It may be the ultimate challenge of executive and bureaucratic entrepreneurship to figure out what the role is and how to make it work.

- *How do policy entrepreneurs sustain themselves psychologically and financially?* Policy entrepreneurship sounds like such a difficult and taxing process, how do entrepreneurs keep themselves going? Is there any respite from the exigencies of the process?

As we mentioned in Chapter Five, the policy entrepreneurs considered entrepreneurship to be their calling and life's work. It was a central part of their identity, and they didn't look for an end or a closure to it. That is why we believe the psychology of public entrepreneurship is important. It takes a certain kind of person to endure the hardships of the innovation process. Not everyone has the requisite drive and level of commitment. As one observer notes, "Innovation in American politics is not always the work of a day, and the pursuit of successful innovation is consequently not a task for those who need quick gratification. Possibly the commonest mistake made by observers and participants who favor innovation is to give up too soon, to measure gains only in the very short run, to become discouraged and to be tempted by tactics that are momentarily gratifying, but self-destructive over the medium term" (Polsby, 1984, pp. 173–174).

On the other hand, it is possible to take advantage of the changing rhythms of the process to restore one's spirit and physical well-being. Idea generation typically has a more leisurely pace, allowing a period of quiet reflection, and successful implementation of an idea enables entrepreneurs to pause and rest before they move on to other things. For some of the policy entrepreneurs, the success of public school choice meant developing follow-on initiatives such as the idea of charter schools, while others sat back to wait for future windows of opportunity to open. It is also possible to take breaks from the frenetic activity during the design and implementation phases of the innovation process. And no one has to be an entrepreneur all the time. One can be selective in choosing one's battles.

Advice from the Entrepreneurs

In our last discussions with them, after they had read the manuscript, we asked the policy entrepreneurs for any final thoughts they would like to share. Each had a slightly different perspective on what he had learned, what he wanted to pass on to other change agents, and what he took issue with in our work.

- *The veteran policy entrepreneur began by reiterating the importance of the ten change heuristics outlined in Chapter Four.* He was concerned that they might be lost among the other details of the case. "Go back to those fundamentals," he said, they are "the heart of the change process." Evolved from years of mistakes, these "profound lessons are important guidelines to follow in the future."

He also underscored the importance of keeping focused on the idea or vision. "People [like the policy entrepreneurs] are not turned on by politics; they don't get enjoyment out of it. They do it because they have to." What they need is a purpose in life to give them the high energy to outwork everybody. That is why it is important to resist co-optation, compromise, and tradeoffs. Better to say no than give up on what you really want, he insisted. Also, be willing to wait for the right conditions, because timing is very important. Most important, be strategic and reframe the issues to put your opponents on the defensive. For example, rather than asking educators to support public school choice, ask them why they deny choice to the poor and point out that the rich can afford to move from one school district to another.

He also cautioned against being a naysayer with younger people. Although "I tried that in 1950, and it doesn't work," may be accurate, "others have to have their trial and error learning too." He has argued with the other policy entrepreneurs that charter schools won't work, believing that traditional education will co-opt them—as he believes current research is now showing. However, he thinks the other entrepreneurs who oppose his view will have to learn that lesson for themselves.

When asked if the letter charging the governor and commissioner with backsliding should have been avoided, the veteran entrepreneur answered by saying that change agents always have inadequate information, time, and knowledge. At that time, the team had lost their good access. In sending the letter, they made a judgment call that it was important to shake up the governor and deliberately call him to task. "But what did it cost us? What did we lose?" the veteran entrepreneur asks. He recognizes that some establishment people may have felt hurt, but adds that he is "still not sure whether things should have been done differently." Instead, he was "impressed with how few screw-ups" they actually made.

When asked if there was anything special about Minnesota that would explain the success of public school choice, the veteran policy entrepreneur elaborated on the importance of the community context, which gave the team many advantages. They could leverage organizations, rely on an "outpouring of dedicated people who believed in something," build on knowledge and skills developed through the Citizens League, and benefit from the proximity factor to get people together for meetings. Most important, the situation in Minnesota was and is not hopeless. "You need confidence to make things happen. We are fortunate to be in a place where there is a chance to do things. We are constantly trying to get better and we have a lot to work with."

His final message to others was drawn from a book titled *A Return to Love*. Drawing inspiration from the book to prepare for his son's wedding celebrations, he thought the following passage also would have meaning for other agents of change.

> We're all assigned a piece of the garden, a corner of the universe that is ours to transform. Our corner of the universe is our own life—our relationships, our homes, our work, our current circumstances—exactly as they are. Every situation we find ourselves in is an opportunity perfectly planned by the Holy Spirit, to teach love instead of fear. Whatever energy system we find ourselves a part of, it's our job to heal it—to purify the thought forms by purifying our own. It's never really a circumstance that needs to change—it's *we* who need to change. The prayer isn't for God to change our lives, but rather for Him to change us [Williamson, 1992, p. 76].

- *The second policy entrepreneur we spoke with emphasized the power of systems thinking, but most of our discussion with him focused on more personal and tactical issues of policy entrepreneurship.* He said he did not need the same things other people needed. He lost an election and found it to be a valuable experience. He learned that there were worse things than losing, such as wasting time. His loss focused him on his core beliefs and values and subsequently enabled him to do things others thought politically dangerous. He sees many politicians as so desperate to hang on to office that they "permit themselves to be jerked around." In contrast, he found— and recommends to others—that people have options. Whatever they are, they "enable one to take strange, impolitic positions." Having another line of work permits some detachment to reflect on what one is doing. That is important, because "introspection is not one of the long suits of politicians."

He also offered tactical advice to other change agents. Claim what you want to happen will happen, he advised. Give people a sense of a foregone conclusion. He cited the "myth of the public school as the embracer of diversity" as a case in point. Our beliefs about the public schools are crumbling, yet he anticipates that we will have public schools for a long time. Future schools will be organized around and by communities, a point of difference he has with another entrepreneur who believes that competition is sufficient to create pride and interest in schools. Wanting organizations that inspire us by reason of membership, we don't have any alternative but to build and rebuild our institutions. Again, claim what you want to happen is inevitable and it will happen.

And finally, he noted the importance of teaching the skills of entrepreneurship and change agentry. He meets people all the time who feel powerless, estranged, and victimized. They need to learn how they can make a difference. He believes this can and must happen for our country to survive.

- *The third policy entrepreneur began our interview by reiterating the importance of systems change and how it differs from organizational change.* Our references to business literature troubled him because he feared readers would confuse the two concepts. From his perspective, business sees everything as a management problem that can be corrected by changing something in the organization— replacing executives, giving people more training, and shifting resources. The policy entrepreneurs are talking about something very different, he said.

To differentiate between the two concepts, he described the effects of dining room rules in the retirement homes where his aunt and his father live. His aunt's home charges people for the meals they eat, while his father's charges a flat dining fee as part of membership. The food they serve is very different; it is much better where his aunt is. Her home makes money only when people come in and eat there. His father's place makes its money by people *not* coming to eat. Complaints to the manager in his father's home and insistence that something be done—better management, better cook, better training—are to no avail. These efforts are wasted, according to the entrepreneur, because the problem is in the system. No amount of tinkering will fix it, because it is behaving as it was built to behave. Unless the incentives and rewards for serving poor meals are changed, the quality will stay low.

From his perspective, businesses are too focused on internal operations—they think of replacing or training the cook, but not of changing the rules of the dining room. It is the rules that must be changed, he insisted. He sees similar problems in education. People "talk about the bad things that should be stopped in education and the good things that ought to be done. . . . *They never ask what is it that explains why the good things are not being done. If they want to change what education does, they have to change what it is.*" The rules, not organizational leadership, staff development, or better curriculum, make the difference. He described one very effective superintendent who came to this conclusion. He was trying to make changes in his district and was being blocked by people who felt the changes would hurt them. So he finally went to the legislature to change the rules of the system.

This policy entrepreneur credited the Citizens League with teaching him and the others about systems and incentives. He cited a sports analogy: "Sergei Bubka, the world's greatest pole vaulter, has broken the record twenty to thirty times, moving the record a foot or so in his career. But notice that he moves the record up by only a quarter of an inch each time. Why? Because he gets paid for each world record he makes." The rules of the game of pole vaulting—Bubka's system and its incentives—affect how high he tries to jump. Other systems work the same way.

Ultimately, however, change is more than incentives. It is about persuading people to change the way they think. Referring to the concept of a *paradigm shift* (Kuhn, 1970), this policy entrepreneur believes that radical change requires a new framework of thought. "You cannot deal with problems in the terms in which they are framed. Change comes from reframing the issues." An interaction between a policy entrepreneur and the head of one of the teachers' unions served as an example. The teacher was having problems with public school choice, fearing it would destroy the system. The policy entrepreneur pointed out that public school choice already existed, but only for the rich. Reframing the issue, he asked how public school choice could be implemented effectively for all, and not just for the few? Thus, cautioned the entrepreneur, we must help our readers understand that radical change is not skipping along on the same road, nor taking big leaps on the same road. *Radical change means getting on a different road altogether.* You have to change the way people think to get them to change their choice of roads. And it is particularly important to get them to think beyond their own self-interest in finding the new road.

Over the years of our association with this policy entrepreneur, he has provided several notable examples of paradigm shifts. One came from New Zealand, where wide-ranging structural economic reforms have been undertaken since 1984. He sent us a *Wall Street Journal* article titled "The Politics of Successful Structural Reform" (Douglas, 1990, p. A20) to illustrate some of his points. The purpose of the article, written by New Zealand's former finance minister (1984–1988), was to challenge assumptions people had of radical change. We highlight some major points here.

- Structural reform requires quality people. Good government in democratic countries needs politicians who can "get their minds around complex issues and the guts to adopt policies" that would result in real reform.
- Define objectives clearly and implement reforms quickly. "Speed is essential." If you move too slowly the consensus supporting reforms will likely collapse before results become evident. "It is uncertainty, not speed, that endangers structural reform programs."

- Package reforms in "large bundles." Real reform is systems reform, not an unrelated "collection of bits and pieces." It is important to see linkages among system parts and use them to enhance all action.
- Keep the momentum going and do not stop until you have completed the total effort. You are vulnerable to attack when challenging vested interests, but a rapidly moving target is much harder for opponents to hit. Stay in front to lead the debate and remove privileges evenhandedly to reduce opposition.
- Maintain confidence and credibility through consistency of policy and communications. Avoid ad hoc decisions and do not waiver from your objectives. "People are unable to cooperate with real reform unless they know where they are going." When feasible, spell out intentions in advance. "Successful structural reform is not possible until you trust, respect, and inform the electors." Tell people and keep telling them what the problem is, how it surfaced, what damage it is doing, what the objective is, how you will achieve the objective, what the costs and benefits will be, and why your approach is better than other options.
- "Don't blink; public confidence rests on your composure." Structural reform demands major changes in attitudes and beliefs. It causes real concern and discomfort. People will be "hypersensitive to any signs of similar anxiety" in those responsible for reforms. If people do not understand the argument, they will judge its merits on their assessment of your mental and emotional state.
- When the pressure becomes extreme and there is the temptation to accept "an easy ad hoc compromise," remember why you are in politics. In a democracy, holding power forever is not the point. Best use the time to do something worthwhile. Genuine reform, without compromise, achieves greater gains than other approaches to decision making.

This policy entrepreneur also cited Jean Monnet, the architect and master builder of the European Economic Community. He found Monnet's achievements remarkable, especially in a person of the peasantry, who lived in a rural region of France and never went beyond high school. There was no way Monnet should have become influential, yet he did. The entrepreneur often recommends Monnet's *Memoirs* to others. Using Monnet as his exemplar, he believes that "if one can come in with creativity and political courage, at least in the early stages, and have some skill to move ideas, it is possible to be effective."

This policy entrepreneur also wanted us to emphasize that as he sees it, the use of management examples and research should not be interpreted to mean the policy entrepreneurs had any grand design or organization in mind. There was no master plan to guide their actions. His impression then and now is that their efforts were ad hoc and reactive, enabling them to take advantage of events as they happened. They had a general sense of what the goal was, but not necessarily a predetermined set of steps to accomplish it. It was more like what Ted Van Dyke (another European Economic Community representative) described when he likened the change process to climbing a mountain. You can see the top of the mountain, but not the path to get there. In fact, there may be a variety of paths. What you do is take one, and as you get a little closer to the top and look down, then and only then are you able to see the paths with a little more clarity.

He found our use of the term public entrepreneurship unfortunate for similar reasons as well. The commercial implications and the connotation of self-interest bothered him. Despite our explanation about the literature and the frequent usage of the term, he remained unconvinced, especially when he read our warnings of the darker side of entrepreneurship. If we were not using the word, he retorted, the problems of accountability and ethics would not be an issue. He preferred to describe his activities as "citizenship," which for him did not carry the same negative connotations. He also found it objectionable that people who supported the status quo, and protected their self-interest, should not be held accountable. Somehow it was only those who wanted to change whose motives were called into question—points well taken, as far as we were concerned.

And finally, as had several other policy entrepreneurs, he noted the importance of the political culture. Having made several trips to Chicago to explain about public school choice, it became apparent to him that some of the things the group had accomplished in Minnesota could not be done in Chicago. "There are certain places where you can grow bananas and certain places where you can't." Minnesota's moralistic political culture made it possible to promote change by calling on the sense of commonwealth among its people.

• *A fourth policy entrepreneur, reflecting on his experience with public school choice, insisted that "nothing beats having a strategy. Hoping for the best isn't good enough."* The strategy must be plausible and "once committed to it, you have to stick with it, no matter what distractions come your way." He observed that many people "get caught up in tactical warfare and get off the strategic track." You must stay "stubbornly focused on what you have set off to do, and don't let anybody drive you from it." "Unless you get exceptionally lucky, this sort of thing requires extraordinary patience and persistence from the moment of the first public statement on the issue." He noted that it took the group nearly three years to get into a position where a major politician would risk taking on the idea. It took another three years to have the idea firmly embedded in law. "There were many opportunities to settle for less, but you just can't do it."

He was not sure what, if anything, the policy entrepreneurs would or could have done differently. "Destiny dealt us better than a fair share." The governor was there when they needed him, and so were other public figures who played a major part. "The constellation of stars were in the right alignment." When asked if the Minnesota context made a difference in the outcome, he agreed that "civic soil has a different chemistry" in each community, and that you can't transplant Minnesota institutions. "The trick is to grow your own within your own traditions and do your own soil test first. Figure out what will grow and then plant it. Get past the transplant question." The so-called gap between Minnesota and the rest of the states is closing fast. "We are a laboratory to be reckoned with." "When 45 percent of the births in the Metropolitan area, and 22 percent statewide, are out of wedlock, the Minnesota difference is shrinking. . . . Pay attention to that shrinking."

His final comments returned to the question of strategy. "Understand," he said, "that the great reform problem is a system problem, not a program problem. That is what distinguishes us— pushing for change in the way the system worked." If you keep that in mind, no way could you settle for less—better grading, class size improvement, even devolving responsibility to the school level. "We wouldn't have been satisfied until the relationships and incentives were changed and there were some reasonable expectations that the system would perform differently." While the policy entrepreneurs came from many different backgrounds, they shared that "implicit bond." He compared their experience in education to the current debate on health care. "Health is not being approached from a systems perspective." "If one were to do it right, despite the fact that health care is more complex than education, one could do the same thing, since the same things are wrong. The answer would be to recreate a delivery system to make it resemble a market." "It would be ten years before you could measure change, but change would occur."

• *The fifth policy entrepreneur underscored the importance of patience and persistence in radical change.* Just having read the recent Supreme Court case involving Kansas City and school desegregation (June 1995), he said it was necessary to plan on "staying in the fray for a long term." "Traditionalists have such a limited view of the world." He predicts there will be many unintended consequences of that decision. Reformers will need to anticipate and deal with them. Radical change is a long, drawn-out process. Few have the courage to stick with it.

• *The sixth entrepreneur agreed, saying "There is absolutely no substitute for persistence."* He also noted that there is no substitute for humor. "If you don't laugh, you will eat yourself up." Radical change is full of unexpected turns and disasters. You can just as easily face an explosion as you can enjoy a success. "Be prepared to laugh, otherwise you will be consumed. Humor is far more effective."

Returning to the issue of managing attention, he believed it was impossible to overestimate the value of real-life stories highlighting problems with the status quo. They provide gripping details with which people can identify. He also emphasized the importance of building coalitions to include groups not necessarily related to the reform in question. The directors of Minnesota community action programs were a good example. Working throughout the state to administer antipoverty programs in both urban and rural areas, they were very familiar with the failure of schools and the insensitivity of administrators to low-income kids. When statements were made by traditional educators that public school choice wouldn't help these kids, they were there to say, "Yes it would!" Of course, using personal ties to forge these connections

is critical. He relied on one of the directors, a former teaching col-
league, to unite the directors and make an important appeal to a
key legislator.

He reiterated the importance of the proximity factor mentioned by the veteran entrepreneur. The Minnesota state capitol is
in the Twin Cities—St. Paul and Minneapolis—a large population
center in the central part of the state. All the policy entrepreneurs
were within a ten to fifteen-minute drive of each other, and could
quickly gather for any emergency or late-breaking activity. In contrast, many other state capitols are located in rural communities
far from major metropolitan centers. Physical separation tends to
give more power to established interests with representatives on
site full time. Outside change agents with limited budgets find it
difficult to handle the costs of hotel bills, airfares, and meals. These
expenses make a day-to-day presence more difficult. In these settings, it will be important for change agents to consider how to get
people physically located in state capitols before they launch a
major change effort.

And finally, noting the comments of several entrepreneurs
about their families, he stressed the importance of a strong, loving
relationship with someone with whom you can talk things over. He
said Paul Ellwood told him, "No matter what else you do, take care
of your family." Happily married for twenty-one years, he believes
that this was very good advice and feels that it certainly had much
to do with his effectiveness as a change agent.

A Theory of Radical Change by Design

We are in between idea systems.
—ANONYMOUS

It is better to emit a scream in the shape of theory than to be entirely insensible to the jars and incongruities of life and take everything as it comes in a forlorn stupidity.
—ROBERT LOUIS STEVENSON, "CRABBED AGE AND YOUTH" (1881)

Theories of radical social change often attribute change to outside factors that provoke shifts within a system. The assumption is that a system will not move on its own; it needs prompting of some sort to push it beyond the established institutional order. Some call this originating factor a jolt or a shock (Schroeder, Van de Ven, Scudder, and Polley, 1989), others a disruptive event (Schön, 1971) or a crisis.

Yet events, by themselves, do not automatically produce change: crises can be ignored, shocks can be weathered, jolts can be minimized. The potential for radical change by design occurs when someone defines the situation, interprets the crisis, constructs an explanation of what it means, and describes how to deal with it. (In some cases, crisis might even be manufactured by social actors and minimally related to outside events.)

Enter the policy entrepreneur. She focuses attention on an idea as a solution to a policy problem and insists that people attend to it. Pushing the idea forward both by design and by deft use of chance opportunities, she builds momentum. If she is successful in attracting enough support and resources to counter the resistance of those opposed to change, the idea ultimately becomes part of accepted practice. Although outside forces may present the occasion, it is the policy entrepreneur who seizes the opportunity and responds to them.

Thus, our analysis leads us to understand radical innovation in terms of individuals who initiate action against the current system. The policy entrepreneurs in our study questioned assumptions; they pushed, probed, and challenged the existing order. From our perspective, they did not react to a crisis or disruptive event as much as they helped create the perception that one would appear if no policy changes were made. They functioned as *catalysts,* and, like chemical catalysts, provoked a reaction around them without themselves being transformed.

We view catalytic agents as essential to radical policy change. Faced with warnings of system malfunction, other participants seek incremental adjustments, but policy entrepreneurs challenge people to move beyond established patterns of thought and action and overcome traditional biases (Cobb and Elder, 1983, p. 184). Their commitment and action help redefine a problem, galvanize public opinion around an issue, and shift the frame of reference from incremental to radical change.

Development of the Theory

We designed this study to develop a grounded theory (Glaser and Strauss, 1967) of policy entrepreneurship and radical change out of our observations, rather than to test a theory framed in advance. As we immersed ourselves in the field data and worked out the first layer of interpretation, we found two concepts useful to explain the dynamics we were observing. The concept of *energy* enabled us to describe what the team was doing—that is, providing a force to push their innovative ideas forward. We also employed the concept of *alignment* to describe the mechanisms constraining or directing the energy and preserving it from dissipation.

At first, we used both concepts as metaphors, comparable to

their usage in the change literature (see, for example, Adams, 1984, and Ackerman, 1984). The concepts allowed us to build the diagram of the change process depicted in Figure C.1. The horizontal dimension represents the innovation process and the vertical dimension represents the entrepreneurial process. Representing two vectors in time and space, these two processes work in tandem to produce an innovation. The entrepreneurial vector tracks the agent who seeks to galvanize energy for and counter resistance to the new idea as it moves through time. The innovation vector tracks the different manifestations of the new idea over time from its initiation through its various translations into practice. The unit of analysis of the innovation process is the idea. The unit of analysis of the entrepreneurial process is the catalytic agent or entrepreneur.

Thus, we came to view entrepreneurship as the engine of transformation and public entrepreneurs as the catalysts of innovative change. Entrepreneurs attract resources, garner support, manage meaning, focus direction and attention, and overcome resistance, all in an effort to gather momentum and push their new ideas forward. Framing their ideas as solutions to policy problems, taking advantage of serendipity, and creating their own opportunities in the political context, they craft strategies to win the backing of others.

We see the stages of the innovation process as an alignment system that constrains the energy and channels it to collective ends. The stages are the institutional and legislative obstacles that an idea must overcome before it can pass into the next phase. In the example of public school choice, *the idea was shaped into a proposal* for the governor. *The proposal was then developed into a bill,* and *the bill eventually translated into a law.* Over time, through administration and evaluation, *the law was translated into an operational program.* At each step, more and more social energy was pulled into the fabric of relations surrounding the idea to propel it through the first three stages of the innovation process—initiation, design, and implementation.

Conceptual Framework

As time went on, energy and alignment took on a deeper meaning for us. We began to consider them as central principles of policy entrepreneurship, rather than as metaphors describing it. Instead of a descriptive framework, the concepts fit into an explanatory

Figure C.1. Conceptual Map of the Change Process.

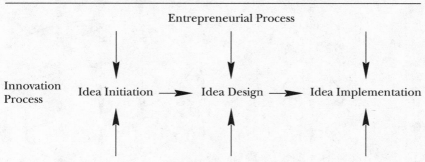

framework that enabled us to specify the conditions under which and the process by which innovation would tend to occur.

Drawing from Lewin's field theory (1951), we found it useful to consider the entrepreneurial process as forming an energy field around an idea to propel it through the phases of the innovation process. The energy field can be considered as a set of relations manipulated by the entrepreneurs to produce action by others to move the idea through the policy system. Innovative ideas that provoke little resistance need a relatively small energy field to move them forward, as we see in Figure C.2. On the other hand, radical ideas that engender a great deal of resistance require a larger amount of social energy to activate a more extensive field of entrepreneurial relations.

Ours was not the first theory built around the two dimensions of energy and alignment. Bradley (1987) uses them to explain the dynamics of social transformation—that is, to describe the relational structures a charismatic system uses to mobilize and regulate the enormous amounts of social energy involved in radical change. Two relational patterns in this process are postulated and empirically verified. First, a system of communion fuses the group together to break down social distinctions and release energy from the existing structure. But communion—and the highly volatile energy that it liberates—is extremely unstable. Unless it is monitored and regulated, it will have destabilizing and often fatal consequences for the group. To survive under these conditions, a

Figure C.2. Energy Fields for Incremental and Radical Change.

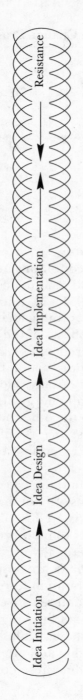

Incremental Change

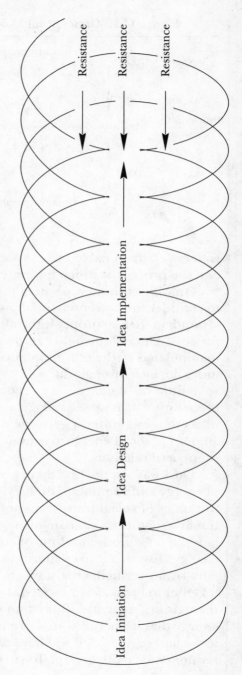

Radical Change

charismatic group requires a strong collective power structure. This structure acts to harness the energy, aligning and channeling it to collective ends.

The first author worked with Bradley to apply the concepts of energy and alignment to both charismatic and noncharismatic systems, and to organizations in varying states of change (Bradley and Roberts, 1989). As Bradley began to elaborate his theory and extend it to biosocial collectives (Bradley and Pribram, 1996), we began to see the differences as well as the points of convergence in our two approaches.

Bradley has examined the relationship between energy and alignment in terms of the efficiency of bounded social systems. We expand the theory to examine the efficiency and internal operation of a partially open social collective and also to explore the effectiveness of the system by examining the extent to which its ideas are viable and survive in the environment. Bradley, in ongoing work with Karl Pribram, has been studying the transfer of energy and information between the neurological, psychological, and sociological levels. We concentrate on the sociological system and explore the dimensions of energy and alignment at the individual, group, and state community levels. Thus, we see our work as an extension of Bradley's research. We examine both internal and external elements—how a collective is able to be stable and efficient *and* how it is able to be effective and survive. We elaborate on Bradley's relational and structural analysis by including other factors in our research, such as environment, personality, community resources, and group dynamics. Our theory was developed to capture the dynamics of radical change, but we also see its application to the dynamics of incremental change, although that aspect is not discussed in detail in this volume.

Propositions

Many propositions can be derived from our consideration of the entrepreneurial process as an energy field and innovation as an energy conversion process.

- *Radical innovative change necessitates an expanded set of entrepreneurial relations to activate enough energy to counter and overcome resistance to the innovative idea.*

The requirements include, but are not limited to creative and intellectual activities to identify performance gaps, generate new ideas, define problems and preferred solutions, and disseminate new ideas; strategic activities to guide the change process, particularly political strategies and heuristics for action; mobilization and execution strategies to establish demonstration projects, cultivate bureaucratic insiders and advocates, collaborate with high-profile individuals and elite groups, enlist elected officials, form and coordinate lobby groups, and cultivate favorable media attention; and support activities for program administration and evaluation.

From this expanded set of relational activities we derive a second proposition:

• *Radical change by legislative design will usually entail collective rather than individual entrepreneurship.*

Collective entrepreneurship can consist either of a group of entrepreneurs working together throughout the process, or of a series of specialists at different phases of the policy process pooling their collective energy to move an innovative idea forward into practice (Roberts, 1992). Specialists can be policy intellectuals, policy advocates, policy champions, and policy administrators. While it is possible that a single individual can possess the requisite analytic, strategic, and behavioral skills, and maintain all the relations necessary to the complete set of activities, we are more likely to find individuals who specialize in a subset of entrepreneurial relations joining forces and working with others. (For example, we anticipate that some will generate ideas while others build coalitions or lobby for support.) Reliance on collective entrepreneurship thus enables policy entrepreneurs to specialize and therefore complement one another during the entrepreneurial process.

Focused commitment from a single policy entrepreneur over a long period of time is much more difficult to sustain than group commitment, which can provide mutual support and backup should a member drop out of the process. Each entrepreneur also brings an independent set of resources to the collective. Taken together, their combined contacts constitute an expanded network of information, political connections, and financial support, dwarfing contributions from a single policy entrepreneur. Collective entrepreneurship has the advantage of building a larger resource base from which to drive the innovation process.

Relations within the collectivity are also important to align the energy and direct it into desired collective action. Thus, we derive a third proposition:

- *Collective entrepreneurship requires attention to the collective's functioning as a separate entity or group, and requires entrepreneurs to address and resolve certain questions.*

The collective must define itself, build a team (specifying who is a member and who is not), decide on its norms and values, manage conflict, structure itself, and coordinate its internal activity and interaction with others. Radical innovation tends to elicit strong passions that can dissipate energy by deflecting attention to issues of group loyalty and external commitments and expectations. Hostility and resistance from external sources may require additional energy to protect group identity and cohesion.

The collective also must develop a capacity to engage in a learning process—to analyze problems, identify potential solutions, pilot test innovative ideas, and redesign the ideas as environmental feedback warrants. Efforts to build a learning system challenge the collective to maintain cohesive and integrated action while the team surfaces alternative plans or pursues different strategies for change. Thus, we postulate:

- *Policy entrepreneurs, working as a collective, are more likely to be successful in the pursuit of radical change to the extent that they develop a parallel learning system independent from the formal apparatus of government to coordinate and direct the energy activated during the change process.*

A fifth proposition derives from our reasoning that radical change is a complex process and that it requires an extensive set of relations to activate and align the energy for collective purposes. Thus, we anticipate:

- *Radical change by design will attract and require certain types of people.*

The entrepreneurial process needs individuals who can employ a systems perspective to diagnose policy problems and who have sufficient cognitive complexity to generate creative solutions to complex, messy social issues. These individuals also must take a long-term view of the policy innovation process and be able to deal with the complex network of relations activated in support of change. Immediate gratification is not and cannot be their reward. Their efforts challenge norms and provoke conflict with those who support the status quo, and they must have the ego strength to be tenacious in their beliefs despite the uncertainty, ambiguity, criticism, and defeat they often face.

Other propositions follow from these major ones; we offer a few as illustration. We anticipate that *radical change will be more likely to be initiated through legislative and judicial design rather than management design in organizations.* The relational networks, tasks, opportunities, and roles of those in the legislative and judicial arena (especially the Supreme Court) give social actors greater latitude to pursue frame-breaking change. The function of those in the legislative branch, for example, is to initiate policy. Contrast the functions of the judicial and legislative branches with those of government bureaus required to implement and execute the law. Although policy can and does evolve through implementation and evaluation, we would not expect radical departures to occur during the latter two phases of the process. Thus, we additionally speculate that *to the extent ideas have a relative advantage, greater trialability and observability, and are more compatible with the existing system, they are more likely to be introduced by organization (bureau) or management design.*

It also follows that *the more an innovative idea deviates from existing practice, the more radical it is likely to seem. The more radical it seems, the more resistance it is likely to engender. The more resistance it engenders, the greater the energy field that must be developed to overcome the resistance.* As in chaotic physical systems, each entrepreneurial activity builds momentum. Taken in combination, the activities create a self-reinforcement process that over time supports each other to propel the idea forward. Negative feedback from the opposition will not be enough to sustain the existing system unless it can counter the momentum of the entrepreneurs. To the extent that the entrepreneurs' field of relations is more extensive than the opposition's, it will release the energy necessary to produce a change in the system and push the system onto a different course.

Radical change also is likely to be successful to the extent that it proceeds quickly and experiments with subparts of the system rather than embarking on change in toto. Without general acceptance of a crisis, it is difficult in a democratic society to justify radical change of a total system. Innovative ideas that can be applied to subsets rather than the entirety of the system have the advantage, as they are likely to provoke less resistance and provide greater opportunity for feedback and learning. This assumes, of course, that there is no crisis. However, *if there is a consensus about a crisis, we anticipate that radical change of a total system can be attempted even in a democratic system.* Under these circumstances, core values and beliefs behind the ideas are expected to be the driving force for radical change.

We also anticipate that *collective entrepreneurship will be more frequent than individual entrepreneurship as the context becomes more turbulent and complex, as in the case of radical change.* Collective entrepreneurship represents a larger field of relations that can activate and gain access to energy. It also helps to have more rather than fewer people to maintain the relational network needed to align the energy for change. For the same reasons, we would expect to see more collective entrepreneurship at the federal level than at the state and local levels. The advantage of collective entrepreneurship also depends on the compatibility of team members, so that energy is not dissipated on internal group issues. The makeup of the group and its complement of individual skills and abilities are as important to the success of the team as the particular traits or profile are to the individual entrepreneur.

Finally, we have proposed a developmental model of public entrepreneurship, comparable to a developmental model of leadership, to differentiate among the different types of public entrepreneurs. As a whole, we expect that *policy entrepreneurs, equivalent to system-level leaders, will have the longest time span of discretion and the most developed cognitive capacity.* Building on this developmental model, we expect that *public entrepreneurs will vary their strategies and behavior depending on their positions in the policy system and the nature of change they pursue.* Those outside the governmental system (policy entrepreneurs), who lack official resources, are more likely to rely on collective entrepreneurship to build their base of support. Free from the constraints of government controls, they also are more likely to pursue radical rather than incremental change. Those inside the government and thus subject to greater oversight, such as bureaucratic entrepreneurs, are more likely to pursue incremental change and more likely to rely on individual entrepreneurship. Cross-functional coordination among organization members tends to be more difficult than unilateral action within a given task domain.

Assessment of the Theory

To demonstrate the explanatory power of the theory of radical change by entrepreneurial design, we subject it to two assessments: the challenge of alternative theories of radical change and the requirements of good process theory (Mohr, 1982).

Alternative Theories of Radical Change

We found three theories that offer different explanations of radical change. As mentioned in the Introduction, these alternatives view radical change as occurring by chance, by learning, or by consensus.

Radical Change by Chance

Kingdon (1984) conceives of three process streams to describe the policy arena: streams of problems, policies, and politics, each largely independent of the others and each developing according to its own dynamics and rules. Policies are generated whether or not they are solving a problem; problems are recognized whether or not there is a solution; and political dynamics move along at their own pace. The greatest policy changes occur when the three streams are joined, or "coupled into a package." (p. 21). This serendipitous linkage often relies on policy entrepreneurs "for coupling solutions to problems and for coupling both problems and solutions to politics" (p. 21). Indeed, "the appearance of a skillful entrepreneur enhances the probability of a coupling" (p. 217). While not completely random, dramatic policy changes rely on "considerable doses of messiness, accident, fortuitous coupling, and dumb luck" (p. 216). They are often prompted by dramatic shifts in the social-political-economic context that alter constraints and opportunities for policy actors.

To what extent does Kingdon's model provide a more accurate account for the radical change in Minnesota? At the macro level of analysis, we found that it did explain much of the case. His view of streams of problems, solutions, and choice opportunities, and of the coupling function of policy entrepreneurs, seemed to capture the fluid, dynamic process we observed. However, over time, at the micro level of analysis, we found the policy entrepreneurs behaving more deliberately and strategically, and with greater conscious planning and orchestration, than Kingdon's model would antici-pate. There seemed to be a logic and an intentionality that guided action and its consequences, a view more in concert with bound-edly rational social actors in pursuit of self-interest. In this domain, the concepts of leadership, strategy, power, choice, coordination, and the ability to manage conflict all had utility. So did the impor-tance of the structural and institutional context in which change occurred.

Rather than wait to take advantage of chance circumstances, the policy entrepreneurs made their own opportunities. They did much more than react to political climate, they created it by stirring up interest and debate for their chosen issue. Their circumstances were not beyond their control; we watched them proactively develop strategies and implement them, based on their assessment of the weaknesses of the system and guided by their vision of what it could become. They employed strategies developed in other policy arenas to provoke the establishment into responding to their challenges. That is, they sponsored experimental programs, convinced high-sta-tus organizations to take up their cause, and took advantage of the institutional context to encourage the introduction of legislation.

Having studied earlier reform movements, they were convinced that successful efforts to reform the educational system would come only from outside, providing of course that some mechanism could be found to activate this renewal. The mechanism they selected was choice, and once set in place, they intended for it to unleash the self-renewing process of change without their direct intervention. In other words, they identified what they thought were important levers to precipitate system response. Their actions were deliberate, strategic, and rational—rational in Simon's sense of maximizing their valued outcomes insofar as their knowledge permitted (Simon, 1957, pp. 76–77).

In sum, through our observations of the entrepreneurial and innovation processes, we came to view them as chaotic and ratio-nal, serendipitous and planned, dynamic and structured. While under certain conditions Kingdon's model may shed some light at the global level, ours may be more appropriate for the micro, group, and structural levels of analysis, and for the global level as well. The major challenge has been to understand this complexity as a coevolutionary process (Jantsch, 1980) interconnecting micro and macro levels, enfolding parts into the whole and the whole into parts (Bohm, 1980). We should also point out that a chaotic system is not an anarchy. A chaotic system is a nonlinear system involving states of highly stable organization separated by regions of turbulence or "chaos." It is a system that produces radical transformations researchers and practitioners have yet to appreciate. Because we are just now learning how to identify this underlying order, we should be careful in attributing randomness to those processes that we do not fully comprehend.

Radical Change by Consensus

Wildavsky (1982; Coyle and Wildavsky, 1987) posits that radical policy change in the United States occurs when the elites of three political cultures find an integrative solution that meets their preferences. (They do not need to agree on why the radical change meets their desires, but only that it does.) These political cultures—defined as "different shared values justifying social relations . . . [that] orient people to political life" (Coyle and Wildavsky, 1987, p. 3)—are *hierarchical collectivism, competitive individualism,* and *egalitarian collectivism.*

To examine the proposition that the radical change in our study was due to consensus among political cultures, not entrepreneurial design, we first had to identify the three cultures and their positions on public school choice.

The label of hierarchical collectivism, representing support for central authority, seemed to fit the traditional educational groups who sought to maintain their authority over the school system. Regarding themselves as the experts, and annoyed by the intrusion of outsiders into education policy making, traditional educators viewed the policy entrepreneurs' radical ideas as a disruption to institutional stability. Their goal was to shore up the system by adding more resources, not to subject it to competition. Not only would collegial decision making and collaboration among professionals be threatened by such action, or so they thought, but the administrative order necessary to run the schools would be disrupted. They preferred equality before the law to assure predictability in the classroom.

Competitive individualism, which seeks to minimize authority through self-regulation, and egalitarian collectivism, which rejects authority in favor of equal influence for each person, were both represented among advocates of public school choice. While "individualists believe in equality of opportunity to undergird competition," and "egalitarians believe in more equal conditions to equal outcomes" (Coyle and Wildavsky, 1987, p. 4), each culture was represented in the policy entrepreneurs' deliberations on public school choice. Indeed, two of the four major rationales policy entrepreneurs used to justify their views drew directly from these two cultures.

Although there was consensus between representatives of competitive individualism and egalitarian collectivism, to what extent did a larger consensus emerge with the culture of hierarchical collectivism? There was a shift toward the benefits of public school choice among educators who came to realize that it could enhance their status as professionals by removing outside mandates and increasing their professional autonomy. However, although this argument did attract some adherents, it did not convince mainstream associations of teachers, superintendents, and school boards to change their views. While overt resistance was muted from the second half of 1985 through the end of the 1988 legislative session, traditional educational groups never did come to view public school choice in terms of what they would gain. They saw themselves as being outflanked in a political process by a governor who had "rewritten the book on strategy." Reluctant participants in the change process at that point, they saw greater harm in overtly opposing public school choice than in waiting and hoping for its demise. Thus, as a whole, we found little evidence that radical change by consensus could account for the changes in Minnesota educational policy.

Radical Change by Learning

Sabatier and Jenkins-Smith (1993) maintain that the interaction of specialists within a policy community can produce radical change if conditions are right. They refer to this interaction as an *advocacy coalition,* a group of people "who share a particular belief system—that is, a set of basic values, causal assumptions, and problem perceptions—and who show a nontrivial degree of coordinated activity over time" (p. 25). Such a coalition can include researchers, analysts, journalists, administrators, interest group members, and elected officials. It generates technical information and conducts formal policy analysis in an attempt to document its viewpoint persuasively. Although interaction between advocacy coalitions often produces a "dialogue of the deaf" (p. 48), it is possible for different advocacy coalitions to have a productive analytical debate and learn from each other. One advocacy coalition may demonstrate such deficiencies in another's core beliefs that a systemwide shift occurs, usually at the instigation of system leaders. However, changes of this magnitude usually require more than internal learning; they tend to be accompanied by an exogenous shock that alters the resources and opportunities of the various coalitions (Sabatier and Jenkins-Smith, 1993, p. 220).

To what extent does the Sabatier and Jenkins-Smith model of change by learning account for the radical change in Minnesota? The advocacy coalition approach to change has much in common with the entrepreneurial approach we describe. Both theories set out to capture the dynamics of change and take a long-term view of the change process. Both connect what heretofore have been separate research streams (such as policy initiation and agenda setting), although the entrepreneurial theory extends to all phases of the policy process. Both assume intentionality and interest in analysis on the part of the social actors. Both stress the importance of ideas and policy proposals, distinct from narrowly defined political interests, as having a major role in driving the change process. Both focus on policy systems or subsystems rather than specific governmental institutions to understand change. Both include actors from all levels of government, including idea generators and disseminators beyond the confines of the government structure. Both deal with the institutional framework of change, including social actors' ability to manipulate other social actors and institutional rules to achieve their policy objectives. Both point to the way policy-oriented learning within coalitions documents performance gaps in the existing system and promotes understanding of the reasons for such gaps. And both acknowledge the importance of factors in the system's environment. It is even entirely appropriate to describe the policy entrepreneurs' network as an advocacy coalition, as defined by Sabatier and Jenkins-Smith (1993). In these instances, the two approaches inform rather than compete with each other.

However, there are some important differences between the two theories. The advocacy coalition approach treats the coalition as the principal vehicle of change, aggregating individuals into a manageable number of units. In radical change by entrepreneurial design, we consider multiple units of analysis—the idea, the group, and the community, as well as the individual entrepreneur and the institutional context. The advocacy coalition approach uses the concept of a belief system as the "template on which change is measured" (Jenkins-Smith and Sabatier, 1993, p. 55), while the entrepreneurial model considers the different manifestations of an idea as it evolves through the innovation process as the template to measure change.

The entrepreneurial approach views change, especially radical change, as a cognitive and political process. The competition among social actors (individuals or coalitions) is viewed as a struggle for ideas and the authoritarian establishment of values to defend those ideas. Policy entrepreneurs are expected to use the instruments of government to support their values and ideas. In contrast, under certain conditions, the advocacy coalition approach expects change to emerge from a productive analytical debate between members of different coalitions. "The indicator of such a debate is that one or both coalitions are led to alter policy core aspects of their belief systems—or at least very important secondary aspects—as a result of an observed dialogue rather than a change in external conditions" (Jenkins-Smith and Sabatier, 1993, p. 48). Simply put, if learning through dialogue can occur, beliefs can change. If beliefs can change, policies can change.

The question before us is whether the radical change in our study occurred through learning or through politics. If learning was the main factor, we would see change facilitated by analysis and exchange of scientific information across coalitions. Politics, on the other hand, would show the policy entrepreneurs working to convince power holders to back their position, displacing the dominant coalition's ideas and beliefs.

The three necessary conditions for learning between coalitions are a moderate level of conflict, an issue with widely accepted theories and quantitative indicators, and a professional forum in which experts from competing coalitions are required to justify their claims before their peers (Jenkins-Smith and Sabatier, 1993, p. 48). One could argue that the first and third conditions were met in the Minnesota example. The level of conflict, while high during the 1985 legislative session, was considerably reduced thanks to the governor's intervention in subsequent years. Additionally, the Governor's Discussion Group provided a forum for both coalitions to share technical information and conduct analyses. During the eighteen-month existence of the GDG, supporters and opponents of public school choice met to exchange information, discuss the givens of the situation, interpret data on educational outcomes, and debate educational reforms.

The second condition, however, is problematic. The issue of public school choice, like other complex issues, is subject to a great deal of uncertainty. Reliant on data and theories that are generally qualitative and subjective, research on school choice provokes enormous debate. Few deny public school choice is an interesting concept, but many question the extent to which research provides evidence that choice is sound public policy. In such instances, according to Jenkins-Smith and Sabatier (1993):

> The complexity and uncertainty are sufficient to admit wholly divergent belief systems whose epistemological foundations are so dissimilar that common bases for evaluating the validity of policy-relevant assertions are lacking entirely. On issues characterized by such fundamental differences in basic beliefs, analysts cannot resolve competing analytical claims by recourse to a common body of analytic knowledge and technique. In effect, there is no overlap—no common ground—across belief systems from which to develop consensual resolution of competing analytical claims. Resolution of the policy debate in such situations awaits change imposed on belief systems, typically from outside the subsystem, such as turnover in system participants through large-scale electoral change [p. 51].

Despite the belief system differences between the coalitions for and against school choice, it might be argued that learning did occur in Minnesota. After all, participants in the GDG signed the final proposal recommending the voluntary extension of choice to all school districts and choice for at-risk children. That agreement suggested at least some changes in secondary aspects of traditional educators' belief system. (Sabatier and Jenkins-Smith (1993) note that learning rarely alters a coalition's core beliefs—and certainly not in such a short period of time.) Despite the brief discussion period, traditional educators acknowledged that they did learn from the policy entrepreneurs and some 6M coalition members did lessen their open resistance to choice initiatives. The traditional educational groups even muted their criticism of public school choice to the point where they had to be encouraged to testify at hearings on it during the 1988 legislative session.

Observing the maneuvering by supporters and opponents of public school choice, however, we are led to question whether any real learning occurred, even at the secondary level. From our vantage point, the process looked very political: the governor's not-so-gentle insistence that all groups stay at the GDG table, which minimized their ability to try end runs in the legislature; the GDG focus on values and fundamentals rather than analytical models and data; the threat from the head of a teachers' union to boycott businesses supporting public school choice; the commissioner's negotiations with the teachers' unions to keep them participating in the GDG; the policy entrepreneurs' threat to bolt the GDG if the idea of public school choice did not stay on the table; the governor's strategy to avoid open confrontation with educators while quietly moving behind the scenes to push public school choice onto the legislative agenda; educators' lessened concern for the consequences of public school choice after the results of the first experiments were reported; and the policy entrepreneurs' continued strategizing to convince the public and its legislators that choice had merit.

We believe these contests reveal more power and politics than learning. While it was the intent of the entrepreneurs to demonstrate major deficiencies in traditional educators' core beliefs so that the majority would acknowledge these deficiencies, they still saw the contest as a political one and developed their change strategies accordingly. Their intent was to use politics to displace traditional ideas, not to enable others to learn from a dialogue. Their interactions with educators over the years had convinced them that dialogue and learning were neither feasible nor desirable. Unwilling to compromise on the fundamentals, they had no intention of giving in on any of their core or even secondary beliefs. They expected and intended that educators would do the changing.

Thus, we concur with the Sabatier and Jenkins-Smith (1993) assessment that there are limits on the extent to which policy actors in competing advocacy coalitions will learn and change their beliefs. The central purpose of an advocacy coalition is not to second-guess its own belief system, but rather to establish or maintain the dominance of its policy ideas. We also find our view more in line with Baumgartner and Jones (1991), who propose that change depends on the extent to which political elites play a major role in forming the coalition and persuading interests to participate. We agree that it is very likely that policy change depends on some political elite's willingness to sponsor and encourage a coalition of interests. And we also concur that the role of policy entrepreneurs and their political will is particularly important for a coalition trying to displace the dominant group.

Requirements of Good Process Theory

Our theory has held up against competing explanations of radical change. Next, we examine its utility and explanatory power against the essential components of good process theory. According to Mohr (1982), process theory deals with discrete states and events that produce a final cause. Time-ordering among the events is expected to be critical for the outcome to occur. Thus, good process theories have three essential components: "(1) necessary conditions and (2) necessary probabilistic processes, which together form the core of the theory, and (3) external, directional forces that function to move the focal unit and conditions about in a characteristic way, often herding them into mutual proximity" (Mohr, 1982, p. 45).

A *necessary condition* is a precursor for the outcome of interest. Thus, process theory depends on the rearrangement or combination of two or more discrete elements to produce the outcome. To understand the outcome, we have to understand what elements have combined. We also understand that the precursor is not sufficient for the outcome. The combination of elements is governed by the laws of chance such that the outcome is produced at least some proportion of the time, but not all the time. Finally, for an outcome to occur, we need a compelling flow of action, an external directional force that explains the outcome.

How does our theory meet these criteria? Table C.1 identifies the criteria and the basic elements of our model.

We begin with the two processes of policy innovation and policy entrepreneurship. Although they appear to be independent,

Table C.1. Application of Mohr's Framework for Assessing Process Theory.

Theory	Focal Unit	Outcome	Necessary Conditions	External Directional Force	Probabilistic Processes	Definition of Outcome
Innovation Process	New Idea	Innovation	1. Idea's compatibility with context 2. Movement through institutional steps	Entrepreneur	Idea competes in marketplace of ideas	Implementation of innovative idea into practice
Entrepreneurial Process	Entrepreneur	Innovation	1. Tenacious, cognitively complex individuals with long time frame who seek change 2. Interventions and strategies to activate and align social energy	Ecology of support for entrepreneurs	Conflict with those who resist ideas to overcome resistance	Implementation of innovative idea into practice

they work in tandem toward the same outcome—innovation, defined as the implementation of an innovative idea into practice.

The focal unit of the innovation process is the novel idea. There are two necessary conditions: the new idea must be compatible with its context, and it must move through the steps required by the governance structure. No idea evolves much beyond its initial formulation unless it fits its context and meets some need or solves some problem. Neither can the idea become part of operational practice unless it has jumped the hurdles of the governance structure to become a proposal, bill, law, and program. All new ideas by legislative design are forced through these same stages. The external force is provided by the policy entrepreneur, who activates and aligns the social energy to propel the idea forward. The resulting competition in the marketplace of ideas is a probabilistic process governed by chance. Many ideas surface as policy solutions; only some survive.

For the entrepreneurial process, the entrepreneur is the focal unit of analysis. There are two necessary conditions: tenacious, cognitively complex individuals with long time frames who seek radical change, and the design of interventions and strategies to generate and align social energy around a new idea. The directional force is provided by the ecology of relations and the support generated by the entrepreneurs' communities. The probabilistic process that governs here is the conflict generated with those who oppose the new idea. Not all resistance will be overcome. Not all entrepreneurs will be successful.

Having identified focal units, outcomes and their definitions, necessary conditions, external directional forces, and probabilistic process, we believe our theory of radical change by design meets Mohr's criteria for good process theory. We view the radical change process as a composite of forces. Motivated by ideas and strategies of design, policy entrepreneurs activate energy and align it to push their new idea into practice. They seek to establish their idea as a better fit with its context and the problems it is attempting to address compared to other proposals competing in the marketplace of ideas. They also design interventions and formulate political strategies to overcome the resistance of their opponents. If successful, their ideas follow a trajectory through proposal, bill, and law to implemented program and accepted practice. Thus, we view policy entrepreneurs as designers of the twin process of innovation and entrepreneurship. They act as intentional, purposive agents who seek solutions to complex problems based on their analysis and study. At the same time, policy entrepreneurs are political actors who engage in power struggles with the dominant advocacy coalition they seek to displace. The question is not whether public entrepreneurs are rational or political. Rather, we ask under what conditions they are rational and political.

Implications and Future Research

We believe the theory of radical change by entrepreneurial design has many implications for future research. Drawing on our discussion in the Appendix of the limitations of case studies, the first is the question of generalizability. Although our theory has evolved to explain and understand educational policy change in a particular situation in Minnesota, we think it is robust enough to generalize to other settings and policy systems. In fact, Chapter Nine specifies how it could be transferred by practitioners who take a capacity-building approach. We invite researchers to apply and assess the theory in other settings and policy domains as well. No doubt there will be modifications; the order of reality is far more subtle and elusive than researchers' models can capture. Yet we hope that we have distilled the essence of how to effect radical change by entrepreneurial design and that others will find our propositions useful in drawing their own maps of change.

In particular, we believe the model can offer insights for wider policy arenas. At the national level, we see policy actors attempting to break out of the constraints of institutional order in health care and environmental concerns. And at the global level, international bodies are forging new policies to govern their relations beyond the constraints of nation states. We would not be surprised to find policy entrepreneurs activating and aligning the energy behind some of these novel ideas.

It also appears that our comprehensive approach is useful, demonstrating the benefits of conducting research on multiple units of analysis and at multiple levels of analysis. The approach has been promising for us and we highly recommend it to others. Taking a systems approach to research may be as important for the researcher as taking a systems approach to change is for the policy entrepreneur.

Now that we have identified some of the key variables in the change process and explored their relationships and dynamics, it may be appropriate to move from a qualitative analysis to a more quantitative one. Our propositions can be tested in other sites and settings, and we look forward to the results of this research. For example, one could explore the proposed developmental model of public entrepreneurship. Alternatively, one could examine the conditions likely to produce modest change versus those likely to be transformative, and so on.

Conclusion: Chaos and Policy Change

We leave the reader with one final and very intriguing implication from our research. Although the comparison enters the metaphoric level of discourse, there are parallels between our conclusions and chaos theory (Prigogine and Stengers, 1984). We define chaos theory in very simple terms as global order out of local chaos. Prigogine and his collaborators, working on a biochemical theory of dissipative structures, have found that *open* (far-from-equilibrium) systems can defy the second law of thermodynamics. Through a process of energy generation and fluctuation, these systems can dissipate entropy, and make a transformational leap to stable, more complex forms of order.

We draw on Bradley and Roberts (1989) for a brief description of how this occurs: As energy fluctuates, the dissipative system creates a catalytic element in a process Prigogine calls *auto-catalysis*. The new catalytic element prompts additional fluctuations and moves the system into a very high energy state. At some point the energy fluctuations no longer average out. Rather, they are amplified to a new and critical level called the *bifurcation point*. At the bifurcation point, the system can jump in any one of a number of different directions. Prigogine maintains that chance determines the order attained.

Beyond the bifurcation point exists a new order that is discontinuous with its predecessor. This new order is stable and resistant until a new round of energy fluctuations begins. To maintain its new order or form, the system must continue to disperse the entropy that builds up. But transformation can occur again with another round of intense energy fluctuations. If this occurs, the system may jump to another new order.

Extending this principle to a policy system, we see the entrepreneurs as auto-catalytic agents. Their goal was to destabilize the existing educational system, counteract the forces that maintained a stable equilibrium, and create such perturbations and oscillations that it would bifurcate and jump to an entirely different order.

If this analogy holds, policy systems must be assumed to share an important property of chaotic systems: when such a system enters a phase transition (bifurcation), no one can say what it will look like once it stabilizes. Chaos theory holds that we can not predict order at the point of a bifurcation. At bifurcation all possible forms of order are theoretically possible—including the real possibility of dissolution. Thus, when policy entrepreneurs are successful as auto-catalytic agents in creating high-energy fluctuations in the policy system and moving some of their ideas into practice, they, along with everyone else, will be unable to predict exactly what the system will look like in the future once these changes coalesce and crystallize into a new order.

This perhaps explains why the policy entrepreneurs were careful not to describe the innovation process as controlled or managed. Understanding it as a long-term effort that was difficult to predict, they saw the disorder of a chaotic system. "You can't manage the process," they warned us on many occasions. On the other hand, we saw them take advantage of, and even create, windows of opportunity. They intervened in the policy system at critical points when it was vulnerable and moving into crisis (instability), and in so doing, capitalized on its increased potential for change. From this perspective, change by design, by intentional action, must work within the constraints of the natural dynamics of a system. As the policy entrepreneurs appreciated, success in design presupposes an understanding of the system's fundamentals. Our efforts in this research have aimed to contribute to such an understanding.

Research Design

We began our research with the question "How do innovations develop from concept to implemented reality?" Our interest was in investigating how innovations actually emerge, develop, grow, or terminate over time. We selected longitudinal field study design (Kerlinger, 1973) and decided to take a process approach (Mohr, 1982; King, 1990). In contrast to the variance approach to innovation (Downs, 1976; Rogers and Shoemaker, 1971), our goal was to understand *how* innovation occurred, not to determine *what* caused it. The process approach was attractive because it gave us a moving picture rather than a snapshot of innovation. Our interest was in the ebb and flow of events and how their sequence and timing might affect the probability of innovation and entrepreneurship in a system. Taking the analogy of cooking, we sought to identify not just the ingredients in the recipe but how the ingredients combined, at what times, and in what order.

The process approach challenged us to conduct research in real time. Retrospective case studies suffer from participants' memory losses, distortions, and after-the-fact sense making. Furthermore, removed in time from actual events, we would not have been involved in the actual innovation process but rather in a reconstruction based on secondary sources. The fewer time-imposed filters of the process approach would permit us to identify and track events as they occurred. We came to appreciate the process approach for its reliance on the laws of chance to make the connections among the elements and events of the innovation process. Given the laws of chance, we did not expect to find innovation all of the time, only when the necessary elements came together (Mohr, 1982, p. 38).

The process perspective on innovation, employing a much longer time horizon than the snapshot of events characteristic of cross-sectional analysis, also demanded a special set of research skills—those of the social anthropologist and social phenomenologist rather than those of the regression analyst. The skills ranged from interviewing, participant observation, and the recording and analysis of nonverbal communication to artifactual analysis, such as content analysis and documentary analysis.

Data Collection

Data collection began in spring 1983 and ended in fall 1988. We employed multiple data collection methods, both qualitative and quantitative: formal interviews, informal contacts, participant observation, archival research, questionnaires, and three psychometric tests given to the policy entrepreneurs.

Formal Interviews. We conducted 134 formal interviews with the policy entrepreneurs, the governor and his staff, the commissioner of education and her staff, executives from governmental agencies, legislators and their staff, educators and lobbyists (representing teachers' unions and associations for primary and secondary school principals and superintendents), parents, school board members, members of various grassroots organizations and interest groups, and the media. The number of interviews breaks out as follows:

Role Matrix of Interviewees

Type	Number of Individuals	Number of Interviews
Executive agency official	6	35
Executive agency staff	11	18
Policy entrepreneur	6	25
Interest group member	15	20
Interest group lobbyist	5	5
Legislator and staff	14	18
Informed other	9	13
Media representative	4	4
Total	70	138

Informal Contacts. We supplemented our formal interviews with frequent informal contacts. Only a twenty-minute drive from the State Capitol, and in close proximity to most of the major actors of the innovation process, we kept up with people and events through phone calls, short meetings, and occasional breakfasts, lunches, or dinners. At other times we traveled with them to educational events and interacted with them at social gatherings, and in the case of the second author, even took a course at the University of Minnesota taught by one of the policy entrepreneurs. Seizing all opportunities to get to know them, understand their ideas, and capture their views of the innovation process, we attended their press conferences, community meetings, legislative hearings, speeches, and presentations.

Participant Observation. Beyond these informal contacts, we were participant observers in the Governor's Discussion Group (GDG), described in Chapter Two. This gave us a natural setting in which to observe the interaction of all of the major participants, including the governor, the commissioner, the policy entrepreneurs, and the formal groups representing educators, as well as parents and community members.

Archival Research. We scanned documents and records from many sources. We studied files from the Minnesota Department of Education, including the commissioner's calendar and meeting minutes, as well as letters and memos. We collected articles and editorials from local, state, and national print media. Colleagues from other departments and universities, who also were observing the innovation process, were generous in sharing their work with us. Our files contain position papers, publications, work in progress, even parts of speeches drafted by the policy entrepreneurs for politicians such as Governor Perpich, Gary Hart, and Ronald Reagan. We have reports from major interest groups in education and legislative records of education bills introduced and passed during this period. We also have several dissertations written about the local community and its support of innovation and change during the period of our study. Besides reading, we watched television debates and heard radio programs on the school choice issue presented by the policy entrepreneurs and other participants in the policy innovation process.

Questionnaires. In order to gather data more efficiently and conserve scarce interview time, we used questionnaires to collect general data and demographic information about the entrepreneurs. The instrument included items about educational attainment, work experience and career path, organizational affiliations, and areas of policy expertise. In addition, it asked policy entrepreneurs to describe their major life accomplishments.

We gave a second questionnaire to leaders and members of education groups to assess the influence of the policy entrepreneurs. Twenty-two returned the instrument, including thirteen GDG members, two Minnesota State Planning Agency staff members, four state educational leaders, and one lobbyist for an educational interest group.

We sent a third questionnaire to GDG members. Having access to the group's reports, meeting agendas, and minutes during their nineteen-month deliberation, we also wanted an assessment of the group's process and its accomplishments. The questionnaire went to all sixty-one participants, who represented twenty-four educational policy stakeholders (that is, groups and organizations with stakes or major concerns about the issue). Most stakeholder groups had two or three participating members in the GDG; the range was from three groups with only a single participant to one group with six. Each stakeholder group formally designated a representative and, when multiple members were involved, an alternate. We received at least one questionnaire from each stakeholder group. All three of these questionnaires are available from the authors.

Psychometric Tests. We administered a battery of psychometric tests to the entrepreneurs: the California Psychological Inventory (Gough, 1987); the Myers-Briggs Type Indicator (Myers and McCaulley, 1985); and the Loevinger Sentence Completion Test for Ego Development (Loevinger, 1976; Loevinger, Wessler and Redmore, 1970). The analysis of the psychometric data was done by psychologists trained in the instrumentation. (See Chapter Six for a more complete discussion of these tests). Three of the six policy entrepreneurs completed the test battery. Those who refused gave reasons such as "I don't believe in test batteries" or "I am too busy at this time to take the tests." The three who did not fill out the assessment instruments were also participants in the initial development of the innovative idea. Educational leaders viewed two of the individuals as sources of innovative ideas and key players in mobilizing support for enactment of the ideas in the legislature.

The third individual was described as a passionate spokesperson for public school choice and a key strategist in moving the idea into practice.

The lack of test battery data from the three individuals is unfortunate, but not unanticipated. It is rare to collect such data in policy studies. In fact, we have found no other research that has done so. The scarcity of this type of data reflects the bias in political science, which tends to view personal characteristics and individual profiles as insignificant in political life. With the exception of the study of the American presidency and its counterparts in other countries (Neustadt, 1960; Bunce, 1981), individual actors are not treated as central participants in the policy drama. And furthermore, the paucity of data gathered tends to rely on retrospective, biographical, and psychohistorical methods. (See, for example, Lewis, 1980; Ramamurti, 1986a, 1986b; and Doig and Hargrove, 1987.) Given this backdrop, we were indeed fortunate to have collected these data at all.

Data Analysis

Data analysis in studies using primarily qualitative data consists of three concurrent streams of activity: data reduction, data displays, and drawing and verifying conclusions (Miles and Huberman, 1984). The ideal model is to intertwine all three streams at the same time when conducting field research. For analytical purposes, each one will be addressed separately.

Data Reduction. "Data reduction refers to the process of selecting, focusing, simplifying, abstracting, and transforming the 'raw' data that appear in written-up field notes" (Miles and Huberman, 1984, p. 21). Raw data in qualitative research appear in the form of words, unlike quantitative data that appear in the form of numbers. The challenge to the qualitative researcher is to take these words and transform them in a way that "sharpens, sorts, focuses, discards, and organizes" (p. 21) them so that the researcher can draw and verify conclusions. Data reduction can take many forms, ranging from contact summary sheets, document summary forms, codes (an abbreviation or symbol applied to words, sentences, or paragraphs to classify the words into categories), reflective remarks, and memos (write-ups that theorize about ideas and codes as one is writing).

Our data collection process used many of these forms: coding transcripts, field notes, archival materials, and questionnaires; writing summaries about the data; grouping and clustering codes to identify themes and patterns; and memo writing to ourselves to help us interpret and integrate the data in more general terms. Our most valuable source was the Miles and Huberman text, *Qualitative Data Analysis* (1984).

Data Displays. A display, according to Miles and Huberman, is an "organized assembly of information" (p. 21). Displays can range from matrices, graphs, and networks, to tables, charts, and causal maps. All are designed to organize information in a way that is more accessible than the pages and pages of field notes. Since information is presented in compressed form, it is easier for the researcher to identify and summarize common themes and trends, and eliminate redundant or extraneous information.

We utilized different types of data displays. For example, we kept a chronology to track the key events in the course of the innovation. An event was defined as a change in the innovative idea, people, transactions, contexts, or outcomes during the innovation process. These events were listed and arranged in time to produced a chronological history of the innovation process. We also devised a role matrix to help us categorize the different types of activities the policy entrepreneurs engaged in while working the innovation process. This matrix can be found in Chapter Three, while the chronology joins the many other displays that were only used to aid us in our data reduction and interpretation.

Drawing and Verifying Conclusions. A third data analysis activity involves drawing conclusions and verifying them. The researcher must say what the data mean, by noting regularities and patterns, and offering explanations and interpretations of the findings. We offer many conclusions throughout the book. These conclusions, while tentative when initially drawn, became more grounded in field data as the study progressed. We also broke the report into two sections. The first, representing first-order analysis, is a narrative of the case in the terms the participants used. The second represents second-order analysis, and explains the first-order analysis in more conceptual terms (Van Maanen, 1979). Then it presents our final conclusions from the five-year field study, attempting to give some theoretical coherence to the overall data and advice to practitioners.

We submitted our conclusions to verification based on the recommendations of Miles and Huberman (1984). Both of us were involved in all facets of the data collection, data reduction, and data analysis. Having two researchers enabled us to cross-check our data, debate our interpretations, and consider alternative and competing explanations of what was happening. As an additional safeguard, we followed the procedures of triangulation whenever we could, collecting different sources of evidence and using different methods to check the validity of our data. For example, upon learning of the centrality of the change agents during interviews with the commissioner, we sought verification from other key educational informants through the use of questionnaires. Or in another instance, developing psychological profiles of the policy entrepreneurs from test instruments, we compared them to our field observations of actual behavior. We constantly searched for negative evidence, asking ourselves if there were data inconsistent with the profiles.

Others provided additional validity checks. As luck would have it, researchers from other departments of the University of Minnesota were also collecting data on the issue of choice in the schools. These researchers graciously read and critiqued the tentative conclusions in our working papers, commenting not only on the facts of the study, but also on our assumptions and interpretations of events. Members of the Minnesota Innovations Research Project also critiqued our work. We attended some of their regular meetings and conferences to present summaries of our data and offer tentative conclusions. Their challenges and cautions helped us avoid some of the pitfalls of qualitative research, such as *going native* (losing the research perspective and being co-opted into the perceptions and explanations of local informants) or falling into the *wholistic fallacy* (seeing events as more patterned and regular than they really are).

Going native had the potential of being a serious problem in this research. The first author was very aware of the danger when she met with the superintendent (later commissioner) of education for the first time. Dynamic and energetic, the superintendent would eventually be described as a charismatic leader. Her accomplishments in her district held everyone in awe, including the members of the original research team. Aware of the threat to researcher objectivity in this situation, the first author brought in a noted expert on charisma, Dr. Raymond Bradley, to serve as a consultant to the project both at the school district level and the state level. He helped verify the presence of charisma in the case of the school district (Roberts, 1985) and the lack of it at the state level (Roberts and Bradley, 1988), and served as an additional validity check for the project.

The informants themselves provided another validity check, reviewing our preliminary papers and reports. For example, the policy entrepreneurs critiqued our paper for a conference and noted omissions and discrepancies in our data. When these discrepancies could not be reconciled, we returned to the field to collect additional data. Some of the differences were over facts of the case, others were due to differing interpretations. We corrected what we believed were errors of omission and commission, and retained our interpretations where we thought appropriate, even when the policy entrepreneurs did not share them. In one instance, this feedback was very important in helping us realign our focus. The policy entrepreneurs accused us of seeing more regularity in the data than the initial phases of the innovation process actually included. Having framed the research to study how the process was being managed, we were looking for the organization sponsoring the change. Thanks to their input, we became more aware of the differences between innovation by management design and innovation by legislative design, and of the fluidity of the innovation process at the state level. We were able to reorient our research accordingly.

Limitations of the Study

The large number of participants of this five-year field study placed constraints on the authors' ability to talk to everyone and to observe all details of the process. Interviewing every person on a regular basis was impossible. While every effort was made to avoid bias and to seek contact with major participants over the course of the five years, it is likely that we have missed a number of people, details, and events. For example, while we enjoyed free and unrestrained access to all formal GDG meetings, we knew that at times some of the participants had informal contacts that may have influenced activities within the group. Without direct access to this information, it was difficult to assess how these outside interactions may have influenced the GDG. Our noncontinuous presence at the state capitol and the legislature also forced us to deduce what was happening when we were not there.

In addition, any researcher who embarks on a field setting is likely "to create social behavior in others that would not have ordinarily occurred." Thus, we have, according to Miles and Huberman (1984), "two possible sources of bias here: (a) the effects of the researcher on the site and (b) the effects of the site on the researcher" (p. 232). We have tried to build in safeguards against self-delusion, researcher bias, and researcher effects by employing second readers, outside consultants, two field researchers, and informant feedback, and by following advice outlined in the text (pp. 233–234). However, there are no guarantees that we were able to avoid all the potential pitfalls and errors of qualitative research. We suggest that the reader beware.

References

Aberbach, J. D., Putnam, R. D., and Rockman, B. A. *Bureaucrats and Politicians in Western Democracies*. Cambridge, Mass.: Harvard University Press, 1981.

Abernathy, W. J., and Clark, K. B. "Innovation: Mapping the Winds of Creative Destruction." *Research Policy,* 1985, *14,* 3–22.

Ackerman, L. S. "The Flow State: A New View of Organizations and Managing." In J. D. Adams (ed.), *Transforming Work*. Alexandria, Va.: Miles River Press, 1984.

Adams, J. D. (ed.). *Transforming Work*. Alexandria, Va.: Miles River Press, 1984.

Adams, J. L. *Conceptual Blockbusting*. Stanford, Calif.: Stanford Alumni Association, 1974.

Adams, J. L. *The Care and Feeding of Ideas*. Stanford, Calif.: Stanford Alumni Association, 1986.

Alinsky, S. *Reveille for Radicals*. New York: Vintage Books, 1989a. (Originally published 1946.)

Alinsky, S. *Rules for Radicals*. New York: Vintage Books, 1989b. (Originally published 1971.)

Anderson, W. R., and Grossman, N. B. *The Governor's Commission on Education for Economic Growth*. St. Paul, Minn.: 1984.

Angle, H. L. "Psychology and Organizational Innovation." In A. H. Van de Ven, H. L. Angle, and M. S. Poole (eds.), *Research on the Management of Innovation*. New York: HarperCollins, 1989.

Angle, H. L., and Van de Ven, A. H. "Suggestions for Managing the Innovation Journey." In A. H. Van de Ven, H. L. Angle, and M. S. Poole (eds.), *Research on the Management of Innovation*. New York: HarperCollins, 1989.

Argyris, C., and Schön, D. *Organizational Learning*. Reading, Mass.: Addison-Wesley, 1978.

Bardach, E. *The Implementation Game: What Happens After a Bill Becomes a Law*. Cambridge, Mass.: MIT Press, 1977.

Barnard, C. I. *Functions of the Executive*. Cambridge, Mass.: Harvard University Press, 1938.

Barron, F. M., and Harrington, D. M. "Creativity, Intelligence and Personality." In M. R. Rosenzweig and L. W. Porter (eds.), *Annual Review of Psychology*. Vol. 32. Palo Alto, Calif.: Annual Review Press, 1981.

Baumgartner, R. R., and Jones, B. D. "Agenda Dynamics and Policy Subsystems." *Journal of Politics*, 1991, *53*(4), 1044–1074.

Behn, R. D. "Management by Groping Along." *Journal of Policy Analysis and Management*, 1988, 7(4), 643–663.

Bellone, C. J., and Goerl, G. F. "Reconciling Public Entrepreneurship and Democracy." *Public Administration Review*, 1992, *52*(2), 130–134.

Berman, P., and Weiler, D. *The Minnesota Plan: The Design of a New Education System*. Vols. 1 and 2. Berkeley, Calif.: Berman-Weiler Associates, 1984.

Bickel, W. E. "Effective Schools: Knowledge, Dissemination, Inquiry." *Educational Researcher*, 1983, *12*(4), 3–5.

Bird, B. *Entrepreneurial Behavior*. Glenview, Ill.: Scott, Foresman, 1989.

Bobrow, D. B., and Dryzek, J. S. *Policy Analysis by Design*. Pittsburgh, Pa.: University of Pittsburgh Press, 1987.

Bohm, D. *Wholeness and the Implicate Order*. New York: Routledge, 1980.

Bollier, D. *Pioneers of Progress: Policy Entrepreneurs and Community Development*. Vols. 1 and 2. Somerville, Mass.: Jobs for the Future, 1991.

Bosso, C. *Pesticides and Politics*. Pittsburgh, Pa.: University of Pittsburgh Press, 1987.

Boyer, E. L. *High School: A Report on Secondary Education in America*. New York: HarperCollins, 1985.

Bradley, R. T. *Charisma and Social Structure: A Study of Love and Power, Wholeness and Transformation*. New York: Paragon House, 1987.

Bradley, R. T., and Pribram, K. H. "Optimality in Biosocial Collectives." In D. S. Levine and W. R. Elsberry (eds.), *Optimality in Biological and Artificial Networks*. Hillsdale, N.J.: Erlbaum, 1996.

Bradley, R. T., and Roberts, N. C. "Relational Dynamics of Charismatic Organization: The Complementarity of Love and Power." *World Futures*, 1989, *27*, 87–123.

Brookfield, S. D. *Developing Critical Thinkers: Challenging Adults to Explore Alternative Ways of Thinking and Acting*. San Francisco: Jossey-Bass, 1987.

Bunce, V. *Do New Leaders Make a Difference? Executive Succession and Public Policy Under Capitalism and Socialism*. Princeton, N.J.: Princeton University Press, 1981.

Burns, R., and Stalker, G. M. *The Management of Innovation*. London: Tavistock, 1961.

Burnside, R. M. "Improving Corporate Climates for Creativity." In M. A. West and J. L. Farr (eds.), *Innovation and Creativity at Work: Psychological and Organizational Strategies*. New York: Wiley, 1990.

Bushe, G. R., and Shani, A. B. *Parallel Learning Structures: Increasing Innovation in Bureaucracies.* Reading, Mass.: Addison-Wesley, 1991.

Caldeira, G. A., and Wright, J. R. "Organized Interests and Agenda Setting in the U.S. Supreme Court." *American Political Science Review,* 1988, *82,* 1109–1127.

California Psychological Inventory. *Test Report.* Palo Alto, Calif.: Consulting Psychologists Press, 1988.

Campbell, J. *Collapse of an Industry.* Ithaca, N.Y.: Cornell University Press, 1988.

Carlson, S. "Students Report Opposition to Exercising School Options." *St. Paul Pioneer Press,* Feb. 2, 1986, p. 13C.

Caro, R. F. *The Power-Broker: Robert Moses and the Fall of New York.* New York: Vintage Books, 1975.

Cartwright, T. J. "Planning and Chaos Theory." *American Planning Association Journal,* Winter 1991, *44,* 44–56.

Chubb, J. E., and Moe, T. *Politics, Markets, and America's Schools.* Washington, D.C.: Brookings Institution, 1990.

Citizens League. *Issues of the '80s: Enlarging Our Capacity to Adapt.* Minneapolis, Minn.: Citizens League, 1980.

Citizens League. *Citizens League Report: Rebuilding Education to Make It Work.* Minneapolis, Minn.: Citizens League, 1982.

Cobb, R. W., and Elder, C. D. *Participation in American Politics: The Dynamics of Agenda Building.* (2nd ed.) Baltimore: Johns Hopkins University Press, 1983.

Coleman, J. "Private Schools, Public Schools, and the Public Interest." *Public Interest,* 1981, *64,* 19–30.

Cook, M. "At Hometown School Perpich OKs Open School." *St. Paul Pioneer Press and Dispatch,* May 7, 1988, pp. 9A, 12A.

Corson, R. "Choice Ironies: Open Enrollment in Minnesota." *American Prospect,* 1990, *1*(3), 94–99.

Cortner, R. C. "Strategies and Tactics of Litigants in Constitutional Cases." *Journal of Public Law,* 1968, *17,* 287–307.

Cowan, R. B. "Women's Rights Through Litigation: An Examination of the American Civil Liberties Union Women's Rights Project, 1971–1976." *Columbia Human Rights Law Review,* 1976, *8,* 373–412.

Coyle, D., and Wildavsky, A. "Requisites of Radical Reform: Income Maintenance Versus Tax Preferences." *Journal of Policy Analysis and Management,* 1987, *7*(1), 1–16.

Daft, R., and Becker, S. *Innovations in Organizations.* New York: Elsevier Science, 1978.

Dalglish, L. "Reformers Claim School Bill Gutted." *St. Paul Pioneer Press and Dispatch,* May 3, 1987, p. 1B.

Derthick, M., and Quirk, P. *Politics of Deregulation.* Washington, D.C.: Brookings Institution, 1985.

Dery, D. *Problem Definition in Policy Analysis.* Lawrence: University of Kansas Press, 1984.

Doig, J. W., and Hargrove, E. C. (eds.). *Leadership and Innovation.* Baltimore: Johns Hopkins University Press, 1987.

Dornblaser, B. M., Lin, T., and Van de Ven, A. H. "Innovation Outcomes, Learning, and Action Loops." In A. H. Van de Ven, H. L. Angle, and M. S. Poole (eds.), *Research on the Management of Innovation.* New York: HarperCollins, 1989.

Douglas, R. "The Politics of Successful Structural Reform." *Wall Street Journal,* Jan. 17, 1990, p. A20.

Downs, A. *Inside Bureaucracy.* Glenview, Ill.: Scott, Foresman, 1967.

Downs, A. "Up and Down with Ecology: The Issue-Attention Cycle." *Public Interest,* 1972, *28,* 38–50.

Downs, G. W. *Bureaucracy, Innovation, and Public Policy.* Lexington, Mass.: Heath, 1976.

Doyle, P. "Open Enrollment Limited by Distance, Desegregation Policy." *Minneapolis Star and Tribune,* Aug. 6, 1987, pp. 1A, 16A.

Dreyfus, H. L., Dreyfus, S. E., and Athansian, T. *Mind over Machine: The Power of Human Intuition and Expertise in the Era of the Computer.* New York: Free Press, 1986.

Duren, E., and Peek, T. *Berman-Weiler Study of Minnesota Student Performance: A Critical Review.* Minneapolis, Minn.: Center for Urban and Regional Affairs, 1984.

Edwards, G. C. *Implementing Public Policy.* Washington, D.C.: Congressional Quarterly Press, 1980.

Ericsson, K. A., and Smith, J. (eds.). *Toward a General Theory of Expertise: Prospects and Limits.* Cambridge: Cambridge University Press, 1991.

Eyestone, R. "Confusion, Diffusion, and Innovation." *American Political Science Review,* 1977, *71,* 441–447.

Farr, J. L. "Facilitating Individual Role Innovation." In M. A. West and J. L. Farr (eds.), *Innovation and Creativity at Work: Psychological and Organizational Strategies.* New York: Wiley, 1990.

Feistritzer, C. E. *The Condition of Teaching: A State-by-State Analysis.* Princeton, N.J.: Carnegie Foundation, 1983.

Ferman, B., and Levin, M. A. "Dilemmas of Innovation and Accountability: Entrepreneurs and Chief Executives." *Policy Studies Review,* 1987, 7(1), 187–199.

Finn, C. E. "The Drive for Excellence: Moving Toward a Public Consensus." In B. Gross and R. Gross (eds.), *The Great School Debate: Which Way for American Education?* New York: Simon & Schuster, 1985.

Foley, E., Smetanka, M. J., and Sturdevant, L. "Perpich School Plan Meets with Caution, Rejection, and Confusion." *Minneapolis Star and Tribune,* Jan. 5, 1985, p. 8A.

French, J. R., and Raven, B. "The Bases of Social Power." In D. Cartwright (ed.), *Studies in Social Power.* Ann Arbor, Mich.: Institute of Social Research, 1959.

Fritschler, L. *Smoking and Politics.* Upper Saddle River, N.J.: Prentice Hall, 1989.

Galbraith, J. "Designing the Innovating Organization." *Organizational Dynamics,* Summer 1982, *10,* 5–25.

Gerlach, L., and Hines, V. *The Dynamics of Change in America.* Minneapolis: University of Minnesota Press, 1973.

Gifford, J. L., Horan, T. A., and White, L. G. "Dynamics of Policy Change." Unpublished paper, George Mason University, 1992.

Gioia, D. A., and Chittipeddi, K. "Sensemaking and Sensegiving in Strategic Change Initiation." *Strategic Management Journal,* 1991, *12,* 433–448.

Giroux, R. M., and others. "A Review of the Minnesota Business Partnership/Berman-Weiler Associates Student Data–Based Assessment of Minnesota Education." Unpublished paper, 1985.

Gladstein, D., and Caldwell, D. "Boundary Management in New Product Teams." *Academy of Management Proceedings,* 1985, 161–165.

Glaser, B. G., and Strauss, A. L. *The Discovery of Grounded Theory: Strategies for Qualitative Research.* Hawthorne, N.Y.: Aldine, 1967.

Golden, O. "Innovation in Public Sector Human Services Programs: The Implications of Innovation by 'Groping Along.'" *Journal of Policy Analysis and Management,* 1990, *9,* 219–248.

Goldstein, S. G. "Organizational Dualism and Quality Circles." *Academy of Management Review,* 1985, *10,* 504–517.

Golembiewsky, R., Billingsley, K., and Yeager, S. "Measuring Change and Persistence in Human Affairs." *Journal of Applied Behavioral Sciences,* 1976, *12,* 133–154.

Goodlad, J. I. *A Place Called School: Prospects for the Future.* New York: McGraw-Hill, 1984.

Gough, H. G. *California Psychological Inventory: Administrator's Guide.* Palo Alto, Calif.: Consulting Psychologists Press, 1987.

Gray, B. *Collaborating: Finding Common Ground for Multiparty Problems.* San Francisco: Jossey-Bass, 1989.

Gray, V. "Innovation in the States: A Diffusion Study." *American Political Science Review,* 1973, *67,* 1174–1185.

Greenberg, J. *Judicial Process and Social Change: Constitutional Litigation.* St. Paul, Minn.: West, 1977.

Greiner, L. "Evolution and Revolution as Organizations Grow." *Harvard Business Review,* 1972, *50,* 39–46.

Gross, N., Giaquinta, J., and Berstein, M. *Implementing Organizational Innovations.* New York: Basic Books, 1971.

Gross, B., and Gross, R. (eds.). *The Great School Debate: Which Way for American Education?* New York: Simon & Schuster, 1985.

Hanson, R. "Legislative Stalemate Poses Basic Questions." *Minnesota Journal,* 1985, *11*(15), 1–4.

Hanushek, E. A. "Throwing Money at Schools." *Journal of Policy Analysis and Management,* 1981, *1*(1), 19–41.

Heclo, H. *Social Policy in Britain and Sweden.* New Haven, Conn.: Yale University Press, 1974.

Hernes, G. "Structural Change in Social Processes." *American Journal of Sociology,* 1976, *82,* 513–547.

Holyoak, K. "Symbolic Connectionism: Toward Third-Generation Theories of Expertise." In K. A. Ericsson and J. Smith (eds.), *Toward a General Theory of Expertise: Prospects and Limits.* Cambridge: Cambridge University Press, 1991.

Hotakinen, R. "55 percent in State Want Kids to Spend More Time in School." *Minneapolis Star and Tribune,* Aug. 12, 1992, p. 1B.

Hunt, J. G. *Leadership: A New Synthesis.* Newbury Park, Calif.: Sage, 1991.

Ingraham, P. W. "Toward More Systematic Consideration of Policy Design." *Policy Studies Journal,* 1987, *15,* 611–628.

Janis, I. L. *Crucial Decisions.* New York: Free Press, 1989.

Jantsch, E. *The Self-Organizing Universe: Scientific and Human Implications of the Emerging Paradigm of Evolution.* New York: Pergamon/Elsevier, 1980.

Jaques, E. "The Development of Intellectual Capability: A Discussion of Stratified Systems Theory." *Journal of Applied Behavioral Science,* 1986, *22,* 361–383.

Jaques, E. *Requisite Organization: The CEO's Guide to Creative Structure and Leadership.* Arlington, Va.: Cason Hall, 1989.

Jenkins-Smith, H. C., and Sabatier, P. A. "The Dynamics of Policy-Oriented Learning." In P. A. Sabatier and H. C. Jenkins-Smith (eds.), *Policy Change and Learning: An Advocacy Coalition Approach.* Boulder, Colo.: Westview Press, 1993.

Jones, C. *Clean Air.* Pittsburgh, Pa.: University of Pittsburgh Press, 1975.

Kanter, R. M. *Men and Women of the Corporation.* New York: Basic Books, 1977.

Kanter, R. M. *The Change Masters.* New York: Simon & Schuster, 1983.

Kanter, R. M. "When a Thousand Flowers Bloom: Structural, Collective and Social Conditions for Innovation in Organization." In B. M.

Staw and L. L. Cummings (eds.), *Research in Organizational Behavior.* Vol. 10. Greenwich, Conn.: JAI Press, 1988.

Katz, R. "Project Communication and Performance: An Investigation into the Effects of Group Longevity." *Administrative Science Quarterly,* 1982, *27,* 81–104.

Katzenbach, J. R., and Smith, D. K. *The Wisdom of Teams.* New York: Harper-Business, 1994.

Kaufman, H. *Limits of Organizational Change.* University: University of Alabama Press, 1971.

Kellogg, C. F. *NAACP: A History of the National Association for the Advancement of Colored People.* Baltimore: Johns Hopkins University Press, 1967.

Kerlinger, F. N. *Foundations of Behavioral Research.* (2nd ed.) Austin, Texas: Holt, Rinehart & Winston, 1973.

Kidder, T. *The Soul of a New Machine.* New York: Little, Brown, 1981.

Kimberly, J. R. "Managing Innovation." In P. Nystrom and W. Starbuck (eds.), *Handbook of Organizational Design.* Vol. 1. Oxford: Oxford University Press, 1981.

King, N. "Innovation at Work: The Research Literature." In M. A. West and J. L. Farr (eds.), *Innovation and Creativity at Work: Psychological and Organizational Strategies.* New York: Wiley, 1990.

King, N., and Anderson, N. "Innovation in Working Groups." In M. A. West and J. L. Farr (eds.), *Innovation and Creativity at Work: Psychological and Organizational Strategies.* New York: Wiley, 1990.

King, P. J. *Policy Entrepreneurs: Catalysts in the Policy Innovation Process.* Unpublished doctoral dissertation, University of Minnesota, 1988.

King, P. J., and Roberts, N. C. "An Investigation into the Personality Profile of Policy Entrepreneurs." *Public Productivity and Management Review,* 1992, *16,* 173–190.

Kingdon, J. W. *Agendas, Alternatives, and Public Policies.* New York: Little, Brown, 1984.

Kluger, R. *Simple Justice: The History of* Brown v. Board of Education *and the Black American Struggle for Equality.* New York: Knopf, 1976.

Kuhn, T. S. *The Structure of Scientific Revolutions.* (2nd ed.) Chicago: University of Chicago Press, 1970.

Lambright, W. H. *Technology Transfer to Cities.* Boulder, Colo.: Westview Press, 1980.

Lambright, W. H., and Teich, A. H. "Policy Innovation in Federal R&D: The Case of Energy." *Public Administration Review,* 1979, *39,* 140–147.

Levin, M. A., and Sanger, M. B. *Making Government Work: How Entrepreneurial Executives Turn Bright Ideas into Real Results.* San Francisco: Jossey-Bass, 1994.

Levy, A. "Second-Order Planned Change: Definition and Conceptualization." *Organizational Dynamics,* Summer 1986, pp. 5–20.

Lewin, K. *Field Theory in Social Science.* New York: HarperCollins, 1951.

Lewis, E. *Public Entrepreneurship: Toward a Theory of Bureaucratic Political Power.* Bloomington: Indiana University Press, 1980.

Lieberman, M. *Privatization and Educational Choice.* New York: St. Martin's Press, 1989.

Lincoln, Y. S., and Guba, E. G. *Naturalistic Inquiry.* Newbury Park, Calif.: Sage, 1985.

Lindblom, C. E. "The 'Science' of Muddling Through." *Public Administration Review,* 1959, *21,* 78–88.

Linder, S. H., and Peters, B. G. "The Two Traditions of Institutional Designing: Dialogue Versus Decision?" In D. L. Weimer (ed.), *Institutional Design.* Boston: Kluwer, 1995.

Linowes, D. F. *Privatization: Toward More Effective Government.* Report of the President's Commission on Privatization. Urbana: University of Illinois Press, 1988.

Loevinger, J. *Ego Development: Conceptions and Theories.* San Francisco: Jossey-Bass, 1976.

Loevinger, J., and Wessler, R. *Measuring Ego Development 1: Construction and Use of a Sentence Completion Test.* San Francisco: Jossey-Bass, 1970.

Loevinger, J. Wessler, R., and Redmore, C. *Measuring Ego Development 2: Scoring Manual for Women and Girls.* San Francisco: Jossey-Bass, 1970.

Lynn, L. E. *Managing Public Policy.* New York: HarperCollins, 1987.

McClelland, D. C. *Human Motivation.* Cambridge: Cambridge University Press, 1987.

March, J. C., and Olsen, J. P. *Rediscovering Institututions: The Organizational Basis of Politics.* New York: Free Press, 1989.

Mayer, R. E. *Thinking, Problem Solving, Cognition.* (2nd ed.) New York: Freeman, 1991.

Mazzoni, T. L. "Educational Choice and State Politics: A Minnesota Case Study." Unpublished manuscript, 1986.

Meyer, A. D., Goes, J. B., and Brooks, G. R. "Organizations Reacting to Hyperturbulence." In G. P. Huber and W. H. Glick (eds.), *Organizational Change and Redesign.* New York: Oxford University Press, 1993.

Miles, M. B., and Huberman, A. M. *Qualitative Data Analysis.* Newbury Park, Calif.: Sage, 1984.

Miller, D., and Friesen, P. H. "Momentum and Revolution in Organizational Adaptation." *Academy of Management Journal,* 1980, *23,* 591–614.

Minnesota Business Partnership. *Educating Students for the 21st Century.* Minneapolis: Minnesota Business Partnership, 1984.

Minnesota Department of Education. *Planning Document No. 5.* St. Paul: Minnesota Department of Education, 1986a.

Minnesota Department of Education. *Postsecondary Enrollment Options Program: Preliminary Report.* St. Paul: Minnesota Department of Education, 1986b.

Minnesota Department of Education. *Postsecondary Enrollment Options Evaluation Report.* St. Paul: Minnesota Department of Education, 1987.

Minnesota Education Association. *Agenda for Educational Excellence: A Teacher Treatise.* St. Paul: Minnesota Education Association, 1984.

Mohr, L. B. *Explaining Organizational Behavior: The Limits and Possibilities of Theory and Research.* San Francisco: Jossey-Bass, 1982.

Monnet, J. *Memoirs.* New York: Doubleday, 1978.

Moore, M. "What Sort of Ideas Become Public Ideas?" In R. B. Reich (ed.), *The Power of Public Ideas.* New York: Ballinger, 1988.

"More Options, More Rigor for High-School Pupils." *Minneapolis Star and Tribune,* Aug. 17, 1985, p. 10A.

Morgan, G. *Images of Organization.* Newbury Park, Calif.: Sage, 1986.

Morris, C. R. *The Cost of Good Intentions.* New York: Norton, 1980.

Myers, I. B. *Gifts Differing.* Palo Alto, Calif.: Consulting Psychologists Press, 1980.

Myers, I. B., and McCaulley, M. H. *Manual: A Guide to the Development and Use of the Myers-Briggs Type Indicator.* Palo Alto, Calif.: Consulting Psychologists Press, 1985.

National Commission on Excellence in Education. *A Nation at Risk: The Imperative for Educational Reform.* Washington, D.C.: U.S. Government Printing Office, 1983.

Nelson, B. J. *Making an Issue of Child Abuse: Political Agenda Setting for Social Problems.* Chicago: University of Chicago Press, 1984.

Neustadt, R. E. *Presidential Power.* New York: Macmillan, 1980.

Nisbett, R., and Ross, L. *Human Inference: Strategies and Shortcomings of Social Judgment.* Upper Saddle River, N.J.: Prentice Hall, 1980.

Nord, W. R., and Tucker, S. *Implementing Routine and Radical Innovations.* Lexington, Mass.: Lexington Books, 1987.

O'Connor, K. *Women's Organizations' Use of the Courts.* Lexington, Mass.: Lexington Books, 1980.

O'Connor, K., and Epstein, L. "The Role of Interest Groups in Supreme Court Policy Formation." In R. Eyestone (ed.), *Public Policy Formation.* Greenwich, Conn: JAI Press, 1984.

Osborne, D., and Gaebler, T. *Reinventing Government: How the Entrepreneurial Spirit is Transforming the Public Sector.* Reading, Mass.: Addison-Wesley, 1992.

Ouchi, W. *The M-Form Society.* Reading, Mass.: Addison-Wesley, 1984.

Pacelle, R. L. "The Supreme Court's Agenda and the Dynamics of Policy Evolution." Paper presented at the American Political Science Association Meetings, San Francisco, Aug. 3–Sept. 2, 1990.

Peek, T. R., Duren, E. L., and Wells, L. C. *MN K–12 Education: The Current Debate, the Present Condition*. Minneapolis: Center for Urban and Regional Affairs, University of Minnesota, 1985.

Peek, T. R., and Wilson, D. S. *Fiscal Constraints on Minnesota—Impacts and Policies: Economic Conditions and Changing Government Policies*. Minneapolis: Center for Urban and Regional Affairs, University of Minnesota, 1983.

Peirce, N. R., and Hagstrom, J. *The Book of America: Inside Fifty States Today*. New York: Warner Books, 1984.

Pehler, J., Nelson, T., McEachern, B., and Nelson, K. *Initiatives for Excellence*. St. Paul: Minnesota Senate, 1985.

Peltz, D. C. "Innovation Complexity and the Sequence of Innovating Stages." *Knowledge: Creation, Diffusion, Utilization*, 1985, *6*, 261–291.

Peltz, D. C., and Andrews, F. *Scientists in Organizations*. New York: Wiley, 1966.

Peltz, D. C., and Munson, F. C. "Originality Level and the Innovating Process in Organizations." *Human Systems Management*, 1982, *3*, 173–187.

Perpich, R. "Access to Excellence." St. Paul: Minnesota Department of Education, 1985.

"Perpich Sort of Recants His Education Heresy." *Minneapolis Star and Tribune*, May 25, 1986, p. 18A.

Peters, G. B., and Hogwood, B. W. "In Search of the Issue Attention Cycle." *Journal of Politics*, 1985, *47*, 238–253.

Peters, T. J. *Thriving on Chaos*. New York: HarperCollins, 1989.

Peters, T. J., and Austin, N. *A Passion for Excellence: The Leadership Difference*. New York: Warner Books, 1985.

Peters, T. J., and Waterman, R. W. *In Search of Excellence*. New York: HarperCollins, 1982.

Pfeffer, J. *Power in Organizations*. Boston: Pitman, 1981.

Pfeffer, J., and Salancik, G. R. *The External Control of Organizations*. New York: HarperCollins, 1978.

Pinchot, G. *Intrapreneuring*. New York: HarperCollins, 1985.

Pincus, F. L. "From Equity to Excellence: The Rebirth of Educational Conservatism." In B. Gross and R. Gross (eds.), *The Great School Debate: Which Way for American Education?* New York: Simon & Schuster, 1985.

Polsby, N. W. *Political Innovation in America: The Politics of Policy Initiation*. New Haven, Conn.: Yale University Press, 1984.

Poole, M. S., and Van de Ven, A. H. "Toward a General Theory of Innovation Processes." In A. H. Van de Ven, H. L. Angle, and M. S. Poole (eds.), *Research on the Management of Innovation*. New York: Harper-Collins, 1989.

Pressman, J., and Wildavsky, A. *Implementation*. Berkeley: University of California Press, 1973.

Prigogine, I., and Stengers, I. *Order out of Chaos: Man's New Dialogue with Nature*. New York: Bantam Books, 1984.

Public School Incentives. "Nine High-Potential Ideas." Unpublished paper, Public School Incentives, St. Paul, Minn., 1984a.

Public School Incentives. "What Is Public School Incentives?" Unpublished paper, Public School Incentives, St. Paul, Minn., 1984b.

Quinn, J. B. "Managing Innovation: Controlled Chaos." *Harvard Business Review*, May–June 1985, pp. 73–84.

Ramamurti, R. "Effective Leadership of Public Sector Organizations: The Case of 'Public Entrepreneurs.'" In S. Nagel (ed.), *Research in Public Policy Analysis and Management*, Vol. 3. Greenwich, Conn.: JAI Press, 1986a.

Ramamurti, R. "Public Entrepreneurs: Who Are They and How Do They Operate?" *California Management Review*, 1986b, *28*(3), 142–158.

Randall, R., and Geiger, K. *School Choice: Issues and Answers*. Bloomington, Ind.: National Educational Service, 1991.

Raywid, M. A. "Synthesis of Research on Schools of Choice." *Educational Leadership*, Apr. 1984, pp. 71–78.

Redman, E. *The Dance of Legislation*. New York: Simon & Schuster, 1973.

Reger, R. K., Gustafson, L. T., Demarie, S. M., and Mullane, J. V. "Reframing the Organization: Why Implementing Total Quality Is Easier Said than Done." *Academy of Management Review*, 1994, *19*, 565–584.

Reich, R. B. "Policy Making in a Democracy." In R. B. Reich (ed.), *The Power of Public Ideas*. New York: Ballinger, 1988.

Reich, R. B. *Public Management in a Democratic Society*. Upper Saddle River, N.J.: Prentice Hall, 1990.

Reich, R. B. *The Work of Nations: Preparing Ourselves for 21st-Century Capitalism*. New York: Vintage Books, 1992.

Reid, T. R. *Congressional Odyssey: The Saga of a Senate Bill*. New York: Freeman, 1980.

Riker, W. H. *The Art of Political Manipulation*. New Haven, Conn.: Yale University Press, 1986.

Ripley, R. B., and Franklin, G. A. *Congress, the Bureaucracy, and Public Policy*. (5th ed.) Belmont, Calif.: Wadsworth, 1991.

"The Reindustrialization of America." *Business Week*, June 30, 1980, pp. 55–142.

Roberts, N. C. "Transforming Leadership: A Process of Collective Action." *Human Relations*, 1985, *38*, 1023–1046.

Roberts, N. C. "Organizational Power Styles: Collective and Competitive Power Under Varying Organizational Conditions." *Journal of Applied Behavioral Science,* 1986, *22,* 443–458.

Roberts, N. C. "Toward a Synergistic Model of Power." In J. M. Bryson and R. C. Einsweiler (eds.), *Shared Power.* Lanham, Md.: University Press of America, 1991.

Roberts, N. C. "Public Entrepreneurship and Innovation." *Policy Studies Review,* 1992, *11*(1), 55–74.

Roberts, N. C. "Dialogue and Deliberation: An Alternative Mode of Strategy Making." Paper presented at the Berkeley Symposium on Public Management and Research, Berkeley, Calif., July 19, 1993a.

Roberts, N. C. "Limitations of Strategic Action in Public Bureaus." In B. Bozeman (ed.), *Public Management: State of the Art.* San Francisco: Jossey-Bass, 1993b.

Roberts, N. C., and Bradley, R. T. "Limits to Charisma." In J. Conger and R. Kanungo (eds.), *Charismatic Leadership: The Elusive Factor in Organizational Effectiveness.* San Francisco: Jossey-Bass, 1988.

Roberts, N. C., and Bradley, R. T. "Stakeholder Collaboration and Innovation: A Study of Public Policy Initiation at the State Level." *Journal of Applied Behavioral Sciences,* 1991, *27,* 209–227.

Roberts, N. C., and King, P. J. "The Process of Public Policy Innovation." In A. H. Van de Ven, H. L. Angle, and M. S. Poole (eds.), *Research on the Management of Innovation.* New York: HarperCollins, 1989a.

Roberts, N. C., and King, P. J. "The Stakeholder Audit Goes Public." *Organizational Dynamics,* Winter 1989b, pp. 63–79.

Roberts, N. C., and King, P. J. "Policy Entrepreneurs: Their Activity Structure and Function in the Policy Process." *Journal of Public Administration Research and Theory,* 1991, *1,* 147–175.

Rogers, E. *Diffusion of Innovations.* (3rd ed.) New York: Free Press, 1983.

Rogers, E., and Kim, J. I. "Diffusion of Innovations in Public Organizations." In R. L. Merritt and A. J. Merritt (eds.), *Innovation in the Public Sector.* Newbury Park, Calif.: Sage, 1985.

Rogers, E., and Shoemaker, F. F. *Communication of Innovation: A Cross-Cultural Approach.* (2nd ed.) New York: Free Press, 1971.

Rogers, T. B., Kuiper, N. A., and Kirker, W. S. "Self-Reference and the Encoding of Personal Information." *Journal of Personality and Social Psychology,* 1977, *35,* 677–688.

Rosenfeld, R., and Servo, J. C. "Facilitating Innovation in Large Organizations." In M. A. West and J. L. Farr (eds.), *Innovation and Creativity at Work: Psychological and Organizational Strategies.* New York: Wiley, 1990.

Rossides, D. W. "The Worthless Debate Continues." In B. Gross and R. Gross (eds.), *The Great School Debate: Which Way for American Education?* New York: Simon & Schuster, 1985.

Sabatier, P. A., and Jenkins-Smith, H. C. (eds.). *Policy Change and Learning: An Advocacy Coalition Approach.* Boulder, Colo.: Westview Press, 1993.

Salamon, L. M. (ed.). *Beyond Privatization: The Tools of Government Action.* Washington, D.C.: Urban Institute, 1989.

Salthouse, T. A. "Expertise as the Circumvention of Human Processing Limitations." In K. A. Ericsson and J. Smith (eds.), *Toward a General Theory of Expertise: Prospects and Limits.* Cambridge: Cambridge University Press, 1991.

Sanger, J. B., and Levin, M. A. "Using Old Stuff in New Ways: Innovation as a Case of Evolutionary Tinkering." *Journal of Policy Analysis and Management,* 1992, *11,* 88–115.

Schein, V. E., and Greiner, L. "Can Organization Development Be Fine-Tuned to Bureaucracies?" *Organizational Dynamics,* Winter 1977, pp. 48–61.

Schön, D. A. *Beyond the Stable State.* New York: Norton, 1971.

Scioli, F. P. "Problems of Controlling the Efficiency of Bureaucratic Behavior." *Policy Studies Review,* 1986, *6*(1), 71–89.

Schneider, A., and Ingram, H. "Behavioral Assumptions of Policy Tools." *Journal of Politics,* 1990, *52,* 510–529.

Schroeder, R. G., Van de Ven, A. H., Scudder, G. D., and Polley, D. "The Development of Innovative Ideas." In A. H. Van de Ven, H. L. Angle, and M. S. Poole (eds.), *Research on the Management of Innovation.* New York: HarperCollins, 1989.

Schumpeter, J. A. *Capitalism, Socialism, and Democracy.* Cambridge, Mass.: Harvard University Press, 1934.

Schumpeter, J. A. *Business Cycles: A Theoretical, Historical, and Statistical Analysis of the Capitalist Process.* (2 vols.) New York: McGraw-Hill, 1939.

Scribner, S. "Studying Working Intelligence." In R. Rogoff and J. Lave (eds.), *Everyday Cognition: Its Development in Social Context.* Cambridge, Mass.: Harvard University Press, 1984.

Senge, P. *The Fifth Discipline: The Art and Practice of the Learning Organization.* New York: Doubleday, 1990.

Shanker, A. "You Can't Have Better Education 'On the Cheap.'" In B. Gross and R. Gross (eds.), *The Great School Debate: Which Way for American Education?* New York: Simon & Schuster, 1985.

Shapiro, S. "If You Won't Work Sunday, Don't Come on Friday." In B. Gross and R. Gross (eds.), *The Great School Debate: Which Way for American Education?* New York: Simon & Schuster, 1985.

Sheldon, A. "Organizational Paradigms: A Theory of Organizational Change." *Organizational Dynamics,* Winter 1980, pp. 61–80.

Simon, H. *Administrative Behavior.* New York: Macmillan, 1957.

Singer, I. "What's the Real Point of *A Nation at Risk?*" In B. Gross and R. Gross (eds.), *The Great School Debate: Which Way for American Education?* New York: Simon & Schuster, 1985.

Sizer, T. R. *Horace's Compromise: The Dilemma of the American High School.* Boston: Houghton Mifflin, 1984.

Smith, D. "Education Focus Shifts to Funding Inequality in District." *Minneapolis Star and Tribune,* Apr. 5, 1987a, p. 1B.

Smith, D. "Fears About College Program Groundless, State Agency Says." *Minneapolis Star and Tribune,* Feb. 7, 1987b, p. 1B.

Smith, D., and Parry, K. "Perpich to Push Schools on Open Enrollment." *Minneapolis Star and Tribune,* May 2, 1987, pp. 1B, 8B–9B.

Smith, R. E., Sarason, I. G., and Sarason, B. R. *Psychology: The Frontiers of Behavior.* (2nd ed.) New York: HarperCollins, 1982.

Snider, W. "The Call for Choice: Competition in the Educational Marketplace." *Education Week,* June 24, 1987, pp. C1–C23.

Stedman, L. C., and Smith, M. S. "Weak Arguments, Poor Data, Simplistic Recommendations." In B. Gross and R. Gross (eds.), *The Great School Debate: Which Way for American Education?* New York: Simon & Schuster, 1985.

Stein, B., and Kanter, R. M. "Building the Parallel Organization: Creating Mechanisms for Permanent Quality of Work Life." *Journal of Applied Behavioral Sciences,* 1980, *16,* 371–388.

Stewart, A. *Team Entrepreneurship.* Newbury Park, Calif.: Sage, 1989.

Stockman, D. A. *The Triumph of Politics.* New York: Avon, 1987.

Stone, C. N. "The Implementation of Social Programs: Two Perspectives." *Journal of Social Issues,* 1980, *36*(4), 13–34.

Sturdevant, L. "Nelson, Olsen Hold Keys to School Bills." *Minneapolis Star and Tribune,* Apr. 1, 1985a, pp. 9C–10C.

Sturdevant, L. "Perpich School Plan Clears House Hurdle." *Minneapolis Star and Tribune,* Mar. 26, 1985b, pp. 1A, 9A.

Sturdevant, L. "Open Enrollment Cut from Bill." *Minneapolis Star and Tribune,* Apr. 4, 1985c, pp. 1A, 11A.

Sturdevant, L. "Open Enrollment Plan Is Hanging by a Thread." *Minneapolis Star and Tribune,* Apr. 25, 1985d, pp. 1B, 4B.

Terry, L. D. "Why We Should Abandon the Misconceived Quest to Reconcile Public Entrepreneurship with Democracy." *Public Administration Review,* 1993, *53,* 393–395.

Thomma, S. "Open Enrollment Plan Suffers Second Defeat." *St. Paul Pioneer Post and Dispatch,* Apr. 25, 1985, pp. 1A, 12A.

Tornatzky, L. G., and others. *The Process of Technological Innovation: Reviewing the Literature.* Washington, D.C.: National Science Foundation, 1983.

Tushman, M., and Romanelli, E. "Organizational Evolution: A Metamorphosis Model of Convergence and Reorientation." In B. M. Staw and L. L. Cummings (eds.), *Research in Organizational Behavior.* Vol. 7. Greenwich, Conn.: JAI Press, 1985.

U.S. Department of Education. *The Nation Responds: Recent Efforts to Improve Education.* Washington, D.C.: U.S. Government Printing Office, 1984.

Van de Ven, A. H. "Central Problems in the Management of Innovation." *Management Science,* 1986, *32,* 590–607.

Van de Ven, A. H., and Angle, H. L. "An Introduction to the Minnesota Innovation Research Program." In A. H. Van de Ven, H. L. Angle, and M. S. Poole, (eds.), *Research on the Management of Innovation.* New York: HarperCollins, 1989.

Van Maanen, J. "The Fact of Fiction in Organizational Ethnography." *Administrative Science Quarterly,* 1979, *24,* 539–550.

Vobejda, B. "The Nation's Schools Get an 'A' for Effort, an Incomplete for Results." *Washington Post National Weekly Edition,* May 2–8, 1988, p. 30.

Vose, C. E. *Caucasians Only.* Berkeley: University of California Press, 1959.

Vose, C. E. *Constitutional Change.* Lexington, Mass.: Lexington Books, 1972.

Walker, J. L. "The Diffusion of Innovations Among the American States." *American Political Science Review,* 1969, *63,* 880–899.

Walker, J. L. "Setting the Agenda in the U.S. Senate: A Theory of Problem Selection." *British Journal of Political Science,* Oct. 1977, pp. 423–445.

Walker, J. L. "The Diffusion of Knowledge, Policy Communities, and Agenda Setting: The Relationship of Knowledge and Power." In J. E. Tropman, M. J. Dluhy, and R. M. Lind (eds.), *New Strategic Perspectives on Social Policy.* New York: Pergamon/Elsevier, 1981.

Watzlawick, P., Weakland, J., and Fisch, R. *Change.* New York: Norton, 1974.

Wedl, R. J. "Value of Postsecondary Options." Presentation to the Task Force on Implementation of Choice, St. Paul, Minn., Feb. 1985.

Weimer, D. L. (ed.). *Institutional Design.* Boston: Kluwer, 1995.

West, M. A. "The Social Psychology of Innovation in Groups." In M. A. West and J. L. Farr (eds.), *Innovation and Creativity at Work: Psychological and Organizational Strategies.* New York: Wiley, 1990.

West, M. A., and Farr, J. L. (eds.). *Innovation and Creativity at Work: Psychological and Organizational Strategies.* New York: Wiley, 1990.

Wildavsky, A. "Choosing Preferences by Constructing Institutions: A Cultural Theory of Preference Formation." *American Political Science Review,* 1987, *81*(1), 3–21.

Wildavsky, A. "The Three Cultures: Explaining Anomalies in the American Welfare State." *Public Interest,* 1982, *69,* 45–58.

Wilhelm, P. M. "The Involvement and Perceived Impact of the Citizens League on Minnesota State School Policymaking, 1969–1984." Unpublished doctoral dissertation, University of Minnesota, 1984.

Williams, W. *The Implementation Perspective.* Berkeley: University of California Press, 1980.

Williamson, M. *A Return to Love.* New York: HarperCollins, 1992.

Wilson, B. "Senate Alternative to Perpich's School Plan Is Presented." *Minneapolis Star and Tribune,* Mar. 23, 1985, p. 7B.

Wilson, B. "2nd Chance Sought for Dropouts." *Minneapolis Star and Tribune,* Feb. 22, 1987, pp. 1B, 2B.

Wilson, B. "State to Give Parents Choice of Public Schools." *Minneapolis Star and Tribune,* May 7, 1988, pp. 1B, 8B.

Wilson, J. Q. "Policy Intellectuals and Public Policy." *Public Interest,* 1981, *64,* 31–46.

Wilson, J. Q. *Bureaucracy: What Government Agencies Do and Why They Do It.* New York: Basic Books, 1989.

Winter, D. *The Power Motive.* New York: Free Press, 1973.

Yin, R. K. *Changing Urban Bureaucracies: How New Practices Become Routinized.* Lexington, Mass.: Heath, 1979.

Zaltman, G., Duncan, R., and Holbek, J. *Innovations and Organizations.* New York: Wiley, 1973.

Zand, D. E. "Collateral Organization: A New Change Strategy." *Journal of Applied Behavioral Science,* 1974, *10,* 63–89.

Zand, D. E. *Information, Organization, and Power.* New York: McGraw-Hill, 1981.

Zegans, M. D. "Innovation in the Well-Functioning Public Agency." *Public Productivity and Management Review,* 1992, *16,* 141–156.

Name Index

Subject Index